MW01609927

Certain Agendas in Architecture

2006: One Year of Student Research at MIT's Dept of Architecture

Editors: Alexander D'Hooghe, Sarah Dunbar

SA+P Press 2007

Introducing the Introduction

At MIT
We are trying to generate new design agendas.
We are trying to openly debate issues.

We have not yet completely inventoried the
intelligence available in our community;
this book is part of that ongoing process.
We are not trying to achieve a unified voice since we
are much too diverse to have one.

Research is in progress.
Reform is in progress.
Thought is in progress.
Architecture is in progress.

With the spirit of change and a disregard of neutrality
(since we are not located in Switzerland), I have
asked my colleague Alexander D'Hooghe to edit this
volume of student design work at MIT along with a
team of students. For the future issues, other faculty
members will be invited to perform the same task.
Therefore, the presentation of student work will
become another platform for discourse.

Yung Ho Chang
Professor of Architecture and Department Head

MIT: A Space of Agendas

The following is a sample of work done at MIT during a single calendar year: 2006. The incredible diversity of MITs prolific agents is hard to summarize: presenting only 'studio projects' would simply not do justice to the design research network at this school. The presence of a multitude of agendas presents its own richness - and challenge. Our editorial team structured this wealth by gathering almost everything produced in 2006 and laying it out. At that moment, a variety of relatively clear agendas presented themselves. Our labor was that of a midwife: to bring out the assorted material, its inherent hypotheses and array these without value judgement.

The architecture department increasingly functions as a flexible and agile group of actors – students, faculty, visitors, and friends. Within these networks, smaller groups coagulate frequently around common research interests. Almost spontaneously, projects appear and emerge. Some of these are formally called 'studio'; many others just happen, and become formalized later. Some investigations go on to change the topography of architectural discourse; many remain just experiments, but in each case, a steep learning curve benefits all involved. The absence of a clear bureaucratic organization allows the individual researcher-entrepreneurs to define how they organize, learn, think, draw, and build.

For that reason, this book does not structure itself along the educational formalities of 'studio', 'workshop', 'independent study' , or 'thesis'; also, it does not search to distinguish between the different degree programs. Finally, the book does not need a structure by geography: that the school is international is by now so evident that nobody even looks up when another research project is launched on the far side of either the Atlantic or the Pacific.

The book presents, therefore, the material according to its own underlying premises. This book is also the result of editorial interpretation. In an effort to unearth some of the debates and discourse currently ongoing in the hallways of MIT, the framing of work may even diverge from the intentions of the authors/ instructors of individual projects.

MIT today does not have a homogenized agenda. It is, rather, the site of a series of debates and differing worldviews. It is a space of agendas. This book is an attempt to capture the space of agendas. It is our belief that a clear formulation of agendas, exposing differences and disagreements, is a highly productive and intellectually necessary operation. In order to clarify what each concept really means, we have decided to structure the book as a series of chapters, each consisting of two oppositional terms. In most cases, these are two sides of the same dialectic. By pulling them apart, we not only arrive at a deeper understanding of each, but also allow ourselves to make further progress along each road.

In going public with this – to publish these agendas, and present them as debating points, we invite the broader research community of architects and intellectuals worldwide to enrich the discussion. Of course, to expose our conjectures and refutations to public scrutiny is also a method to advance the discussion in general and the learning at MIT in particular. Publicness, as Karl Popper once argued, is a requirement for scientificness. We hope that you will enjoy the graphic content structured according to the various belief systems presented here, and welcome you to the MIT spirit.

On behalf of the editorial team,

Alexander D'Hooghe
Assistant Professor of Architectural Urbanism

Yung Ho Chang, professor of Architecture and Department Head

02.14.2006 - competition deadline

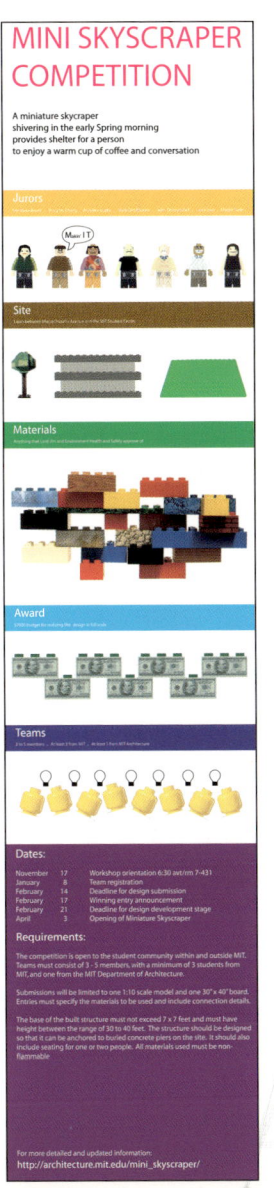

mobile landscape
mobile landscape
mobile landscape

digital_minim al

MINI SKYSCRAPER COMPETITION

A miniature skyscraper
shivering in the early Spring morning
provides shelter for a person
to enjoy a warm cup of coffee and conversation

Jurors

Site

Materials

Award

Teams

Dates:

November	17	Workshop orientation 6:30 am/rm 7-431
January	8	Team registration
February	14	Deadline for design submission
February	17	Winning entry announcement
February	21	Deadline for design development stage
April	3	Opening of Miniature Skyscraper

Requirements:

The competition is open to the student community within and outside MIT. Teams must consist of 3 - 5 members, with a minimum of 3 students from MIT, and one from the MIT Department of Architecture.

Submissions will be limited to one 1:10 scale model and one 30" x 40" board. Entries must specify the materials to be used and include connection details.

The base of the built structure must not exceed 7 x 7 feet and must have height between the range of 30 to 40 feet. The structure should be designed so that it can be anchored to buried concrete piers on the site. It should also include seating for one or two people. All materials used must be non-flammable

For more detailed and updated information:
http://architecture.mit.edu/mini_skyscraper/

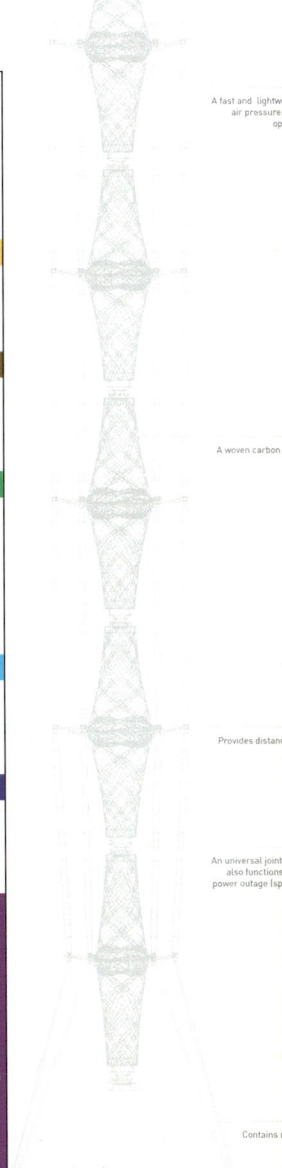

A fast and lightwe
air pressure
op

A woven carbon

Provides distance

An universal joint
also functions
power outage (sp

Contains r

photo by Peter DePasquale
drawing by John Snavely

7

Craig Dykers of Snøhetta lectures on his work.
02.14.2006

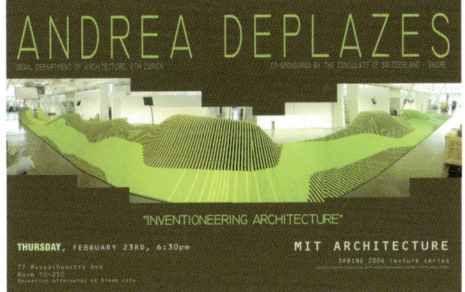

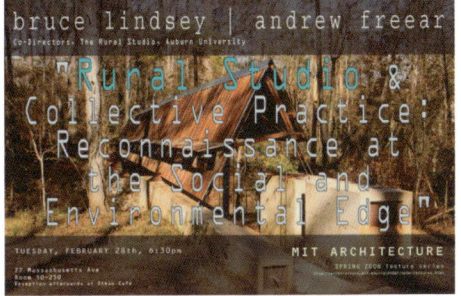

Swiss architect Andrea Deplazes lectures about the ETH and recent projects.
02.23.2006

02.28.2006

03.07.2006

03.10.2006

COMBAT ARCHITECTURE
7:30 p.m., Thursday, March 2nd, 2006
MIT, Room 34-101
BERNARD KHOURY/ DW5

Sponsored by the Lebanese Club at MIT, Department of Architecture, and the AKPIA

VISUAL ARTS PROGRAM
MASSACHUSETTS INSTITUTE OF TECHNOLOGY

presents a lecture by
Matt Mullican
MARCH 7, 2006
7:30 PM
BARTOS THEATER
MIT MEDIA CENTER
Wiesner Building, E15
20 Ames Street

Computation Group (CG) Lecture Series, Spring 2006
MIT Department of Architecture

Lars Hesselgren Friday, March 10th,
12:00 - 1:30

Geometry as Design Driver

03.14.2006

03.17.2006

TUESDAY, March 14TH, 6:30pm

thom mayne
MORPHOSIS | santa monica, ca [www.morphosis.net]

"Continuities of the Incomplete"

MIT SCHOOL OF ARCHITECTURE AND PLANNING
The 13th Pietro Belluschi Lecture

77 Massachusetts Ave | Room 10-250
Reception afterwards at Steam Cafe
architecture.mit.edu/calendar/sp06/lectures.html

NOTE: Please arrive early. We will admit
members of the MIT community from 5:45-6:15pm,
and the General Public at 6:15pm.

Computation Group SIG Lecture Series, Spring 2006

Friday, March 17th,
Room 3-133
12:00 - 1:30

HIGHLY EVOLVED
USELESS THINGS
IN ACTION

Allen Sayegh

Lecturer in Architecture
Graduate School of Design
Harvard University

Thom Mayne is the 13th guest of the Pietro Belluschi Lecture series.
03.14.2006

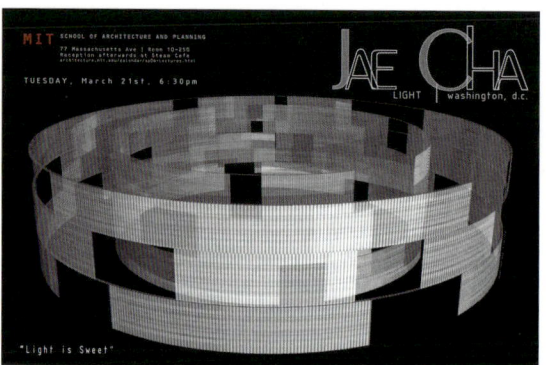

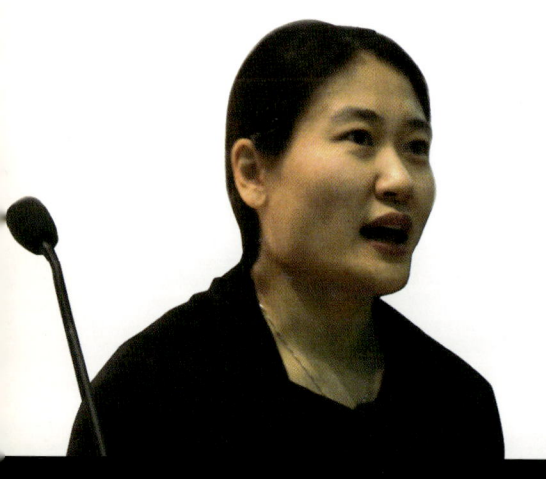

Korean-American architect, Jae Cha, lectures on recent projects done in Bolivia and Honduras. - 03.21.2006

Steven Holl sports a Simmons Hall t-shirt while lecturing on his work.
04.04.2006

"Sustainable Construction in Community"
TUESDAY, April 11th, 6:30pm

MIT architecture

YING-CHUN HSIEH
architect | taiwan

Computation Group (CG) Lecture Series, Spring 2006

Dennis Shelden Friday, April 14th,
Chief Technology Officer 12:00 - 1:30
Gehry Technologies Room 3-133

**Tectonics,
Economics and
the Reconfiguration
of Practice**

Taiwanese architect Sheng Yuan Huang lectures.
04.25.2006

04.21.2006

04.25.2006

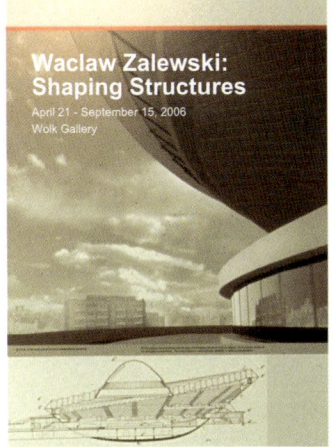

Waclaw Zalewski:
Shaping Structures
April 21 - September 15, 2006
Wolk Gallery

MIT architecture

SHENG-YUAN HUANG
ARCHITECT | TAIWAN   TUESDAY APRIL 25th 6:30pm   "In-Between Breaks"

Taiwanese architect Ying-Chun Hsieh lectures on building for low-income clients in mainland China. - 04.04.2006

04.28.2006

05.01.2006

05.02.2006

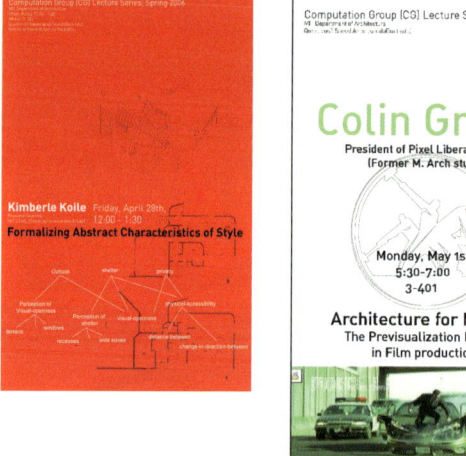

Computation Group [CG] Lecture Series, Spring 2006

Kimberle Koile Friday, April 29th
12:00 - 1:30
Formalizing Abstract Characteristics of Style

Computation Group [CG] Lecture Series, Spring 2006
MIT Department of Architecture

Colin Green

President of Pixel Liberation Front
(Former M. Arch student)

Monday, May 1st
5:30-7:00
3-401

Architecture for Movies
The Previsualization Proces
in Film production

MIT architecture

The 18th Arthur H. Schein Memorial Lecture
Massachusetts Institute of Technology, Department of Architecture

Tuesday, May 2, 2006   6:30pm   Room 10-250

WIEL ARETS | CURTAIN
Architect, Maastricht + Amsterdam

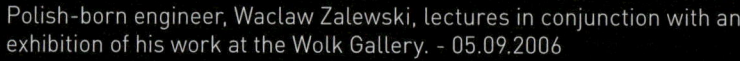

Polish-born engineer, Waclaw Zalewski, lectures in conjunction with an
exhibition of his work at the Wolk Gallery. - 05.09.2006

05.09.2006

05.09.2006

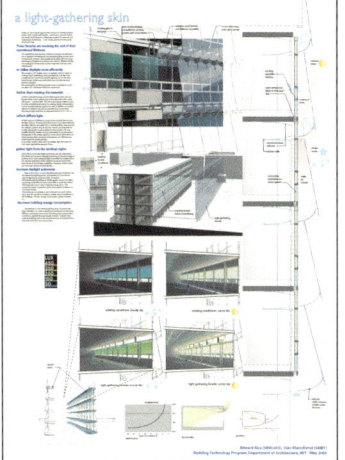

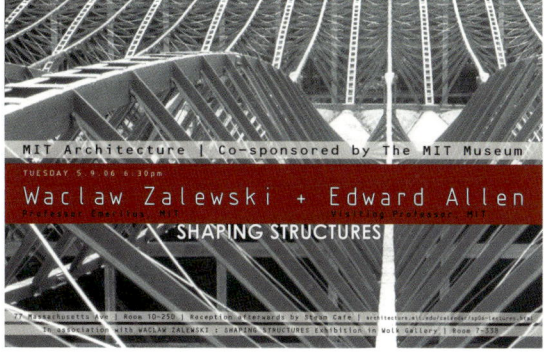

MIT Architecture | Co-sponsored by The MIT Museum

TUESDAY 5.9.06 6:30pm

Waclaw Zalewski + Edward Allen

SHAPING STRUCTURES

Dutch architect Wiel Arets lectures on recent projects. - 05.02.2006

**ARCHITECTURE
THESIS EXTRAVAGANZA!**
MIT DEPARTMENT OF ARCHITECTURE SPRING 2006
MAY 19, 2006 / 1:00-5:00

on to the Fall →

Visual Arts Program
Monday Nights @ VAP

Günther Selichar
Who's afraid of Blue,
Red and Green?

Mon 09/11/06
7–9pm

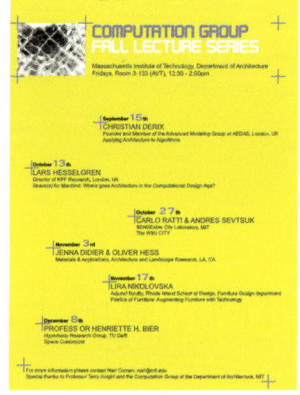

COMPUTATION GROUP
FALL LECTURE SERIES

Massachusetts Institute of Technology, Department of Architecture
Fridays, Room 3-133 (AVT), 12:30 - 2:00pm

September 15th
CHRISTIAN DERIX
Founder and Member of the Advanced Modeling Group at AEDAS, London, UK
Applying Architecture to Algorithms

October 13th
LARS HESSELGREN
Director of KPF Research, London, UK
Reason(s) for Mantric: Where goes Architecture in the Computational Design Age?

October 27st
CARLO RATTI & ANDRES SEVTSUK
SENSEable City Laboratory, MIT
The WIKI CITY

November 3rd
JENNA DIDIER & OLIVER HESS
Materials & Applications, Architecture and Landscape Research, LA, CA.

November 17th
ILRA NIKOLOVSKA
Adjunct faculty, Rhode Island School of Design, Furniture Design department
Poetics of Furniture: Augmenting Furniture with Technology

December 6th
PROFESS OR HENRIETTE H. BIER
Hyperbody Research Group, TU Delft
Space Customize!

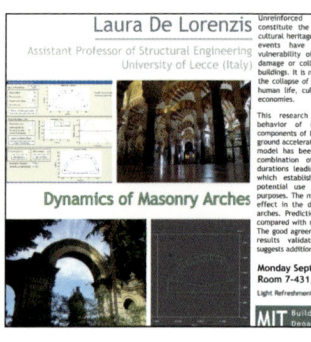

Laura De Lorenzis
Assistant Professor of Structural Engineering
University of Lecce (Italy)

Dynamics of Masonry Arches

Unreinforced masonry (URM) structure constitute the vast majority of the buil cultural heritage of the world. Recent seism events have further proved the hig vulnerability of URM construction, causir damage or collapse of invaluable historic buildings. It is necessary to better understan the collapse of masonry structures to prote human life, cultural resources, and regior economies.

This research investigates the dynamic behavior of masonry arches typic components of URM structures subjected ground acceleration impulses. A new analytic model has been developed to predict t combination of impulse magnitudes a durations leading to collapse of the arc which establishes the failure domain potential use for design and assessmen purposes. The model also interprets the sca effect in the dynamic behavior of masonr arches. Predictions of the model have bee compared with results of numerical modelin The good agreement between the two sets results validates both approaches, a suggests additional work for the future.

Monday Sept 18, 12:30 - 2:00 pm
Room 7-431, AVT

Light Refreshments served.

MIT Building Technology Progra.
Department of Architectur

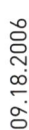

09.18.2006

Fall 2006

09.19.2006

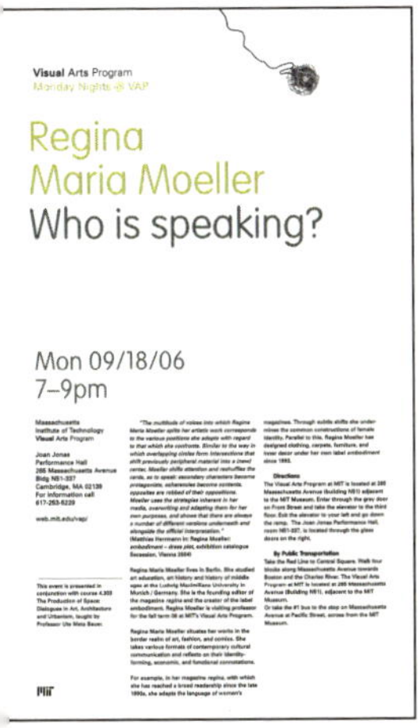

Visual Arts Program
Monday Nights at VAP

Regina
Maria Moeller
Who is speaking?

Mon 09/18/06
7–9pm

Massachusetts
Institute of Technology
Visual Arts Program

09.28 __ 6.30 pm
_room A-133

Prof. Jessica Jaques

_Professor of Aesthetics,
Universitat Autònoma de
Barcelona

Picasso in Gósol, 1906:
A Summer for Aesthetics

10.19 __ 6.30 pm
_room A-155

Prof. William Craft Brumfield

_Professor of Slavic Studies,
Tulane University

Contemporary Moscow:
the Advent of Retro-Moderne

*11.09 __ 6:00 pm
_room A-155

Prof. Rey Chow

_Andrew W. Mellon Professor
of the Humanities,
Brown University

Mimesis, Sacrifice, and Victimhood

HTC Forum Lecture Series
fall
2006

* co-sponsored by MIT
Comparative Media
Studies Program

Massachusetts Institute of
Technology

School of Architecture
and Planning

Department of Architecture

History, Theory and Criticism
of Architecture and Art

TUESDAY, SEPTEMBER 19, 6:30 PM, ROOM 10-250

OLAFUR ELIASSON ARTIST, BERLIN
RELATIVITY OF REALITY

ARCHITECTURE OR REVOLUTION.
CAN BE AVOIDED.

MIT ARCHITECTURE LECTURE SERIES. FALL 2006. REVOLUTION

23

Policy and Design for Housing:
Lessons of the Urban Development
Corporation 1968-1975
September 20 - December 22, 2006
Wolk Gallery

FRONT + BACK:
Investigating a Renaissance
Drawing
September 29, 2006 – December 22, 2006
MIT Museum

Structural engineer and MIT alum, Guy Nordensen, lectures on his work.
10.03.2006

Leith Sharp
Director of Harvard Green Campus Initiative

Harvard Vision 2020
a bridge to campus sustainability

April 27-29, 2006

Faculty, Staff, Students & Alumni

Harvard Green Campus Initiative
A Mission Driven, Business Based Model for Campus Sustainability

Ms Sharp will describe the effort of Harvard University to initiative a long term effort to reduce resource consumption on the campus.

Environmental sustainability is a moving target that requires a rapid and wide reaching escalation in the pace of organizational change across every university. At its heart, the challenge posed by the environmental imperative is an organizational change challenge. We must increase the rate at which our universities are able to innovate in the ways they operate. And this increase in the rate of innovation must be both sustained and successfully leveraged to ensure an optimal rate of continuous improvement.

The Harvard Green Campus Initiative, which began in 2000, has been built in partnership with thousands of individuals across the University, into a business that currently generates over $5 million of annual savings and over 60 million pounds of annual greenhouse gas emissions.

Monday October 2, 12:30 - 2:00 pm
Room 7-431, AVT

Light Refreshments served.

MIT Building Technology Program
Department of Architecture

TUESDAY, OCTOBER 3, 6:30 PM, ROOM 10-250

GUY NORDENSON STRUCTURAL ENGINEER, NEW YORK

STRUCTURE OR REVOLUTION

ARCHITECTURE OR REVOLUTION.
CAN BE AVOIDED.

MIT ARCHITECTURE LECTURE SERIES FALL 2006: REVOLUTION

the gasket project
new sculpture by charles mathis
october 6 - 30

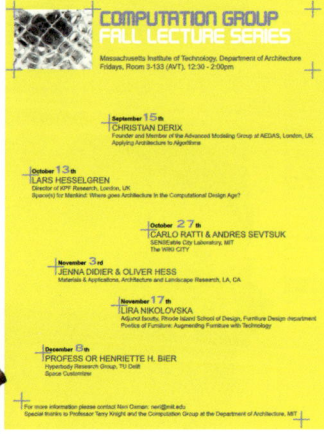

COMPUTATION GROUP
FALL LECTURE SERIES

Massachusetts Institute of Technology, Department of Architecture
Fridays, Room 3-133 (AVT), 12:30 - 2:00pm

September 15th
CHRISTIAN DERIX
Founder and Member of the Advanced Modeling Group at AEDAS, London, UK.
Applying Architecture to Algorithms

October 13th
LARS HESSELGREN
Director of KPF Research, London, UK
Space(s) for Mankind: Where goes Architecture in the Computational Design Age?

October 27th
CARLO RATTI & ANDRES SEVTSUK
SENSEable City Laboratory, MIT
The WIKI CITY

November 3rd
JENNA DIDIER & OLIVER HESS
Materials & Applications, Architecture and Landscape Research, LA, CA.

November 17th
LIRA NIKOLOVSKA
Adjunct faculty, Rhode Island School of Design, Furniture Design department
Poetics of Furniture: Augmenting Furniture with Technology

December 8th
PROFESSOR HENRIETTE H. BIER
Hyperbody Research Group, TU Delft
Space Customizer

For more information please contact Neri Oxman: neri@mit.edu
Special thanks to Professor Terry Knight and the Computation Group at the Department of Architecture, MIT

Roman Building Technology:
Materials and Structure in Ancient Rome

Lynne Lancaster
Associate Professor of Classics, Ohio University

Monday, October 16, 2006, 12:30
MIT Room 7-431

This seminar will focus on the development of vaulting in Rome during the imperial period with a particular emphasis on bath technology. The spread of the bathing habit throughout the Roman Empire was a major catalyst for technological developments and dissemination. The development of these large vaulted structures, which required both fireproof and waterproof materials, prompted advances in the use of hydraulic concrete and terracotta building elements as well as in the way the vaults were combined to ensure structural stability. By looking at the context in which these developments occurred we gain insight into some of the motivating forces at work within Roman society and how they changed over time.

Lynne Lancaster earned her B.Arch. from Virginia Polytechnic Institute and an M.Phil. and D.Phil. in Classical Archaeology from Oxford University. Her articles have focused on the construction of buildings in imperial Rome, particularly the Colosseum (*Journal of Roman Archaeology*), Trajan's Column and Trajan's Markets (*American Journal of Archaeology*). Her recent book is entitled *Concrete Vaulted Construction in Imperial Rome: Innovations in Context* (Cambridge University Press 2005).

Light refreshments offered.
Please email Prof. John Ochsendorf [jao@mit.edu] for further information.

Lecture co-sponsored by: MIT Building Technology Program
MIT Archaeological Materials Program

Nicholas Negroponte, founder of the Media Lab and MIT SAP alum, speaks about the 'One Laptop per Child' initiative. - 10.19.2006

THURSDAY, OCTOBER 19, 6:30 PM, ROOM 34-101 (50 VASSAR ST)

ARCHITECTURE OR REVOLUTION.

CAN BE AVOIDED.

NICHOLAS NEGROPONTE
PROFESSOR OF MEDIA ARTS & SCIENCES, MIT

ONE LAPTOP PER CHILD

MIT ARCHITECTURE LECTURE SERIES FALL 2006: REVOLUTION

Axel Kilian
Postdoctoral Associate, MIT Dept of Architecture

Design Exploration between
Form Finding and Design Discovery

Form finding has a rich history related to structural optimization and the notion of organic forms. While early work in the field was using physical form finding techniques recent developments in digital solvers have made the interactive solving of large meshes through particle spring models and other techniques possible. The removal of constraints of the physical model opens up unique possibilities in extending form finding to an environment for design discovery through the integration simulated forces and constraints.
Examples of different environments and approaches will be presented based on ODE (open dynamics engine) and processing using a library by Simon Greenwold. The talk is based on work conducted for the author's PhD titled "Design Exploration through Bidirectional Modeling of Constraints".

Monday October 23, 12:30-2:00 pm
Room 7-431, AVT
Light Refreshments served.

MIT Building Technology Program
Department of Architecture

Axel Kilian, a post-doc in Computation, lectures on generative techniques for form-finding as part of the Building Technology lecture series. - 10.23.2006

27

10.23.2006

10.24.2006

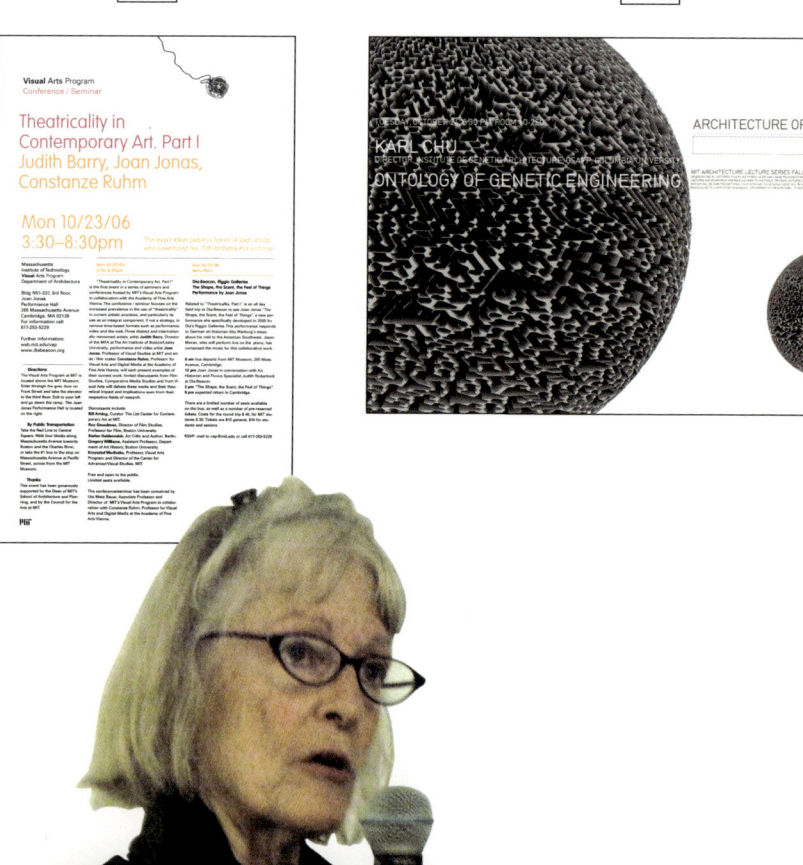

Visual Arts Program
Conference / Seminar

Theatricality in Contemporary Art. Part I
Judith Barry, Joan Jonas, Constanze Ruhm

Mon 10/23/06
3:30–8:30pm

ARCHITECTURE OR REVOLUTION.

CAN BE AVOIDED.

KARL CHU
ONTOLOGY OF GENETIC ENGINEERING

Professor Joan Jonas speaks at the 'Theatricality in Contemporary Art' conference - 10.23.2006

COMPUTATION GROUP
FALL LECTURE SERIES

Massachusetts Institute of Technology, Department of Architecture
Fridays, Room 3-133 (AVT), 12:30 - 2:00pm

September 15th
CHRISTIAN DERIX
Founder and Member of the Advanced Modeling Group at AEDAS, London, UK
Applying Architecture to Algorithms

October 13th
LARS HESSELGREN
Director of KPF Research, London, UK
Space(s) for Mankind: Where goes Architecture in the Computational Design Age?

October 27th
CARLO RATTI & ANDRES SEVTSUK
SENSEable City Laboratory, MIT
The WIKI CITY

November 3rd
JENNA DIDIER & OLIVER HESS
Materials & Applications, Architecture and Landscape Research, LA, CA

November 17th
LIRA NIKOLOVSKA
Adjunct faculty, Rhode Island School of Design, Furniture Design department
Poetics of Furniture: Augmenting Furniture with Technology

December 8th
PROFESSOR HENRIETTE H. BIER
Hyperbody Research Group, TU Delft
Space Customizer

For more information please contact Neri Oxman: neri@mit.edu
Special thanks to Professor Terry Knight and the Computation Group at the Department of Architecture, MIT

Marilyne Andersen
Assistant Professor of Building Technology
MIT Department of Architecture

A New Daylighting Laboratory at MIT

Daylighting, or more generally lighting, is one of the fundamental components of the built environment. In addition to revealing and structuring volumes and producing visual effects, it must adequately respond to our needs for visual comfort, for a connection to the outside world and for a healthy environment, and must be carefully planned to be ecologically viable.
In terms of a building's environmental impact, the potential for saving energy using daylight is undisputable considering that 40% of a building's energy consumption is generally dedicated to lighting and that a careful management of solar gains can allow significant reductions in cost and energy use for warming and cooling.

Marilyne Andersen will present an overview of the various research projects she and her students are developing to answer the increasing incentive to design buildings that take a better advantage of daylight, including new design tools and instrumentation for advanced materials.

Monday October 30, 12:30 - 2:00 pm
Room 7-431, AVT
Light Refreshments served.

MIT Building Technology Program
Department of Architecture

Karl Chu lectures on his work.
10.24.2006

10.31.2006

10.13.2006

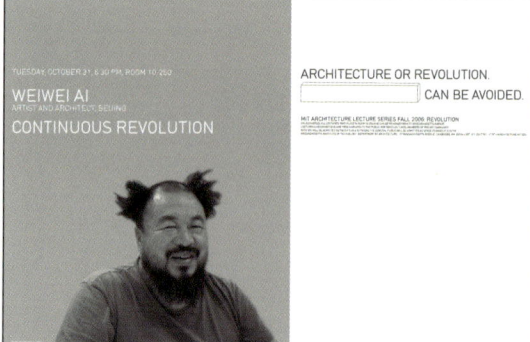

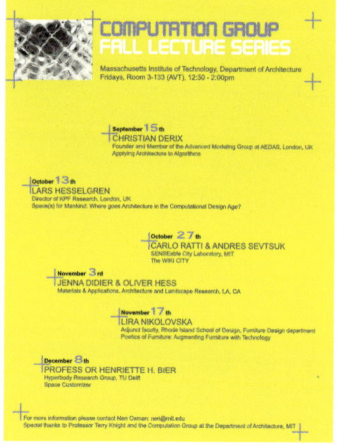

Chinese artist Ai Wei Wei snaps photos of Sanford Kwinter as he begins his talk.
10.31.2006

Steven Lockley

Assistant Professor of Medicine,
Harvard Medical School

In addition to visual function, the human (or more generally mammalian) eye detects light for a range of behavioral and physiological responses separate and apart from sight, collectively termed 'non-visual' or 'non-image forming' responses and sometimes grouped under the term 'circadian photoreception'.

These effects of light were shown to be mediated primarily via activation of a novel opsin, melanopsin, located in cells that are spread across the retina.

The talk will review the basic studies underlying the discovery of this novel photoreception system and will demonstrate how short-wavelength light preferentially stimulates non-visual responses to light, for example the acute alerting effects of light, in humans. While our understanding of the biological mechanisms mediating these responses is growing, the next challenge is to translate this research into architectural and lighting design that is optimized for both visual and non-visual effects of light, thereby maximizing the beneficial effects of light for human health.

Circadian photoreception: more than meets the eye

Monday November 6, 12:30–2:00 pm
Room 7-431, AVT

Light Refreshments served.

Building Technology Program
Department of Architecture

MIT Visual Arts Program
Monday Nights @ VAP

Krzysztof Wodiczko
Projections and Instrumentations

Mon 11/06/06
7–9pm

Rem Koolhaas in discussion with Mark Jarzombek and Alexander D'Hooghe.
11.28.2006

MIT Visual Arts Program
Monday Nights @ VAP

Gustavo Artigas
Game, Risk,
Disaster

Mon 11/13/06
5:30–7pm

Massachusetts
Institute of Technology
Visual Arts Program
Department of Architecture

Bldg N51-337, 3rd floor,
Joan Jonas
Performance Hall
265 Massachusetts Avenue
Cambridge, MA 02139
For information call
617-253-5229

Further information:
web.mit.edu/vap/

Open to the general public.

This event is presented in conjunction with course 4.209 The Production of Space: Dialogues in Art, Architecture and Urbanism, taught by Professor Ute Meta Bauer.

"Are we here to play or to be serious? And in all seriousness what is of playing or games for what matter? [...]

Directions
The Visual Arts Program at MIT is located above the MIT Museum. [...]

TUESDAY, NOVEMBER 14, 5:00 PM, ROOM 10-250

ARCHITECTURE OR REVOLUTION.

REM KOOLHAAS
ARCHITECT, ROTTERDAM

CAN BE AVOIDED.

LAGOS

MIT ARCHITECTURE LECTURE SERIES FALL 2006 REVOLUTION

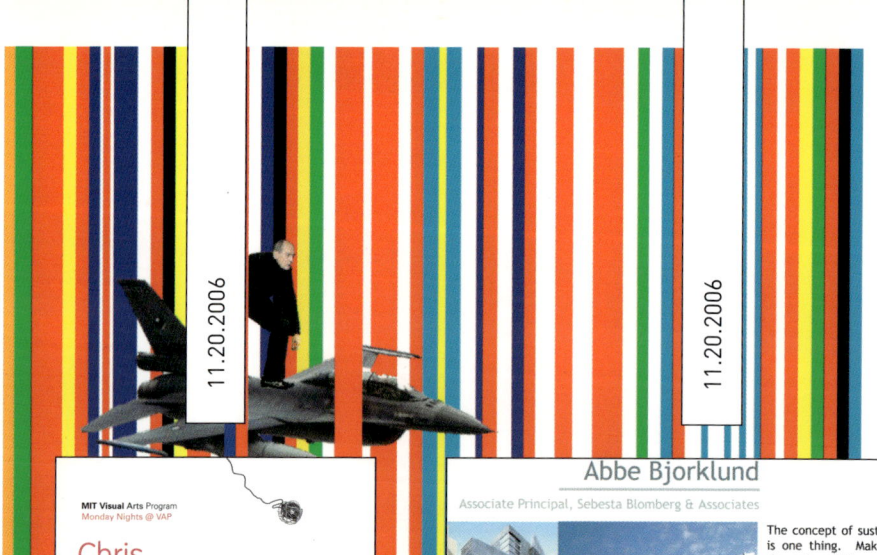

11.20.2006

11.20.2006

MIT Visual Arts Program
Monday Nights @ VAP

Chris
Csikszentmihalyi
Politechnics

Mon 11/20/06
8:30-10pm

A Double Lecture
with Powers/Sequeira – Popwatch
7-8:30pm

Massachusetts
Institute of Technology
Visual Arts Program
Department of Architecture

Bldg N51-337, 3rd floor,
Joan Jonas
Performance Hall
265 Massachusetts Avenue
Cambridge, MA 02139
For information call
617-253-5229

Further information:
web.mit.edu/vap/

Open to the general public.

Politechnics: Political Technologies from the Computing Culture Group.
All technology is politics, but most technologies (and technologists) won't admit it. For five years the Computing Culture Group at the MIT Media Lab has been developing technologies for personal and societal politics. Mixing research from the humanities and social sciences with techniques from engineering, we develop systems and prothods for unique applications, such as how to spy on the government, how to invent military technologies, or how to reverse the gender of kitchen appliances. These systems demonstrate the inherent ideologies in existing technologies, but also point to alternate directions. The talk will be a review of past projects, and a description of future research topics.

Chris Csikszentmihalyi (MFA UC San Diego, BFA Art Institute of Chicago) is the Muriel Cooper Associate Professor of Media Arts and Sciences and directs the Computing Culture Group at the MIT Media Lab. He has worked in the intersection of new technologies, media, and the arts for 15 years. Lecturing, showing new media work, and presenting installations in four continents and one subcontinent, he is interested in cultural narratives, and his work typically aims to create a new technology to embody some kind of particular social agenda.

Directions
The Visual Arts Program at MIT is located above the MIT Museum. Enter through the grey door on Front Street and take the elevator to the third floor. Exit to your left and go down the ramp. The Joan Jonas Performance Hall is located on the right.

By Public Transportation:
Take the Red Line to Central Square. Walk four blocks along Massachusetts Avenue towards Boston and the Charles River, or take the #1 bus to the stop on Massachusetts Avenue at Pacific Street, across from the MIT Museum.

MIT

Abbe Bjorklund
Associate Principal, Sebesta Blomberg & Associates

The concept of sustainable design is one thing. Making it work in the real world is another.

Ms. Bjorklund will provide examples from some of her firm's projects (including one at MIT!) of the barriers to making sustainable designs a reality, and how they were (or were not) overcome.

Real World Experiences
With Sustainable Design

Monday November 20
12:30-2:00 pm
Room 7-431, AVT

Light Refreshments served.

MIT Building Technology Program
Department of Architecture

11.20.2006

11.21.2006

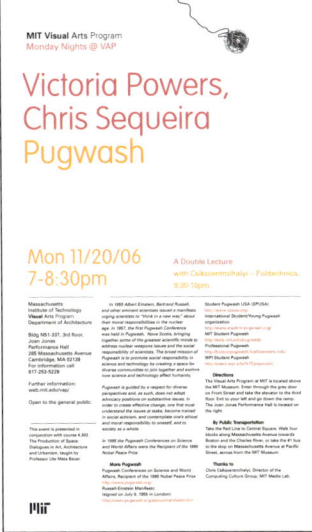

MIT Visual Arts Program
Monday Nights @ VAP

Victoria Powers,
Chris Sequeira
Pugwash

Mon 11/20/06
7-8:30pm

A Double Lecture
with Csíkszentmihályi - Fodsztechnick,
8:30-10pm.

Massachusetts
Institute of Technology
Visual Arts Program
Department of Architecture

Bldg N51-337, 3rd floor,
Joan Jonas
Performance Hall
286 Massachusetts Avenue
Cambridge, MA 02139
For information call
617-253-5239

Further information:
web.mit.edu/vap/

Open to the general public.

This event is presented in
conjunction with course 4.302
The Production of Space
Dialogues in Art, Architecture
and Urbanism, taught by
Professor Ute Meta Bauer.

In 1955 Albert Einstein, Bertrand Russell,
and other eminent scientists issued a manifesto
urging scientists to "think in a new way" about
their moral responsibilities in the nuclear
age. In 1957, the first Pugwash Conference
was held in Pugwash, Nova Scotia, bringing
together some of the greatest scientific minds to
address nuclear weapons issues and the social
responsibility of scientists. The broad mission of
Pugwash is to promote social responsibility in
science and technology by creating a space for
diverse communities to join together and examine
how science and technology affect humanity.

Pugwash is guided by a respect for diverse
perspectives and, as such, does not adopt
advocacy positions on substantive issues. In
order to create effective change, one first must
understand the issues at stake, become trained
in social issues and ethics, and contemplate one's ethical
and moral responsibility to oneself, and to
society as a whole.

In 1995 the Pugwash Conferences on Science
and World Affairs were the Recipient of the 1995
Nobel Peace Prize.

More Pugwash
Pugwash Conferences on Science and World
Affairs, Recipient of the 1995 Nobel Peace Prize
http://www.pugwash.org /
Russell-Einstein Manifesto
(signed on July 9, 1955 in London)
http://www.pugwash.org/about/manifesto.htm

Student Pugwash USA (SPUSA)
http://www.spusa.org
International Student/Young Pugwash
organization
http://www.student-pugwash.org/
MIT Student Pugwash
http://web.mit.edu/sdpugwash
Professional Pugwash
http://iisdmmt.gweb.hubblecosmos.info
MIT Student Pugwash
http://web.mit.edu/MITpugwash/

Directions
The Visual Arts Program at MIT is located above
the MIT Museum. Enter through the grey door
on Front Street and take the elevator to the third
floor. Exit to your left and go down the ramp.
The Joan Jonas Performance Hall is located on
the right.

By Public Transportation
Take the Red Line to Central Square. Walk four
blocks along Massachusetts Avenue towards
Boston and the Charles River, or take the #1 bus
to the stop on Massachusetts Avenue at Pacific
Street, across from the MIT Museum.

Thanks to
Chris Csíkszentmihályi, Director of the
Computing Culture Group, MIT Media Lab.

MIT

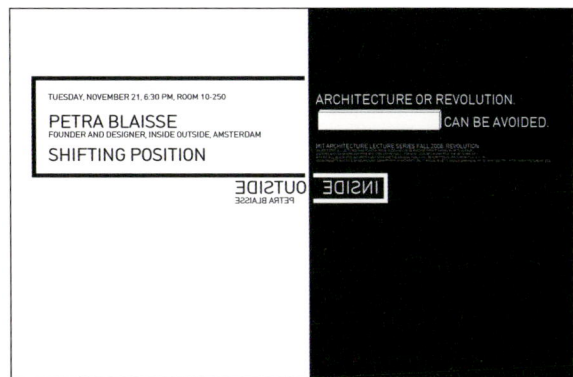

TUESDAY, NOVEMBER 21, 6:30 PM, ROOM 10-250

PETRA BLAISSE
FOUNDER AND DESIGNER, INSIDE OUTSIDE, AMSTERDAM

SHIFTING POSITION

ARCHITECTURE OR REVOLUTION.
CAN BE AVOIDED.

MIT ARCHITECTURE LECTURE SERIES FALL 2006, REVOLUTION.

OUTSIDE INSIDE
PETRA BLAISSE

Sarah Dunbar and Casey Renner present 'Rem Traceur' as an introduction to
the discussion between Koolhaas, Jarzombek, and D'Hooghe. - 11.28.2006

11.27.2006

11.28.2006

Japanese architect Sou Fujimoto lectures on his recent projects.
11.28.2006

11.29.2006

12.08.2006

Petra Blaisse, of Inside Outside, speaks about her work with textiles and landscape design.11.21.2006

Saud Sharaf presents his thesis 'MEGAPORT: Architecture in Infrastructural Environments' to reviewers. - 12.18.2006

PROJECT

Mapping has been one of architecture and urbanism's primary medicines against what used to be called an illness: modernism. Against Modernism's abstract templates and precepts, which increasingly served as an excuse to raze and destroy entire urban neighborhoods, urbanists and architects during the 1960s – and continuing up until today – developed an antidote called 'mapping.' Mapping assumes that the value of what can be found in the everyday life of the city is at least as great as whatever architecture or urbanism can bring to it. Mapping is, of course, an older practice, related to ethnography, exoticism and the curiosity of Europeans when colonizing other civilizations that were alien to them. It is striking that our own cities and their life have become so alien to us that we now bring this practice to any site or city.

Therein lays the quintessential difference with the notion of a 'project': mapping, while exposing unexpected patterns and phenomena, ultimately confirms the status quo, whereas a Project, by its very etymological definition, aims to radically transform it. The notion of the Project lies at the very root of architecture: to define a structure to be superimposed; there is no escape from this hard and ethically compromising fact. Even the gentlest attempts at participationism in architecture have, throughout the 1970s, whenever they led to buildings, resulted in artifacts with a considerable amount of rigidity: the rigidity which is required to vanquish gravity. As an act of foundation, every building, every urban plan, presents its own complete worldview and can exist only by demolishing the previous contents of the site it operates on. The production of the project is nevertheless softened by the existence of what in

MAPPING

French sociology is called 'second production': the tactics of appropriation, use and participation in the daily making and using of a space, in a manner deviant form the initial plan.

So which is the lesser evil? To risk losing oneself in the analysis of current conditions, or to seemingly superimpose a new reality, at the expense of the vitality of everyday life in the city? Without mapping, there is no reality-based project; only fiction or worse, pure aggression. However, without project, there is no discipline of architecture or urbanism: for these fields are, by their very definition, about altering the topography of civilization.

In recent MIT research, mapping develops, just like Robert Venturi did when studying Las Vegas in the 1970s, a series of alternative maps of urban context, aiming to understand more fully the experiential structure of a given site, in order to eventually derive a project from the unique properties discovered through mapping. MIT Projects assert the a priori much more forcefully: what is it that the architect brings to to the site, and what is the most optimal template to be deployed? How does it change the status quo for the better?

MIT's research projects take on both viewpoints and articulate the value of each. Like any of the dialectics structuring this book, ultimately one will require the other.

PROJECT

Post-Industrial Venice/ Turin
J. Meejin Yoon, Instructor
MArch Level II Studio 4.143

Venice Biennale
J. Meejin Yoon, Instructor
MArch Level II Studio 4.143

Swell : A Proposition for Coastal Metropolises in the Age of Rising Seas and Distributed Centralization
Talia Dorsey
MArch Thesis

The Shanghai Studio:
An Architecture of Tactical Refractions
Ann Pendleton-Jullian, Instructor
MArch Level III Studio 4.156

Post-Industrial: Venice/ Turin

J. Meejin Yoon, Instructor
Saeed Arida, TA
MArch Level II Studio 4.143
Fall 2006

For its participation in the Venice Biennale, MIT chose
to work on the most seemingly benign and least
extreme of the 16 cities, Turin, Italy. Architecturally
famous for its Baroque and Modern Architecture,
post-Fiat, Turin has sought to redefine itself through
key projects (including the 2006 Winter Olympics) and
the redevelopment of former industrial sites on their
outskirts as residential and leisure-led pieces of city.
The iconic Lingotto FIAT factory, designed by Matte
Trucco and cited as a prime example of Modernism
in Le Corbusier's Vers une Architecture, is now a
shopping mall renovated by Renzo Piano. Given the
fact that over 83% of Italy's energy is imported, the
studio was used as an opportunity to re-examine
these modern white elephants of the city, in a
plausible future when all energy imports to Italy will
be terminated-- speculating on Turin 2050 as the first
post industrial sustainable city.

model by James Graham and Thaddeus Jusczyck

James Graham
MArch II

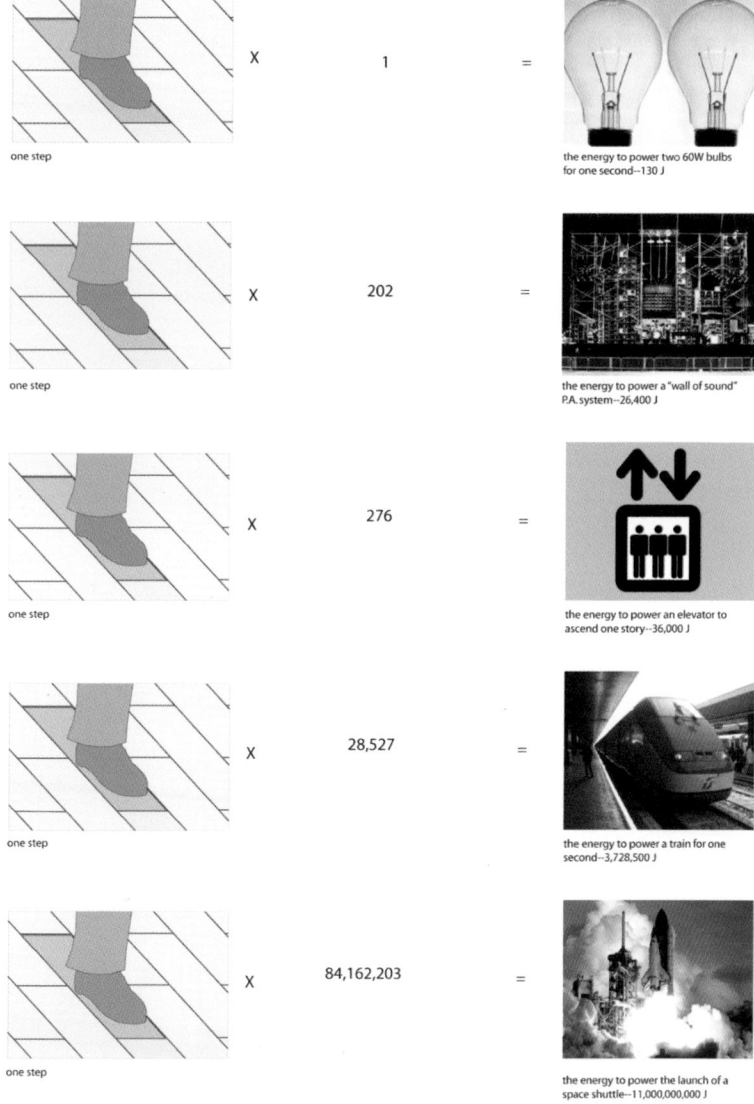

one step	X	1	=	the energy to power two 60W bulbs for one second--130 J
one step	X	202	=	the energy to power a "wall of sound" P.A. system--26,400 J
one step	X	276	=	the energy to power an elevator to ascend one story--36,000 J
one step	X	28,527	=	the energy to power a train for one second--3,728,500 J
one step	X	84,162,203	=	the energy to power the launch of a space shuttle--11,000,000,000 J

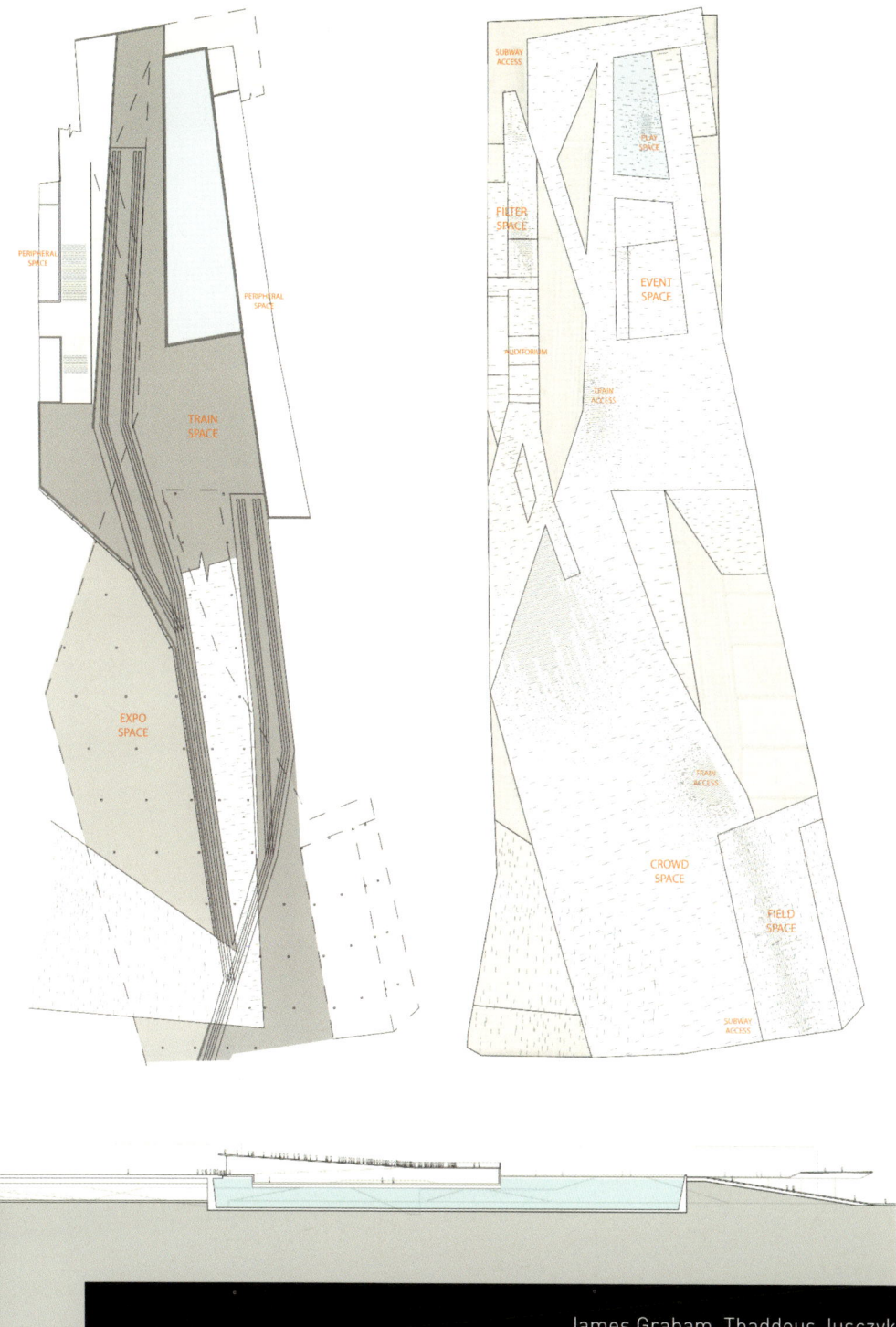

PERIPHERAL
SPACE

PERIPHERAL
SPACE

TRAIN
SPACE

EXPO
SPACE

SUBWAY
ACCESS

PLAY
SPACE

FILTER
SPACE

EVENT
SPACE

AUDITORIUM

TRAIN
ACCESS

TRAIN
ACCESS

CROWD
SPACE

FIELD
SPACE

SUBWAY
ACCESS

James Graham, Thaddeus Jusczyk
MArch II

James Graham, Thaddeus Jusczyk
MArch II

2006 Venice Architecture Biennale Exhibition

J. Meejin Yoon, Instructor
Saeed Arida, TA
MArch Level II Studio 4.143
Fall 2006

MIT was one of 12 international institutions invited by the Venice Biennale to participate in an International Design Studio/Workshop entitled "Learning from Cities" as part of the Venice Biennale 10th International Architecture Exhibition: Cities, Architecture and Society. The respective studios from the various architecture schools around the world looked at one of 16 cities pre-selected by the 10th International Architecture Exhibition. Addressing four themes: mobility, workplaces, dwelling and public space, the Biennale featured Shanghai, Mumbai, Tokyo, Caracas, Mexico City, Bogotá, São Paulo, Los Angeles, New York, Johannesburg, Cairo, London, Barcelona, Berlin, and Milano-Torino. Each school was asked to select a city that was not in their own continent and to engage design research projects that re-examine the core theme of the Cities, Architecture and Society exhibition, culminating in a 'counter exhibition' displayed in the Padiglione Italia as part of the Venice Biennale.

The MIT students' mixed-use Energy Farms on the Porta Nuova train station site were offered as a critique to the Biennale's exhibition on the post industrial, leisurely, and infrastructurally sophisticated future of Turin. Displayed on vertical bands that wrapped from the wall to the floor, culminating in operable mobile stools which served as demo's of energy models (such as a kinetically powered stool which lights when sat on), the students engaged in speculative research on technology, architecture, landscape and urbanism, to create a new vision for Turin 2050.

photo by Thaddeus Jusczyck

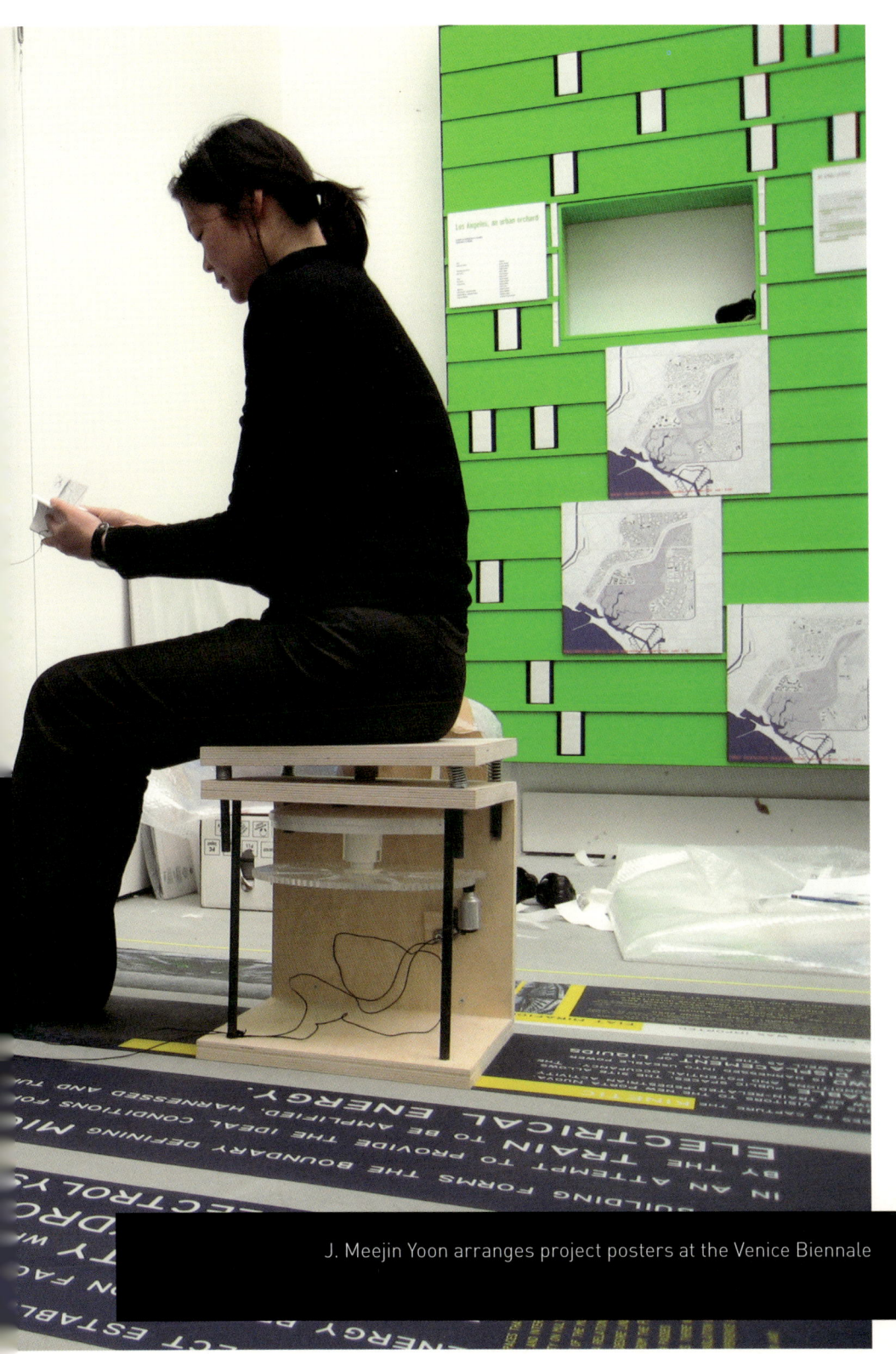

J. Meejin Yoon arranges project posters at the Venice Biennale

Swell: A Proposition for Coastal Metropolises in the Age of Rising Seas and Distributed Centralization

Talia Dorsey
MArch Thesis
Alexander D'Hooghe, Advisor
J. Meejin Yoon and Sanford Kwinter, Readers
Spring 2006

Premised upon the certain realities of the rise of urban sprawl, globalized dynamic networks, and sea levels, this thesis seeks to mobilize the inherent potentials that lie within their intersections. Is contemporary urban form appropriate to contemporary urban culture? Do developing trends within network dynamics offer new potentials for spatial form? Does the forecasted flooding of coastal metropolises offer new grounds for such speculations? How might design begin to actively operate within such a scenario? Aligned within a tradition of visionary conceptions rooted in such considerations, this thesis project is a synthetic proposition of a new urban paradigm for dynamic water-based expansion -- one driven by and resulting from the particularities of its contemporary cultural position.

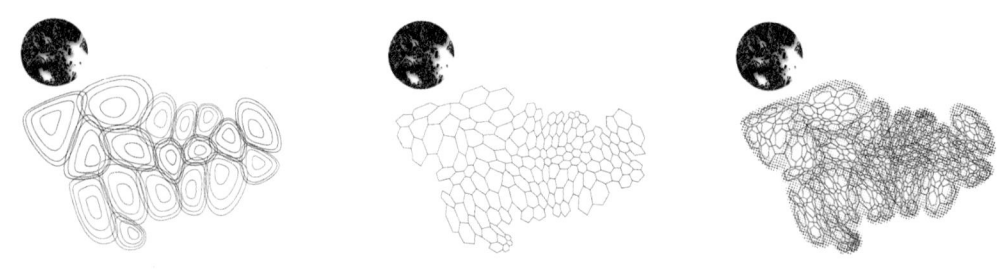

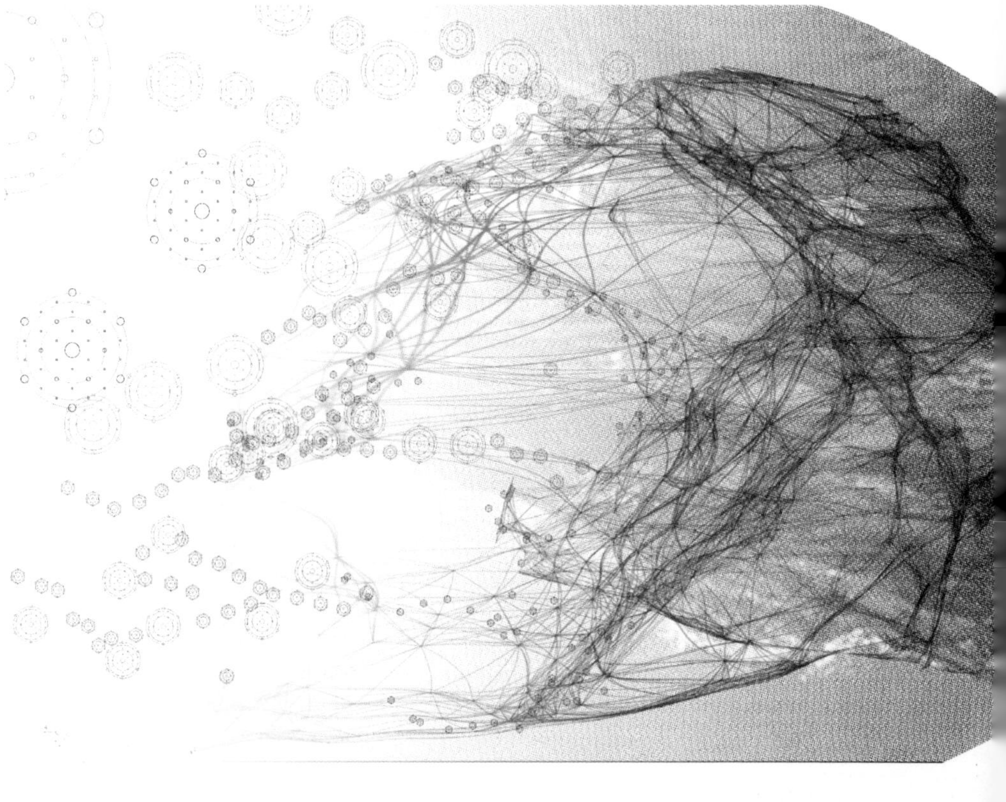

PROJECT | ~~MAPPING~~

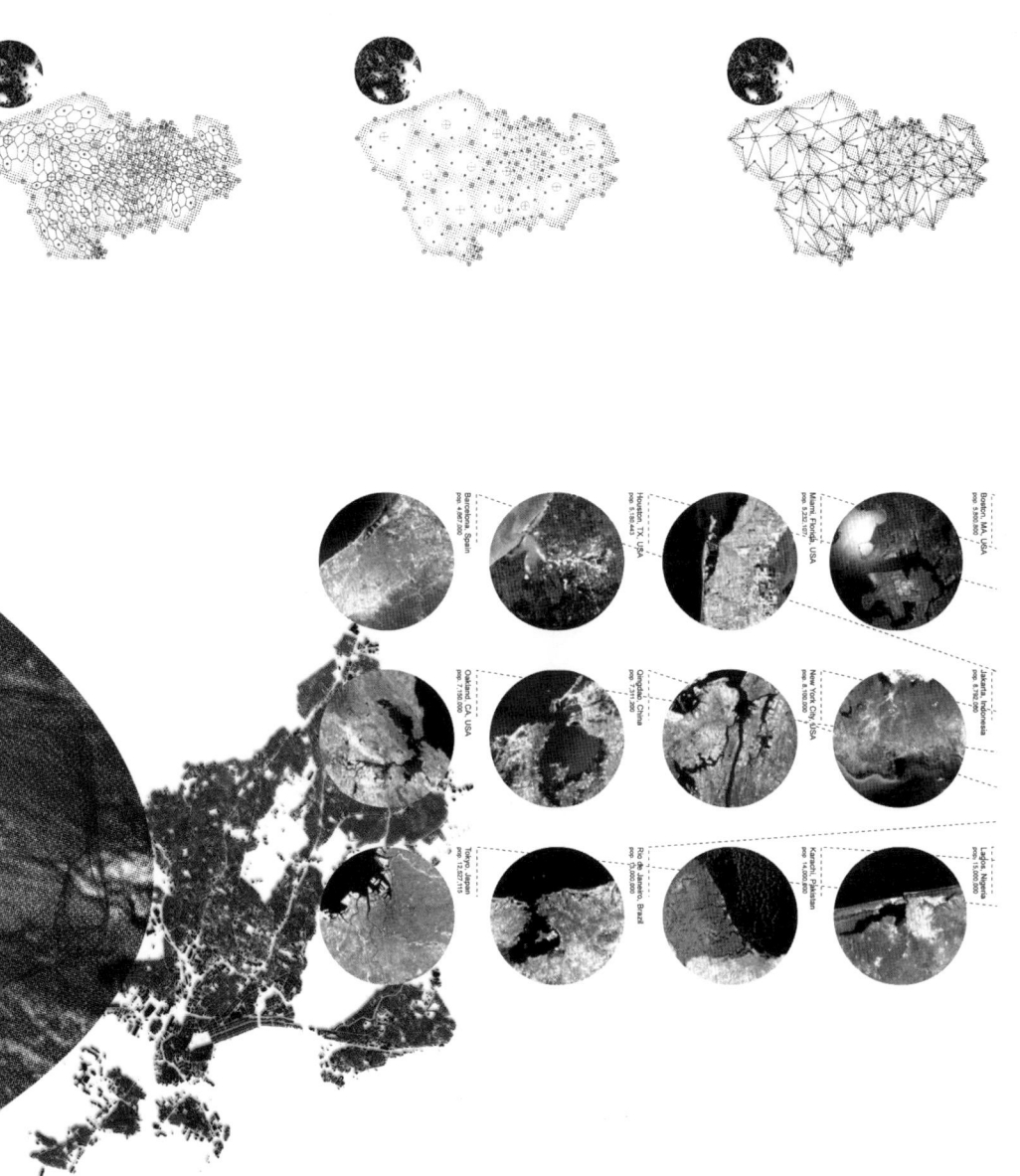

Barcelona, Spain
pop. 4,667,000

Houston, TX, USA
pop. 5,180,443

Miami, Florida, USA
pop. 5,332,1271

Boston, MA, USA
pop. 5,500,000

Oakland, CA, USA
pop. 7,150,000

Qingdao, China
pop. 7,311,200

New York City, USA
pop. 8,100,000

Jakarta, Indonesia
pop. 6,782,000

Tokyo, Japan
pop. 12,537,115

Rio de Janeiro, Brazil
pop. 9,000,000

Karachi, Pakistan
pop. 14,000,000

Lagos, Nigeria
pop. 13,500,000

Swell: A Proposition for Coastal Metropolises in the Age of Rising Seas and
Distributed Centralization - Talia Dorsey, MArch Thesis

59

Swell: A Proposition for Coastal Metropolises in the Age of Rising Seas and Distributed Centralization - Talia Dorsey, MArch Thesis

The Shanghai Studio: An Architecture of Tactical Refractions

Ann Pendleton Julian, Instructor
Neeraj Bhatia, TA
MArch Level III Studio 4.156
Spring 2006

In The Practice of Everyday Life, Michel de Certeau insists that the polarization of mind and body, or of public and private, is non-productive in the discussion of how we construct meaning in space, and ultimately how we constitute culture. He maintains that spatial engagements, both habitual in nature and sporadically practiced, aim at overcoming the alienation that is associated with conceptual/abstract space. "Space occurs as the effect produced by the operations that orient it, situate it, temporalize it, and make it function in a polyvalent unity of conflictual programs or contractual proximities . . . space is practiced place." In this position, there is a strong distinction made between abstract geometrical space and occupied anthropological space. Cultural identity is not a product of form that happens to accommodate space. Instead, "belonging" is constructed through the appropriation of space as a dynamic field of behavior. The architect's role then is anticipation of this dynamic field of behavior, the inlaying of new space into this field, and even inventing new possibilities for modes of appropriation.

The proposed studio will begin from this premise and focus on the relationship of architecture, city, and landscape in Shanghai. The site for the studio is along

the Suzhou River just north of the center of Shanghai. It is an area of tremendous diversity in program and development patterns, containing three existing warehouses that are significant from an historical vantage point because they belonged to the three principal banks of the colonial era. We will study the site from a programming perspective first and then take on the design of particular sites within the site at scales to be determined by each student. We will involve ourselves with issues of infrastructure, density, creative programming, and talk about complexity and variability within a discourse on micro-urbanism.

To take on this task in a manner in which abstract pattern making and rote programming are downplayed within the design process, we started the studio with a two-and-a half-week exercise on game strategy and game play. Through game playing, analysis and then the design of a strategically oriented game, it is intended that each student will develop a certain skill for rule based thinking, which can then be applied to thinking about the existing parameters of the Shanghai site, new intentions, and the inlay of new rules and program pieces relative to these existing parameters and conditions. After this preliminary stretch, the studio traveled to Shanghai (February 24 - March 5) to visit and study the site, "on the ground," and to make first contact with our twin studio that is taking place in Tongji University.

model by Stephen Perdue

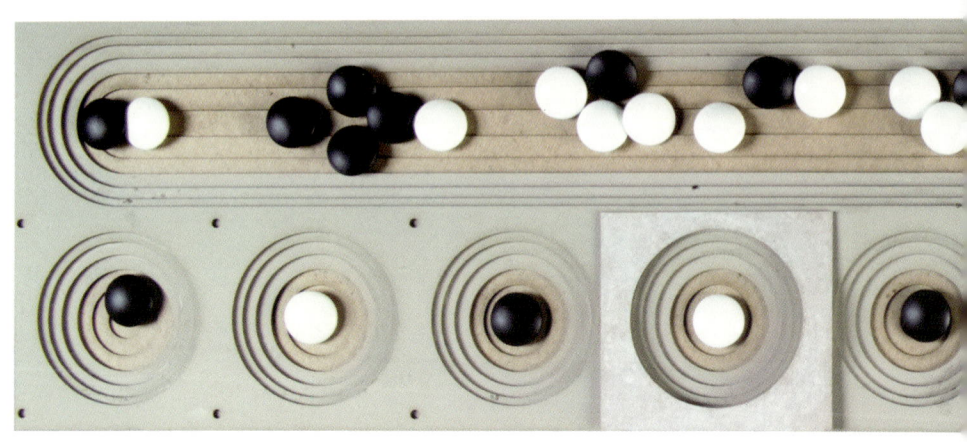

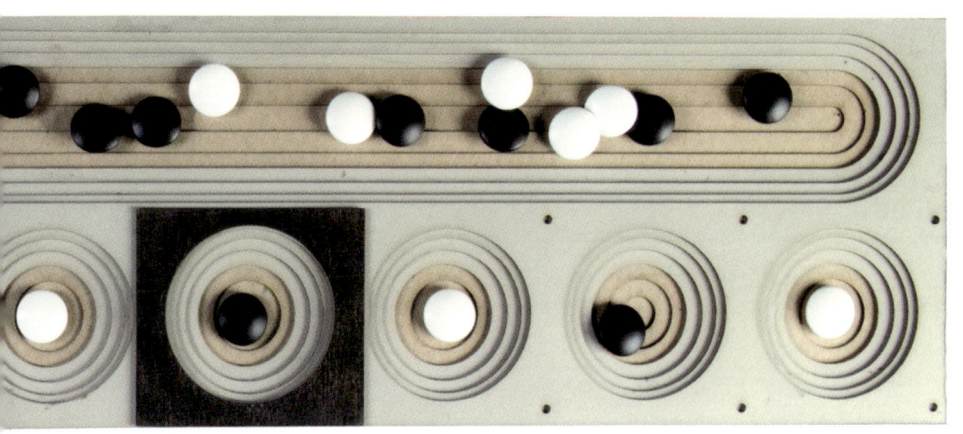

Strategic Game
Ophelia Wilkins, MArch III

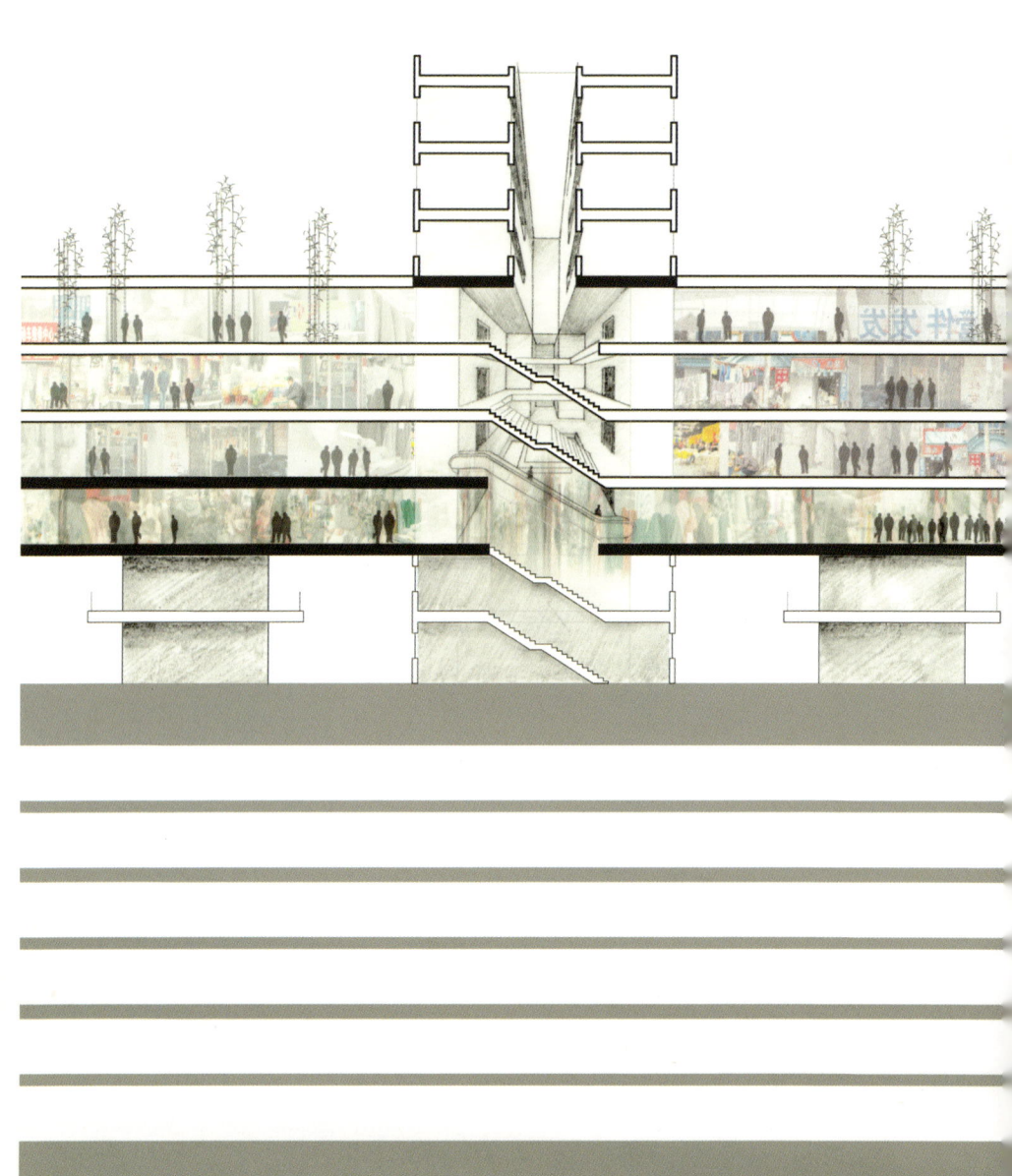

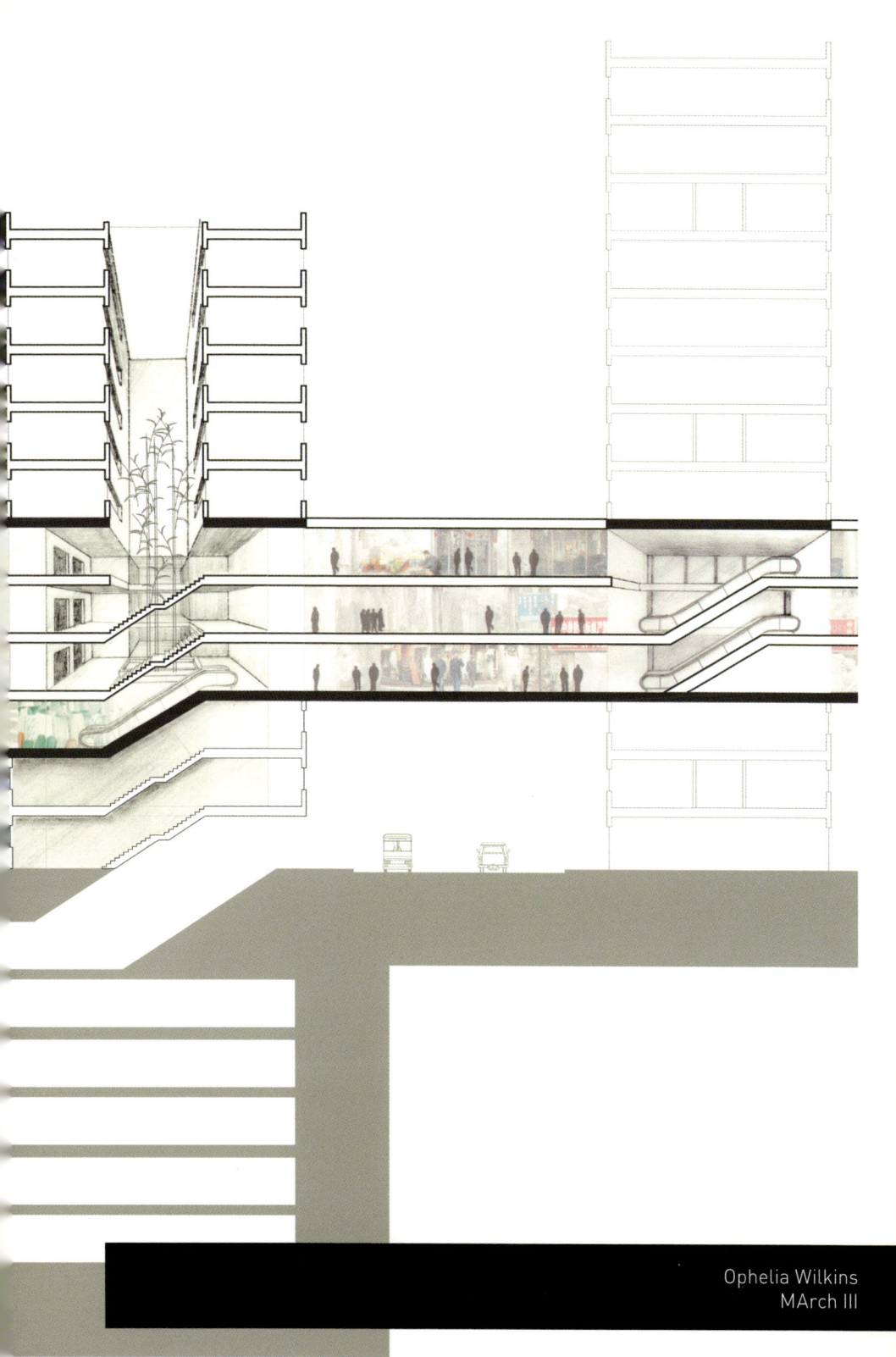

Ophelia Wilkins
MArch III

Stephen Perdue
MArch II

MAPPING

Inside the Sponge
Talia Dorsey and Carlo Ratti, Curators
Exhibition at the Canadian Centre for Architecture

In the quest of an adaptable built form :
studying transformations in the MIT Campus
Maria Zafeiriadou
SMArchS Thesis

digital_minimal
Carlo Ratti, Laura Knott, Gary Van Zante, Curators
Exhibition at the Wolk Gallery

Veneto Experience
Shun Kanda, Instructor
Undergraduate Design Workshop

Inside the Sponge

An Exhibition at the Canadian Centre for Architecture
Montreal, Quebec
Talia Dorsey and Carlo Ratti, Curators
Sarah Dunbar, David Foxe, Guy Hoffman, Jeff Roberts,
Researchers
Liang Hong '06, Ji-Eun Park '07, Jennifer Wong '06,
Simmons Hall Students
Ellen and John Essigmann, Simmons Hall
Housemasters

Simmons Hall is an award-winning university
dormitory designed by architect Steven Holl on
the MIT campus in Cambridge. Inspired by the sea
sponge and the concept of porosity, the building is
radical in structure and ambitious in its program to
encourage social interaction. Inside the Sponge is an
investigation of Simmons Hall from the perspective
of its residents, giving voice to MIT's student body
to draw a unique description of the building's life. It
proposes a dialogue between architectural intentions
and the process by which a community appropriates
space.

The exhibition features original materials and
research by Simmons Hall residents, including videos,
t-shirts, photographs, comics, and entries from the
popular student design competition to modify the
building, "How to Drill a Hole in Simmons Hall." New
technologies were deployed by the students to
analyze the demographics and patterns of activity
of the building's community, including the mapping
of wireless Internet usage, and the use of time-
bracketed photography to suggest the evolving quality
of the site over time. Presented in complement to the
students' work are original watercolors, drawings,
and a model from Steven Holl Architects which
describe the concept and development of the building.

photo by Guy Hoffman

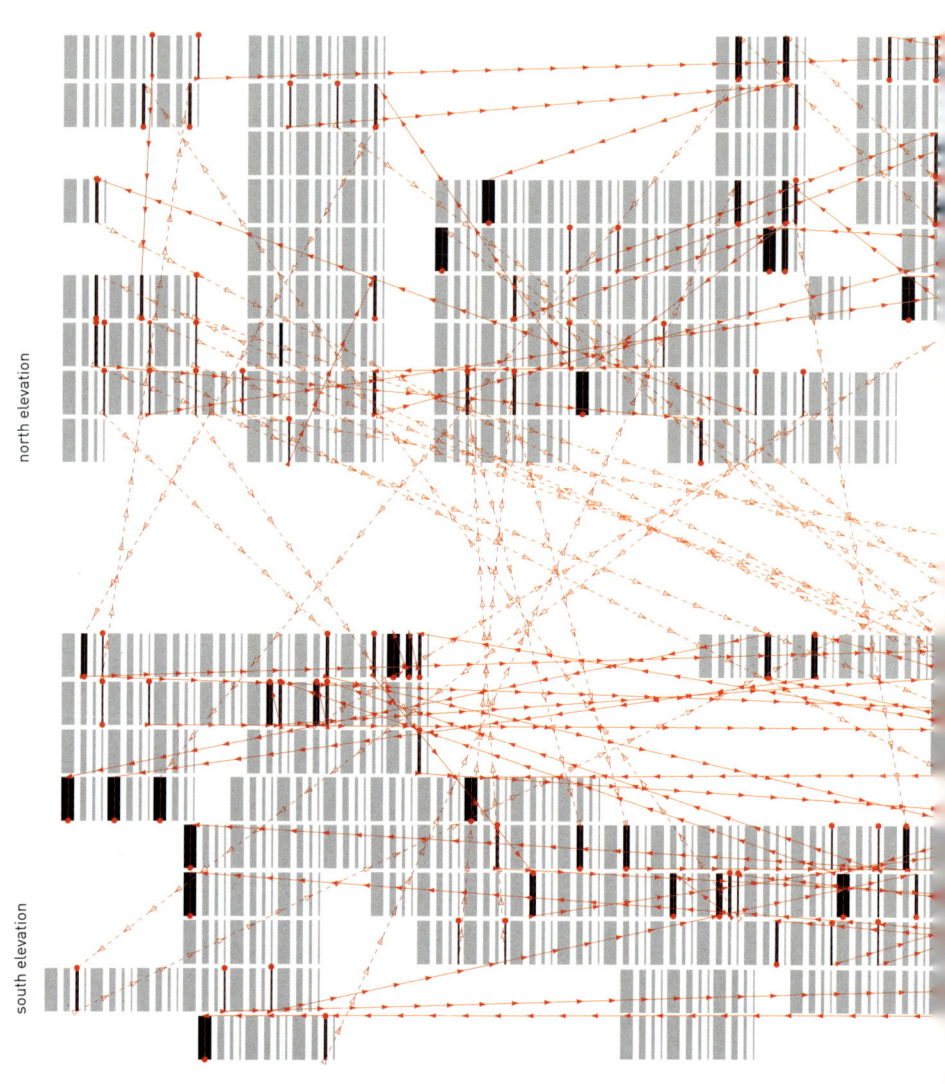

north elevation

south elevation

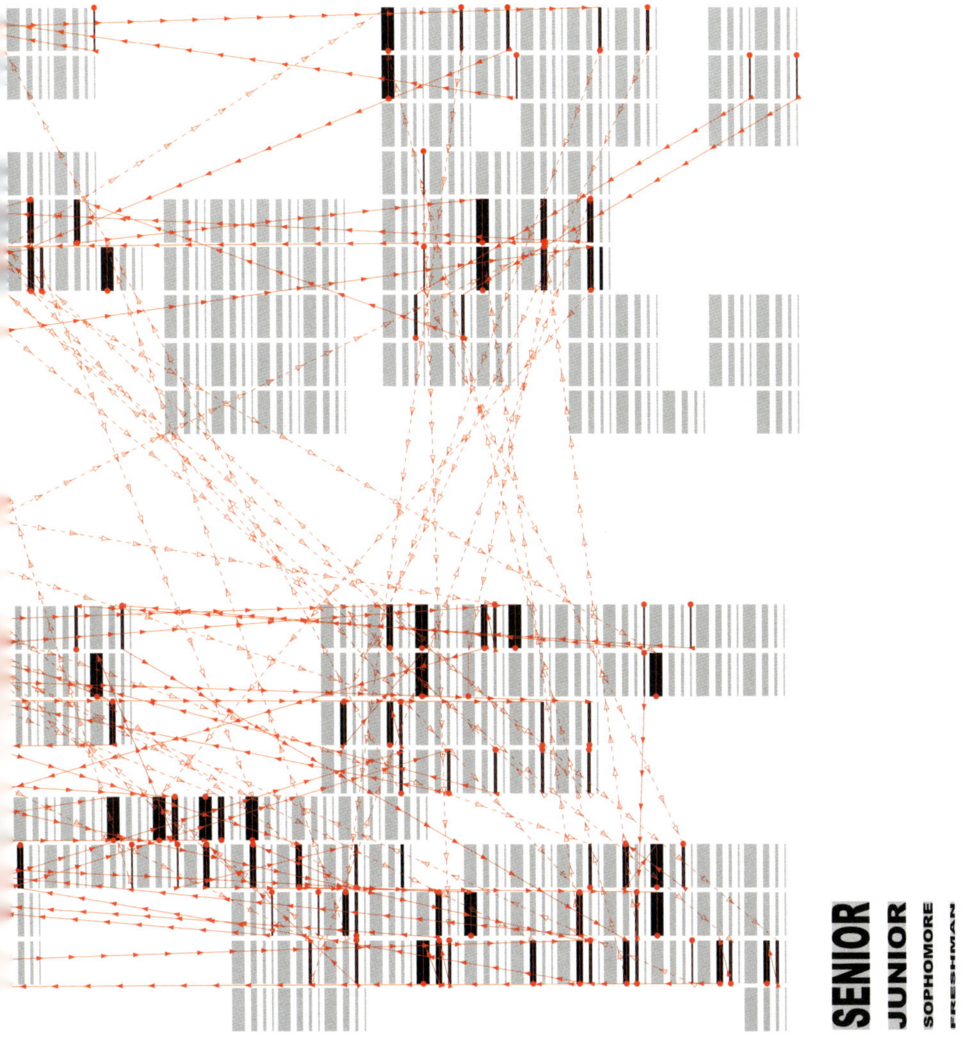

SENIOR
JUNIOR
SOPHOMORE
FRESHMAN

Movement of one class over four years
Talia Dorsey & Sarah Dunbar, MArch II

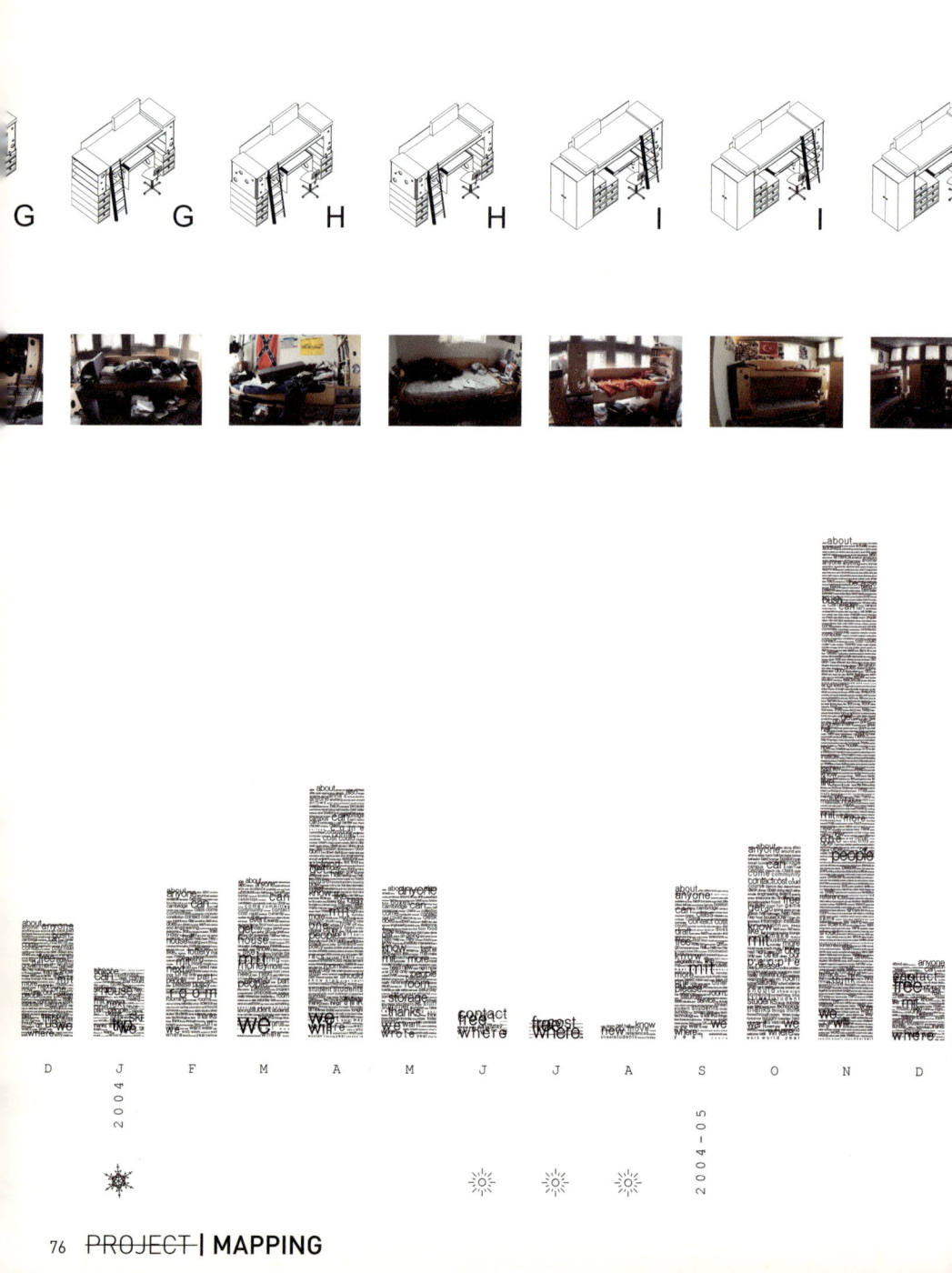

G G H H I I

D J F M A M J J A S O N D

2004

2004-05

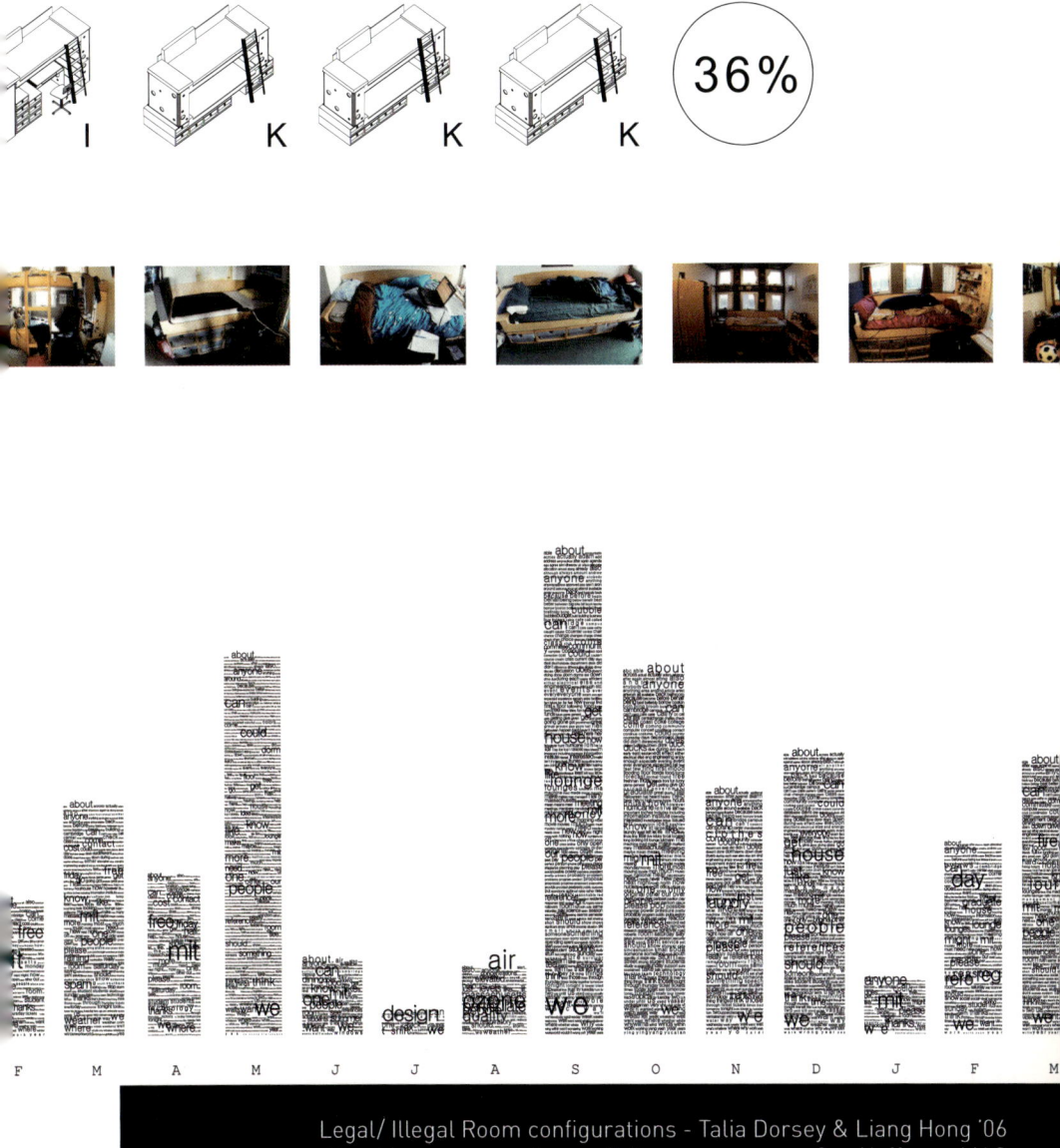

36%

I K K K

Legal/ Illegal Room configurations - Talia Dorsey & Liang Hong '06
Word frequency on SpongeTalk over one year - Guy Hoffman, MAS

In the quest of an adaptable built form : studying transformations in the MIT Campus

Maria Zafeiriadou
SMArchS Thesis
Julian Beinart, Advisor
John de Monchaux, Reader
Spring 2006

Adaptability of the built form has for a long time been the concern of many designers. Driven by different motives such as the accommodation of "uncertainty," the pursue of an "economical space", the restoration of the user's "control" over the form, and the pursue of "fit," designers and scholars have proposed various formal means in order to achieve an architecture that would provide for change. The purpose of this thesis is to add to this discussion, proposing particular design strategies. In order to do this, transformations are documented and measured in the Main Buildings of the MIT Campus, which have often been cited for their ability to accommodate change. The thesis hypothesizes that the buildings in question contained in their body a certain DNA that enabled them to transform easily and effectively. Through the analysis of the original system of buildings and its transformations, which are divided into the two categories of growth and internal change, this DNA is exposed and juxtaposed to the formal means that have been suggested in the ideas of designers and scholars.

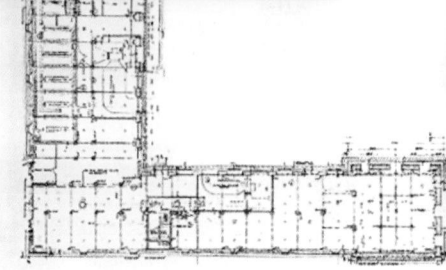

(cont.) The DNA is argued to consist of stems, knuckles, "unit-sections," courts, add-on facades and an underlying circulation system. The result of this thesis is a tested, in terms of effectiveness, series of specific formal means, comprised of MIT's DNA and the other designers' propositions, which can be outlined as three general strategies; provision of extra space, "open- endedness" and delineation of a comprehensive framework along which transformations can take place. At the same time, a physical history of the early years of the Cambridge Campus is produced, ranging from 1912 to 1933.

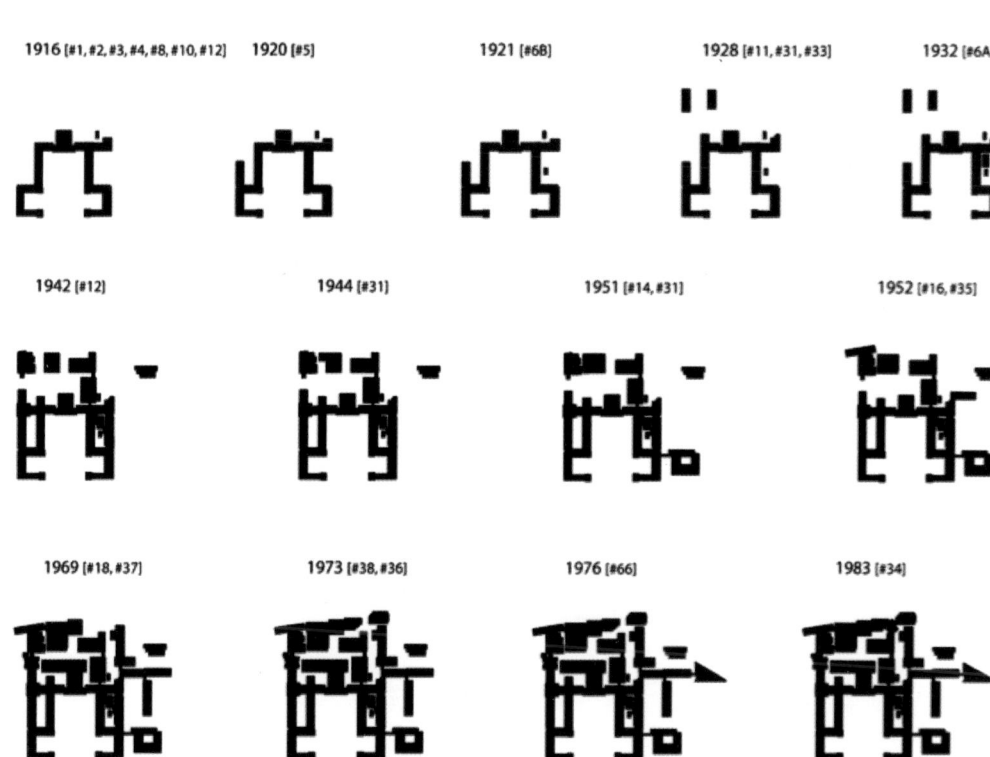

1916 [#1, #2, #3, #4, #8, #10, #12]   1920 [#5]   1921 [#6B]   1928 [#11, #31, #33]   1932 [#6A]

1942 [#12]   1944 [#31]   1951 [#14, #31]   1952 [#16, #35]

1969 [#18, #37]   1973 [#38, #36]   1976 [#66]   1983 [#34]

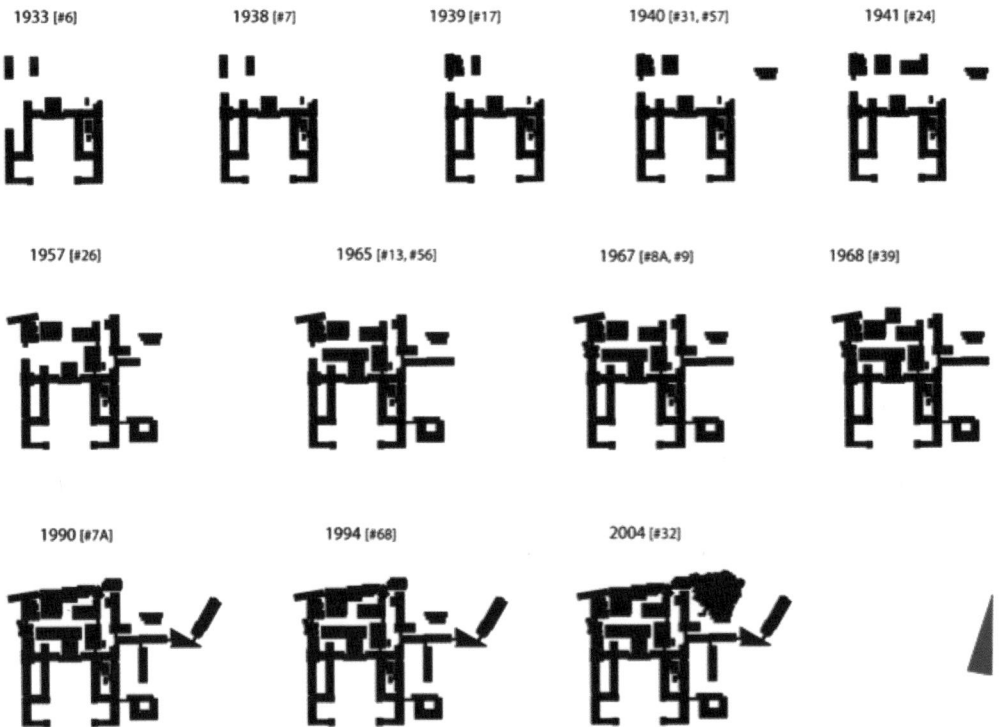

1933 [#6]　1938 [#7]　1939 [#17]　1940 [#31, #57]　1941 [#24]

1957 [#26]　1965 [#13, #56]　1967 [#8A, #9]　1968 [#39]

1990 [#7A]　1994 [#68]　2004 [#32]

In the quest of an adaptable built form : studying transformations in the MIT
Campus - Maria Zafeiriadou, SMArchS Thesis

81

Although the new MIT was a unified mega- structure, the buildings were designed separately [20]. Each building had its own number, this enumeration being different than it is today, and the overall number of the buildings without the wings that got built was 12. At the points where these buildings met, namely on the vertices of the invisible grid of the initial scheme, the staircases and elevators were located. The only exceptions were an elevator in Building 8 and a staircase in Building 1. This created a system of spaces that concentrated vertical movement, namely **joints or knuckles**, and of spaces that were void of any permanent structure of such nature, namely **stems [21- 22] [Quote 3]**. The types of stems that finally got built were 3, less that in the initial scheme.

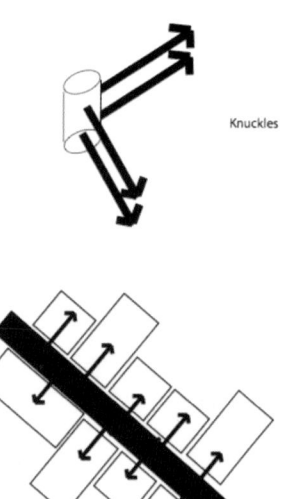

Knuckles

Stems

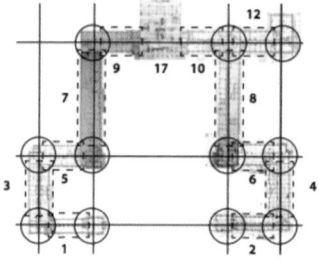

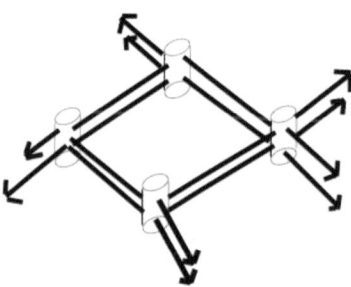

Fig. 33: Circulation System Diagram

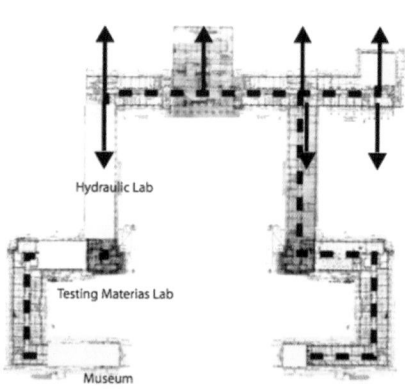

Hydraulic Lab

Testing Materias Lab

Museum

Fig. 34: Circulation System on the First Floor.

In the quest of an adaptable built form : studying transformations in the MIT Campus - Maria Zafeiriadou, SMArchS Thesis

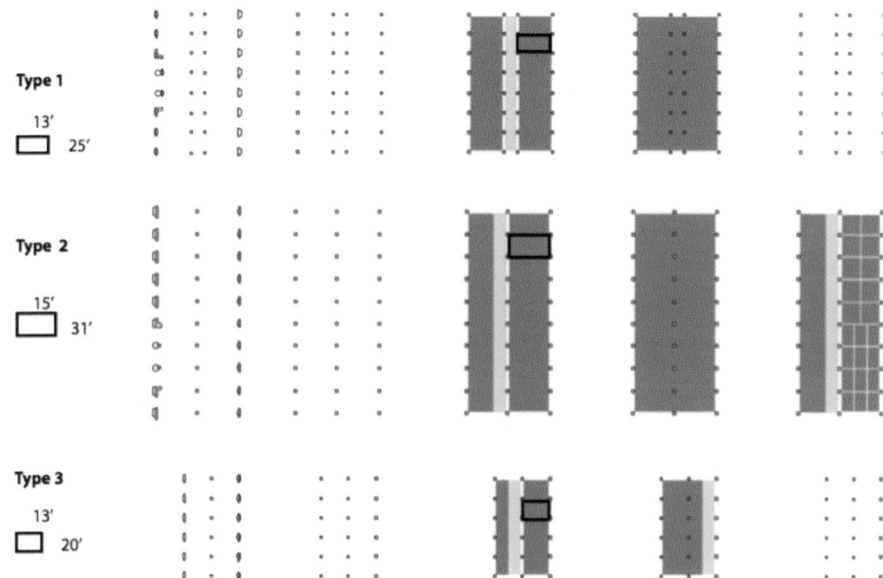

Type 1

13'
☐ 25'

Type 2

15'
☐ 31'

Type 3

13'
☐ 20'

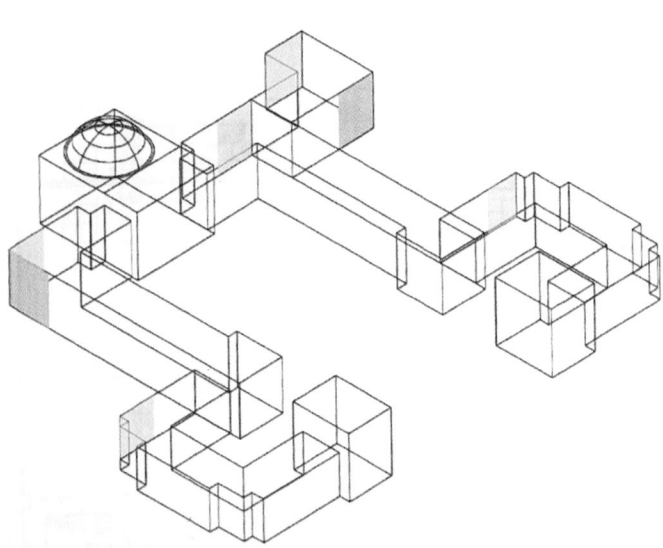

Diagrams of methods and means for growth.
Maria Zafeiriadou, SMArchS Thesis

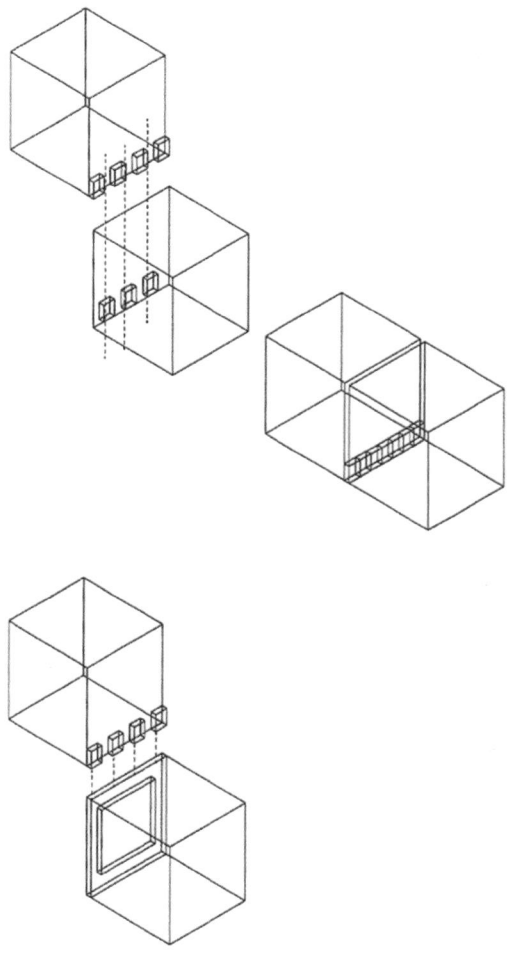

Add-on facades
Different degrees of elaboration permit different degrees of growth.

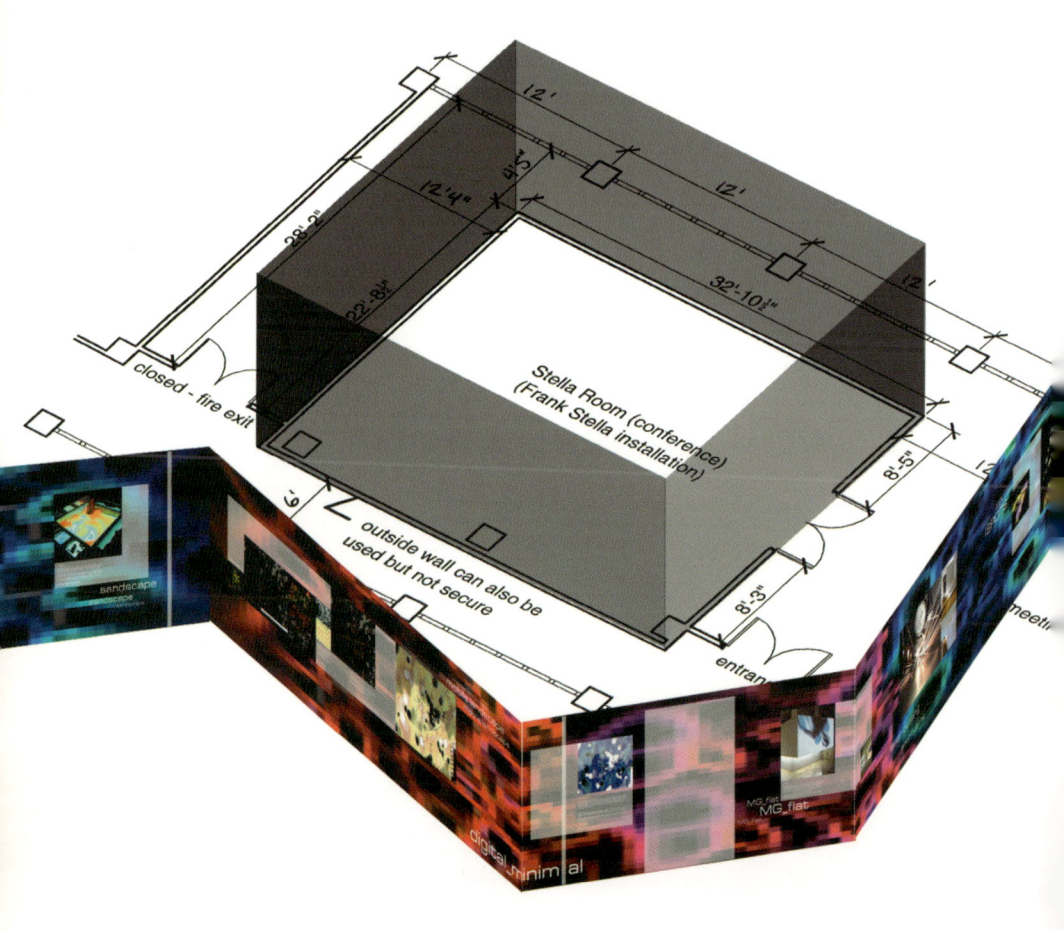

closed - fire exit

12'

12'4"

28'-2"

22'-8½"

8'

12'

32'-10½"

12'

Stella Room (conference)
(Frank Stella installation)

8'-5"

9'

7'

outside wall can also be
used but not secure

entran

meeti

3'-3"

8'

sandscape

digital_minim al

MG_flat
MG_flat

digital_minimal

Carlo Ratti, Laura Knott, Gary Van Zante, Curators
Projects by: SENSEable city lab, **carloratti**associati
February 10th- March 29th 2006

What will be the legacy of the digital revolution in architecture and planning? In the past few years the academic and professional debate has focused primarily on form-making. The digital_minimal exhibition explores a number of possible future directions, from the use of mobile devices that describe urban space in real-time to new tangible user interfaces that redefine the design process.

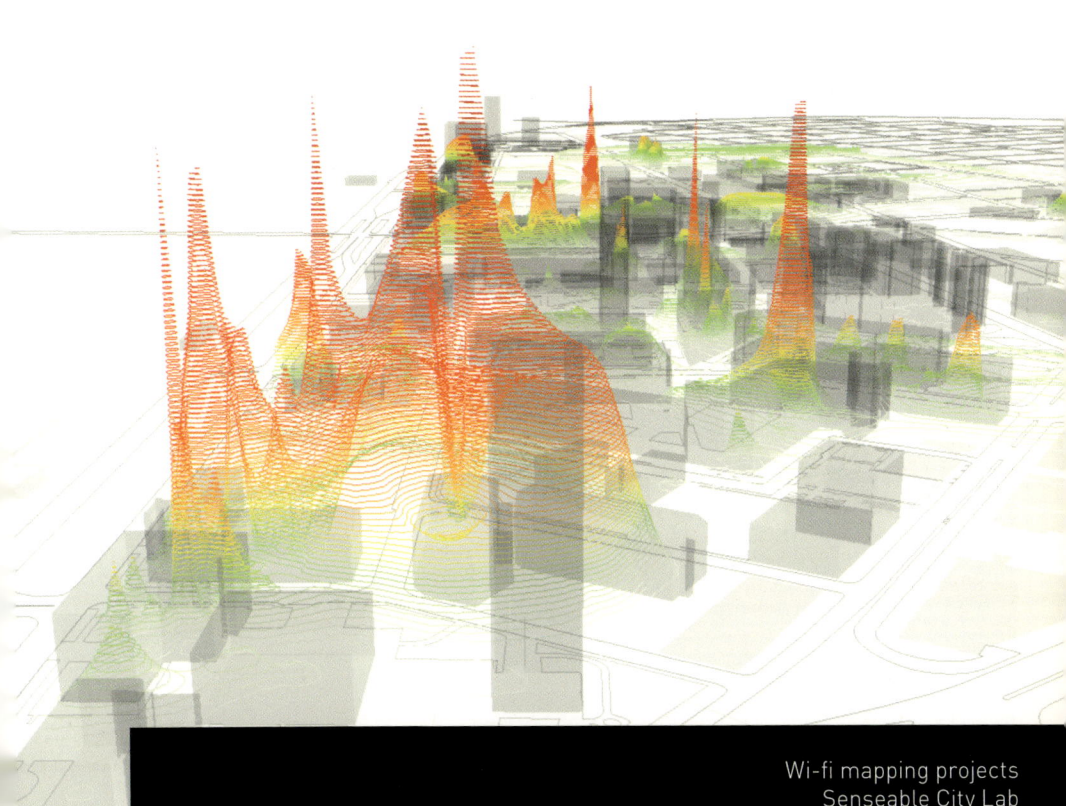

Wi-fi mapping projects
Senseable City Lab

Veneto Experience

Shun Kanda, Instructor
Undergraduate Design Workshop
Summer 2006

The pedagogy of the Veneto Experience flows
essentially from focusing on the intricate and
profound relationship between the life-work of
Venetian architect Carlo Scarpa (1906-1978)
and Venice, each embodied in the other. In the
process we will discover much more, including
the intersections of formal synthesis and
phenomenology; of space, time and place;
of inspired creativity and production.

The Veneto Experience is offered for students
interested in design at diverse scales of
architecture, landscape and city design. By
engaging in extensive fieldwork in and around
Venice, with particular conversion on three
projects by Scarpa, the program provides
opportunities to develop critical thinking in
relating the power of place to design. Various
students and faculty from MIT and other
international universities collaborate on design
exercises, presentations and documentation
during a three-week sojourn in Veneto, Italy.

The workshop is held annually in Winter, Summer
and Fall. The Veneto Experience is directed by
Professor Shun Kanda of the Department of
Architecture at MIT, assisted by other faculty,
professionals and artisans in Venice.

PROPAGANDA

Propaganda focuses on the broadcasting, as eloquent and convincing as possible, of a proposition in architecture. Although associated with totalitarian regimes, propaganda is also essential to architectural discourse. Architects relentlessly need to convince their clients of the desirability, yes the outright necessity of the unconventional, possibly innovative, non-standardized solution they propose. Propositions in architecture assert themselves primarily through design projects. Propaganda, therefore, deploys statements, through forms that take advantage of the full spectrum of aesthetic techniques required to pervasively get across an a priori message: the architectural intent or parti that structures the entire project.

The study of Process does the opposite: it questions whether the propositions we come up with as architects are not within themselves extremely limited, bounded by bureaucratic codes, architectural conventions, social consensus and older technologies. Investigations into process aim to take apart these imprisoning standards in order to arrive at a capacity to produce propositions that lie beyond the realm of historical precedent.

If propaganda is about eloquence in speech, process is about the structure of language itself. While propaganda studies rhethoric, process focuses on the development of a critical path along which previously inconceivable propositions can, almost by accident, by discovered. Both agendas are equally scientific (or not).

PROCESS

Theoretically, one would argue that process comes first, and only after does one develop a propaganda apparatus to make the case for the idea. However, history proves otherwise. Entire lineages of architectural history up until the present have developed their ideas primarily by building an apparatus of propaganda: the building of the external message coincided with the construction of the template of the project itself. The modernist movement, as it canonized itself through the CIAM conferences, provides a crystal clear example. So in architecture too, the medium becomes the message. Just as a concept only enters consciousness and is fully grasped at the moment when it is eloquently worded, so also an architectural proposition can only be understood when eloquently phrased. Therein lies the basic disciplinary autonomy of architecture.

Process suggests experimentation with form, program, and technology, with a pre-set goal – its focus is to find unexpected discoveries on the experiment's trajectory. Propaganda assumes that a priori templates that we already possess deserve clear articulation first. Process assumes an almost objective autonomy of the forms discovered and assumes no value judgments; Propaganda accepts that architecture exists only in a realm of value judgments, and that architectural discourse is simply a conversation, going on through centuries, where each participant attempts to clarify a point of view and convince other debaters to join up. Of course, process and propaganda are both part of an architecture of integrity. They are two parts of the same dialectic.

PROPAGANDA

Boston Metabolism
Instructors, Alexander D'Hooghe, Mark Jarzombek
Workshop 4.181

New Radiant City
Instructors, Yung Ho Chang, Alexander D'Hooghe,
Mark Jarzombek
MArch Level III Studio 4.155

**M49-- Machine for the Living : a performance broad-
cast through an interfering FM radio transmission**
Max Goldfarb
SMVisS Thesis

Studio Seminar in Public Art
Instructor, Antonio Muntadas
Workshop 4.367

Boston Metabolism

Alexander D'Hooghe, Mark Jarzombek, Instructors
Workshop 4.181
Spring 2006

Architectural urbanism has, over the last two decades, regressed into complacency. It is now suffering from endless compromise, a stifling desire to please everybody, and as a result has given up its own propellant, which was to provide an alternative to the status quo of (post) urban development.

In this partnership between critical and projective thought, we will search to liberate ourselves from this hideous consensus. We will propose a series of radical revisions of the form of the city, In order to do so, we need to return to the moment preceding the complacent turn: late modernism.

In the 1960s, Kenzo Tange taught at MIT where he worked out ideas of Metabolism and Brutalism that lay behind his famous "Plan for Tokyo 1960." The studio he taught at MIT was entitled "25,000 People Over Boston." We think it is time to return to some of these ideas and critically assess them, but also to see in what way a "mega-structure-city," or a "floating city" can reinvigorate urban thinking. The knitting together of infrastructure and urbanism is a necessity, but why does it have to be subservient to gravity, especially in an era of rapid population growth and rising land prices? And why not right here in Boston, known as one of the most conservative architectural cities in the world!

The workshop will use techniques of surrealism, including montages of popular culture and found objects, to drive the development of a quasi-realistic urban project. It will thus place itself in a long and honorable tradition of architectural contemplation about the status quo of the city, as found in the works of Fluxus, Archigram, Superstudio, etc.

The apocalypse is happening: It is just that we haven't noticed. Boston's endless low-quality housing stock has become too expensive for its citizens; many of its public infrastructures are in abysmal shape; in short it is a city stuck in the 19th century completely unequipped for the destabilizations of the 21st century. Pre-emptive action is necessary without further delay.

image by Saba Ghole

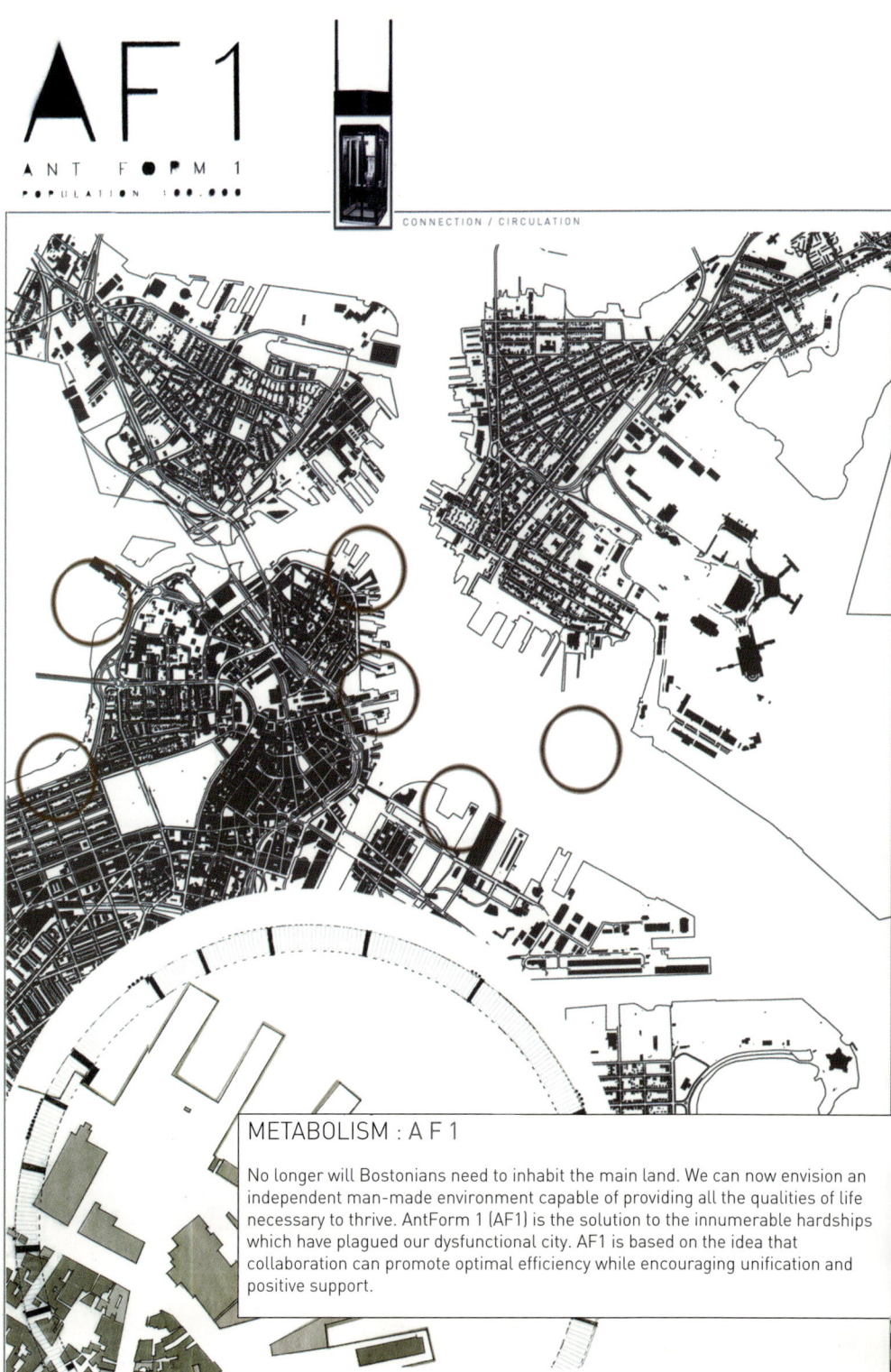

AF 1

ANT FORM 1

POPULATION 100,000

METABOLISM : A F 1

No longer will Bostonians need to inhabit the main land. We can now envision an independent man-made environment capable of providing all the qualities of life necessary to thrive. AntForm 1 (AF1) is the solution to the innumerable hardships which have plagued our dysfunctional city. AF1 is based on the idea that collaboration can promote optimal efficiency while encouraging unification and positive support.

AF1
ANT FORM 1
электрификация всей страны

METABOLISM : AF1
Justin Shea, MArch II

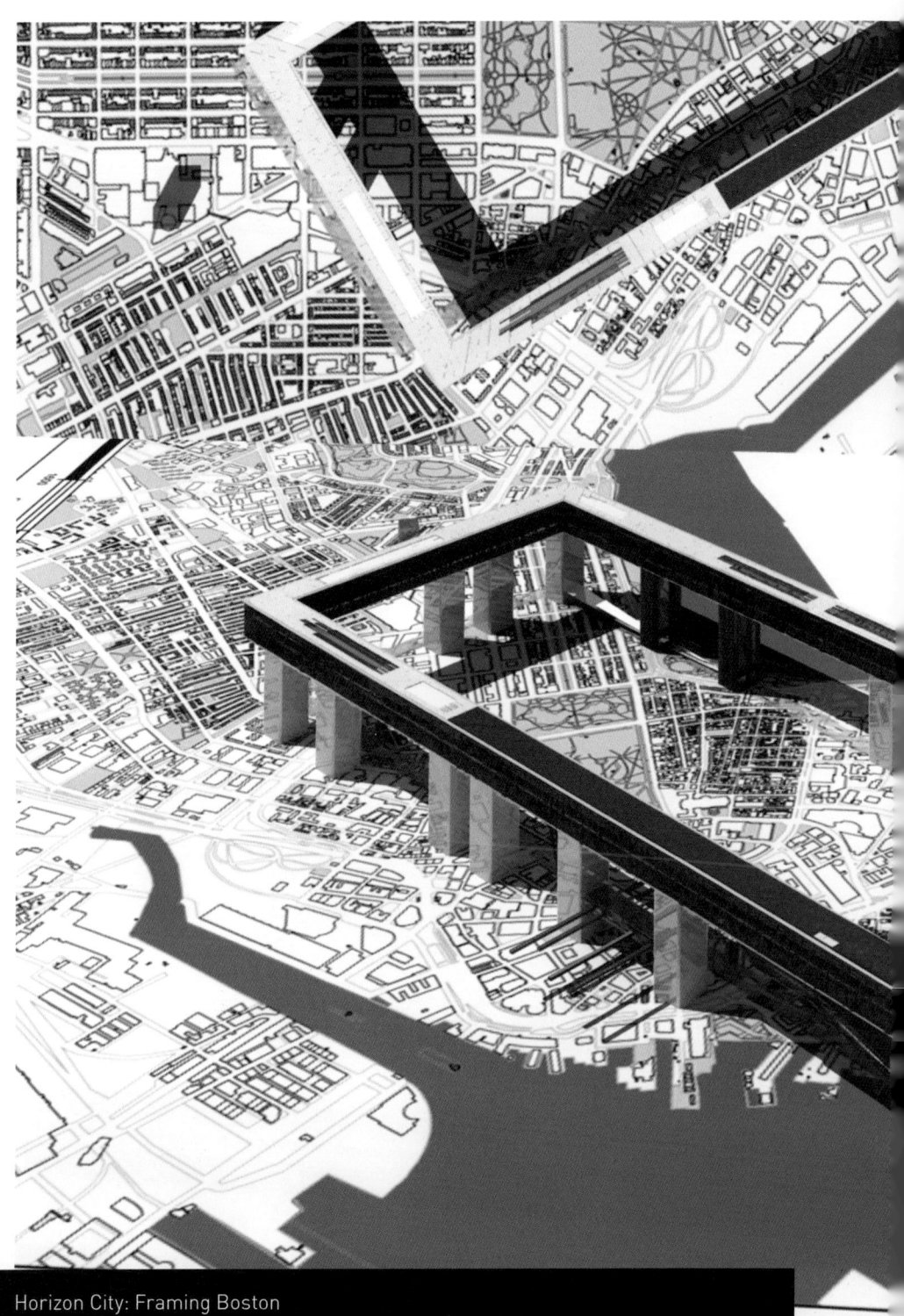

Horizon City: Framing Boston
Saba Ghole, SMArchS

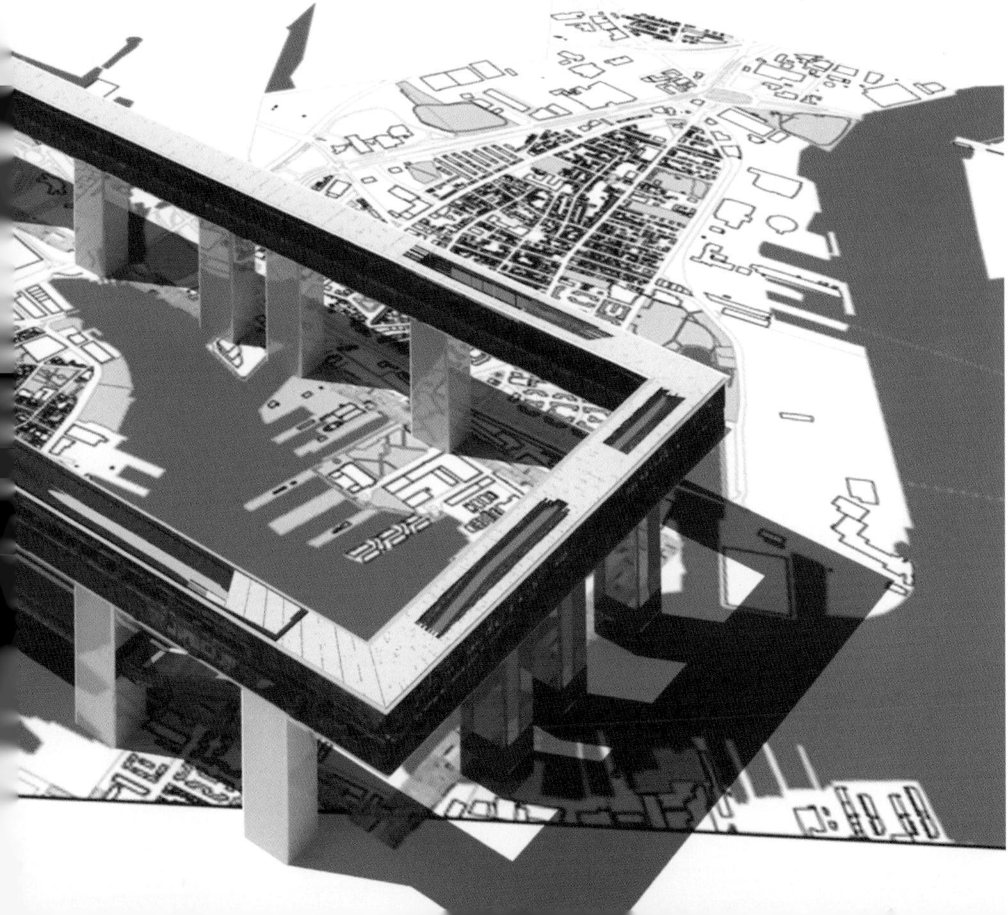

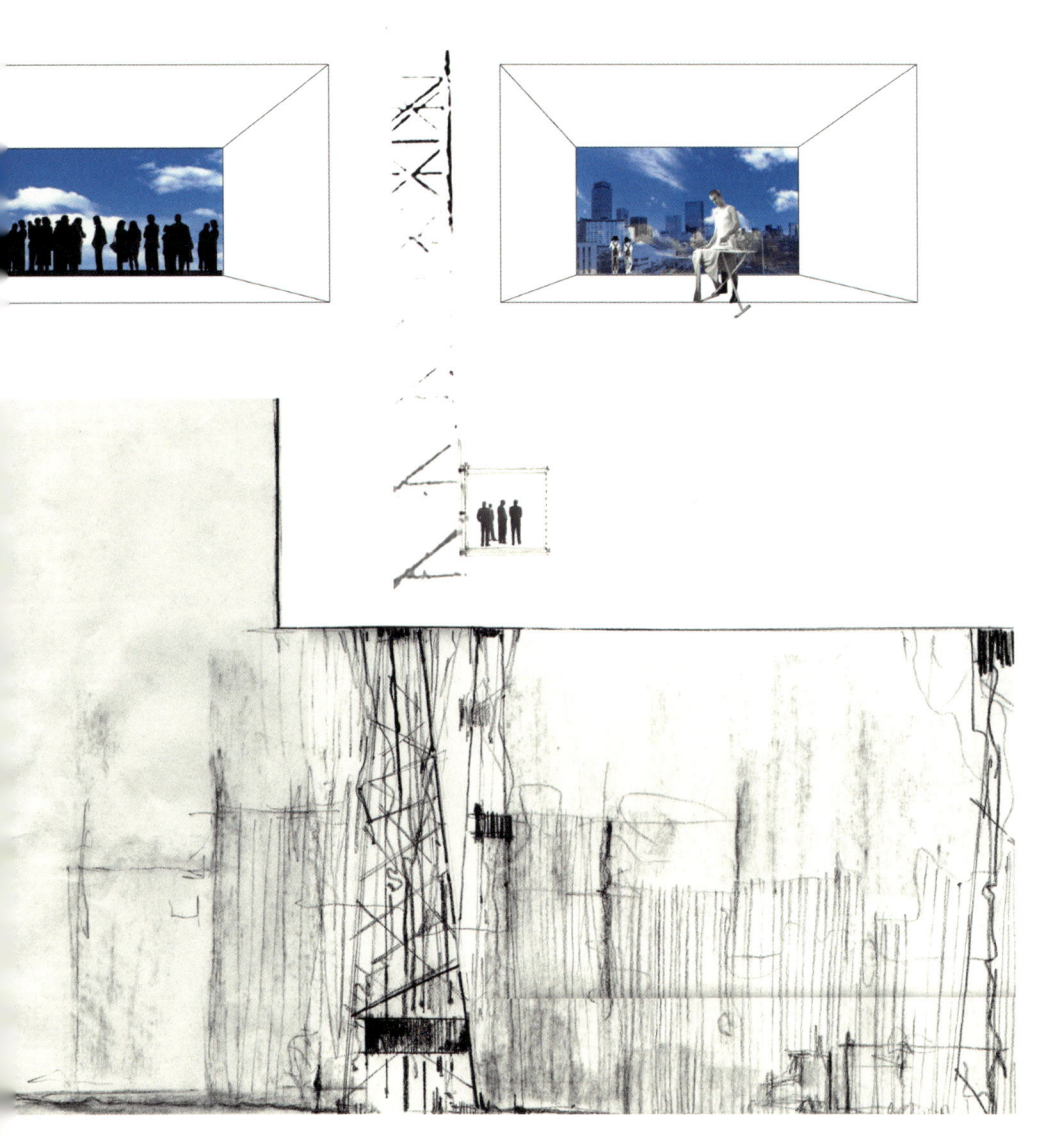

Rebecca Edson
MArch III

New Radiant City

Yung Ho Chang, Alexander D'Hooghe and
Mark Jarzombek, Instructors
MArch Level III Studio 4.155
Fall 2006

Le Corbusier's Radiant City of 1925 broke the hold of emotionalism on the city. Curved streets, picturesque layouts, alleés and majestic civic structures were X-ed out. Instead the city was seen through the lens of science and pragmatism corresponding to the precepts of the modern age. It was a powerful moment in the history of thinking about urban design. Le Corbusier looked at the city not as just an improvement or clarification of older prototypes, but with new categories all together: living, work, traffic and leisure. At the center was the modern Man.

Though this served at the time as an excellent strategy to dismember the nineteenth century city, it did not create a new unity. The failure of Le Corbusier's urbanism - and of CIAM principles in general – lay in the circumstance that it assumed that leisure was separate from work, living separate from industry, and the city separate from the rural.

In the 1960s, with the failures of cities looming over history, cities' developed Masterplans as a way to restore confidence in the future, to create a sense of destiny and common purpose. Traditionally, the Master Plan had been merely the basis upon which the zoning ordinance, site usage regulations were defined. Now they began to include questions of tourism and local culture. City centers were no longer to be torn down arbitrarily, but were to be preserved as cultural environments. In that sense, the ideals of

2006

1980

the modernist city came to be fused with the
remnants of the traditional city. Holding this together
was the image of a city that was not too modern
and not too old. THIS became the prototype of the
contemporary Masterplan that is still in use today,
part rationalism, part neo-sentimentality. But the
Masterplan always promised more than it could
deliver. Most preserved the notion of static square
blocks; most preserved the notion of individual
buildings conforming to conventions of land
ownership. Most Masterplans did not accept their
artificiality, aspiring as they do to simulate organic
modernity. It is against this equation that we protest.

Thinking back to Le Corbusier's Radiant City,
there is one aspect that we admire: the critique of
sentimentality. In our design for the New Radiant City
we want to challenge the sentimentality that has crept
back into the equation in most Masterplans since the
1970s.

The New Radiant City does not even have to determine
all that is built or even how it is built. The New Radiant
City does, however, have to commit itself to the
principles of OUR age. The new city is both a scientific
project and an imaginary one. It is confirmed in the
languages of knowledge and projected in the images
of the mind.

The New Radiant city, therefore, is a project for a
NEW ideal city for 200,000+ people, based on a series
of categories that can replace those of the CIAM
movement. The essence of the task is the grafting of
a large-scale settlement figure, thus establishing a
territorial order that effectively structures form but
does not micromanage program.

Shenzhen Population Growth
by Sarah Dunbar
*each square represents 1000 people

The solid block building envelope

A series of Fluxspaces are subtrac
from the massing for direct appro
tion beyond the reach of authority

The city is stratefied into three
distinct layers.

Residential Program
Private and communal residences and hotels

Narrow Programs
Leisure activities, commercial
enterprises, offices and institutions

Broad Programs
Industry, agriculture,
infrastructure and storage

Guangming New Radiant Hyper-Dense City
Coryn Kempster, MArch III

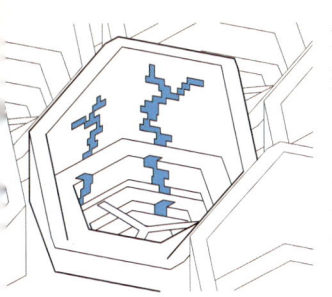

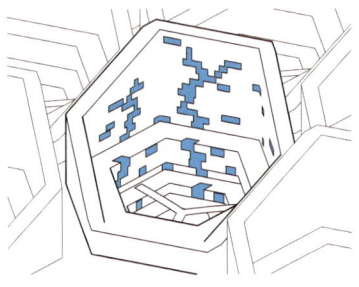

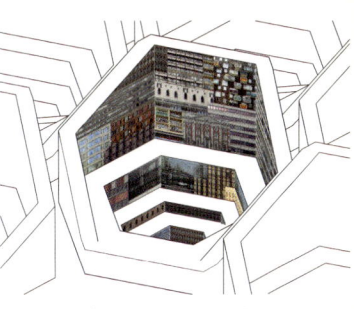

etwork of Mixspace is subtracted
n the massing of the typical block
eate public circulation throughout
eight; a Vertical Groundplane

The resulting porous block built for
navigation and appropriation

Liberated from the groundplane, de-
velopers may build out any contiguous
volume within the building envlope

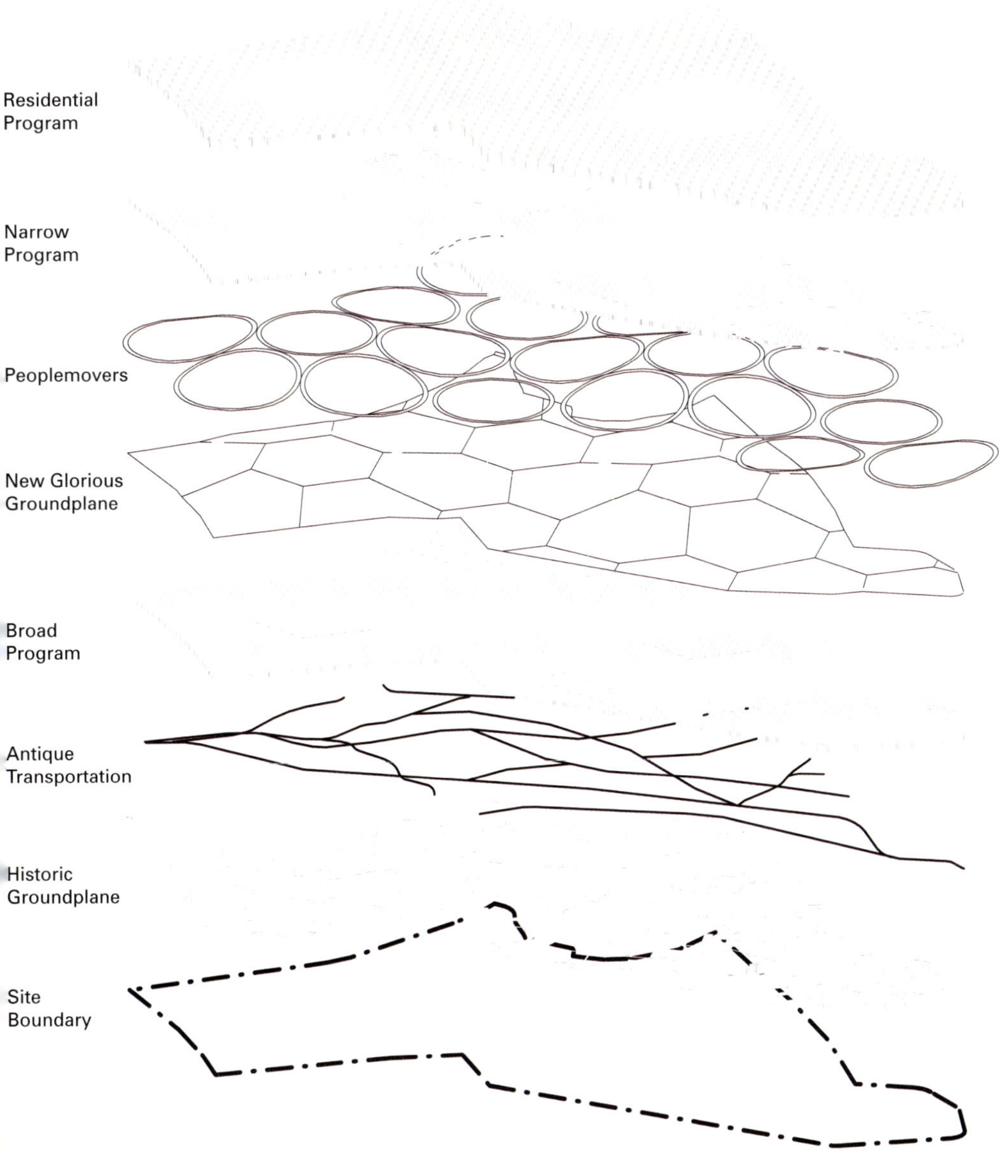

Residential
Program

Narrow
Program

Peoplemovers

New Glorious
Groundplane

Broad
Program

Antique
Transportation

Historic
Groundplane

Site
Boundary

Courtyard Urbanism
the city is arranged as a network
of dense, public courtyards

Guangming New Radiant Hyper-Dense City
Coryn Kempster, MArch III

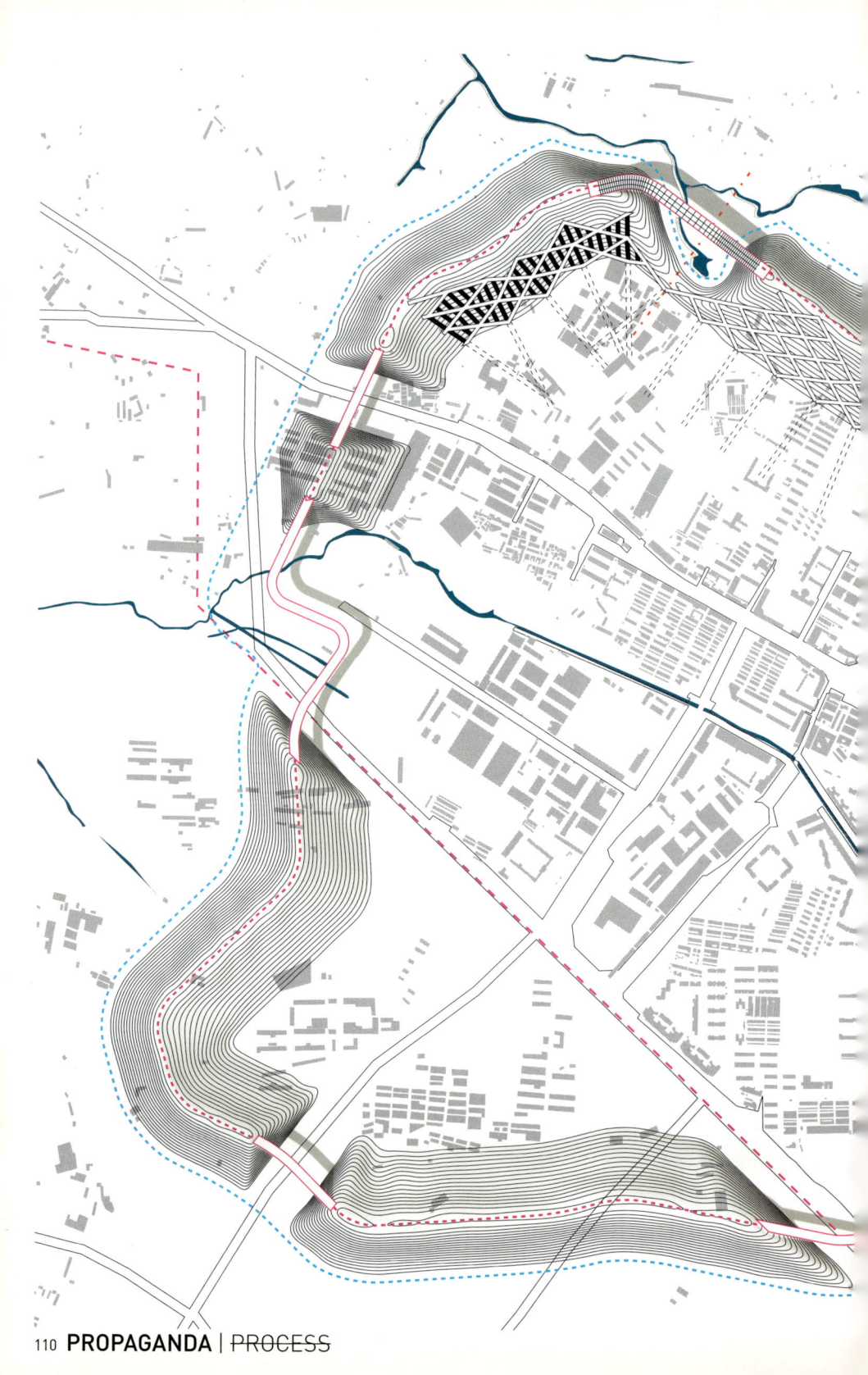

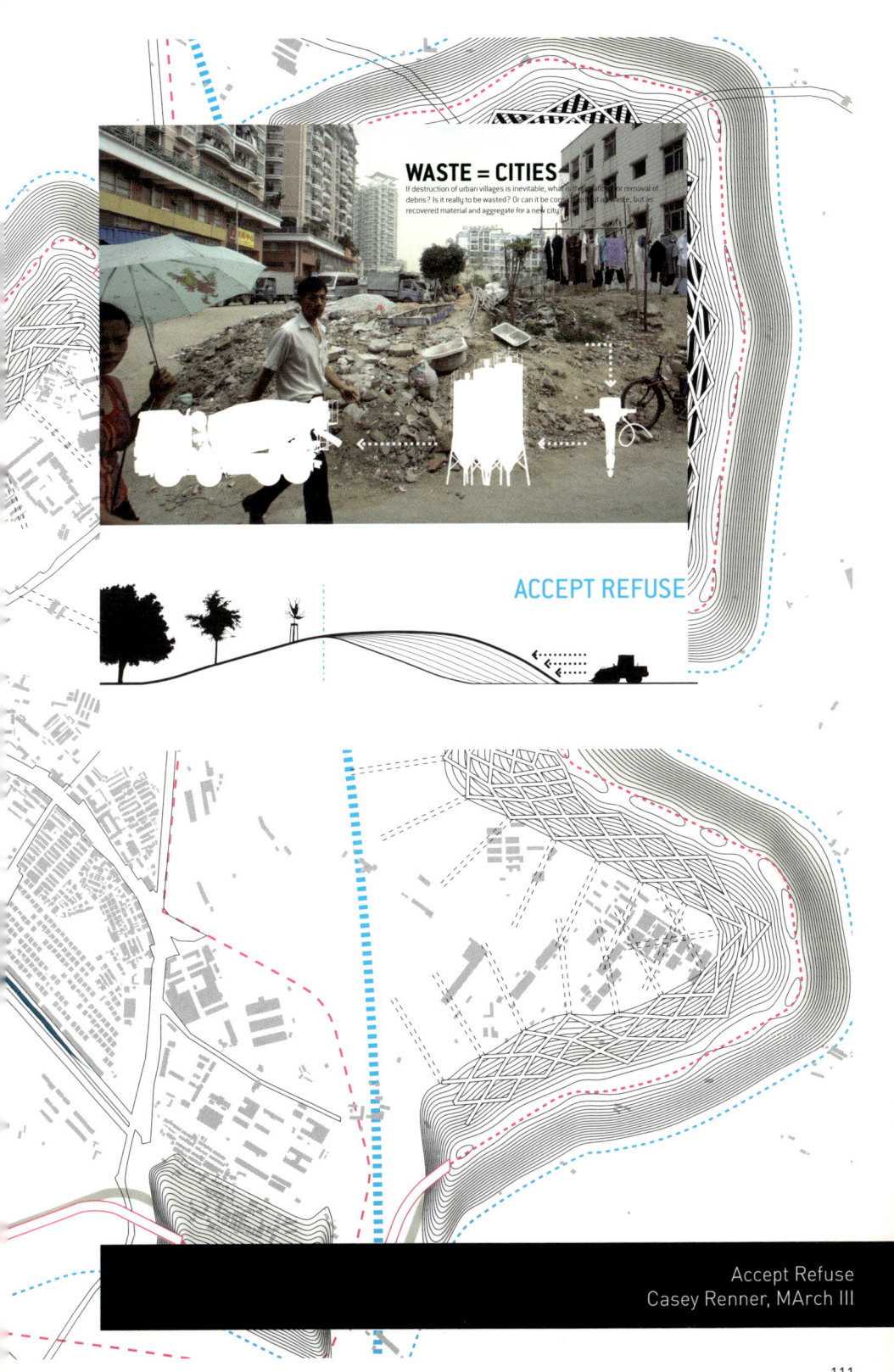

WASTE = CITIES

If destruction of urban villages is inevitable, what is the fate of or removal of debris? Is it really to be wasted? Or can it be conceived of as waste, but as recovered material and aggregate for a new city?

ACCEPT REFUSE

Accept Refuse
Casey Renner, MArch III

Accept Refuse
Casey Renner MArch III

M49: Machine for the Living
A Performance Broadcast through an Interfering FM Radio Transmission

Maximilian M. Goldfarb
SMVisS Thesis
Joan Jonas, Advisor
Fall 2006

The focus of the M49: Machine For The Living project is a performance work that considers the omnipresence of layered communications, which extend, yet supersede corporeal space of the individual. M49 creates a framework to reveal the convergence of immaterial communication with the built environment through an interfering radio transmission. The performance elucidates conceptual boundaries revealed in the breakdown of a system. The project investigates effects of the sub-visible ambiance that overlaps and engulfs structures of urban inhabitation. "What appears in the cathedral of radio noise is an image of the individual as a machine making meaning in a feedback loop between human and alien forces. Without any point of reference or authority, the individual must decode the ether daily, or at least what is transmitted through the so-called ether for human ends. Daily, we work at separating meaning out from the multi-dimensional ether-sphere with its uncanny plenitude of signals that surround us, while the actual electromagnetic lattices beyond our inelegant organic makeup spin a deeper mystery." Joe Milutis, Ether.

Studio Seminar in Public Art

Antoni Muntadas, Instructor
Benjamin Wood, TA
Workshop 4.367
Spring 2006

This course focuses on the production of projects for public places.

The studio seminar will look at ways in which the contemporary urban landscape is shaped by a preoccupation with fear, and insecurity that manifests itself in design for security systems, gated communities, and protected public places. How can we create public art projects that responsibly and proactively respond to this construction of fear? How do we create spaces for discourse and community rather than defensive generic urban spaces?

Public art is a concept that is in constant discussion and revision, as much as the evolution and transformation of public spaces and cities are. Public interventions are created not to impose and be temporary, but as forms intended to activate discourse and discussion. Considering the concept of art and architecture as a public device and also how to search for new ways of avoiding generic identities, we will deal with the concept of Fear and the End of Public Spaces. These dialogues in Public Space should be considered as a point of departure to propose a personal individual construction that will be developed from the initial concept, to a publicly diffused project.

image by Rajesh Kottamasu

PROCESS

Design Explorers
Axel Kilian, Instructor
Workshop 4.596

High Performance Center for NYC
Lise Anne Couture, Instructor
MArch Level III Studio 4.156

'Springy Thingy Design Tool' Workshop
Mark Goulthorpe, Instructor
Workshop 4.184

Tycho Brahe Institute
Mark Goulthorpe, Instructor
MArch Level II Studio 4.144

Sinthome CAD/CAM Research Sculpture-Fabrication
Phase of actual sculpture for Art OMI Outdoor
Sculpture Park
Mark Goulthorpe, Instructor
Workshop 4.183

Design computing of complex-curved geometry
using digital fabrication methods
Kenfield A. Griffith
SMArchS Thesis

Design Explorers (Part II)
Axel Kilian, Instructor
Workshop 4.593

Peter DePasquale

Design Explorers

Axel Kilian, Instructor
Workshop 4.596
Spring 2006

A design explorer is a construct for externalizing
design intention. This workshop investigated the
design process as an exploration with distinct stages.
The exploration was modeled through iterative
computational and physical representations. The
goal is to develop alternatives to the use of geometry
as literal form. We will investigate other criteria as
drivers for design concept and form in architecture.
Depending on the design problem these might be
performative, programmatic or conceptual in nature.

The workshop is organized around a number of
architectural design studies, which incorporate
physical and digital prototypes resulting from the
design exploration, culminating in a final project.

Sarah Dunbar

121

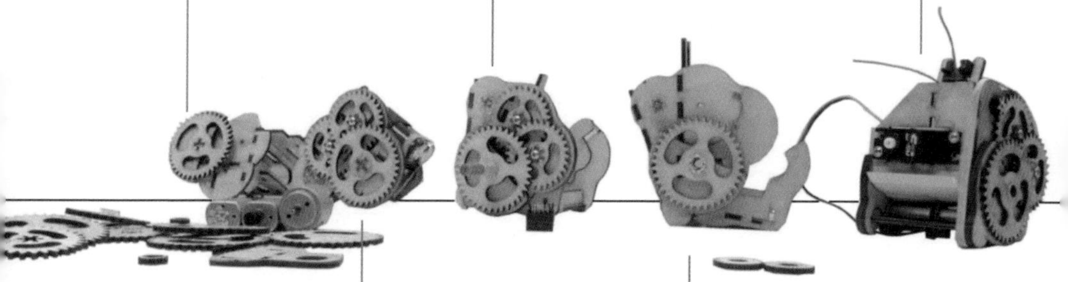

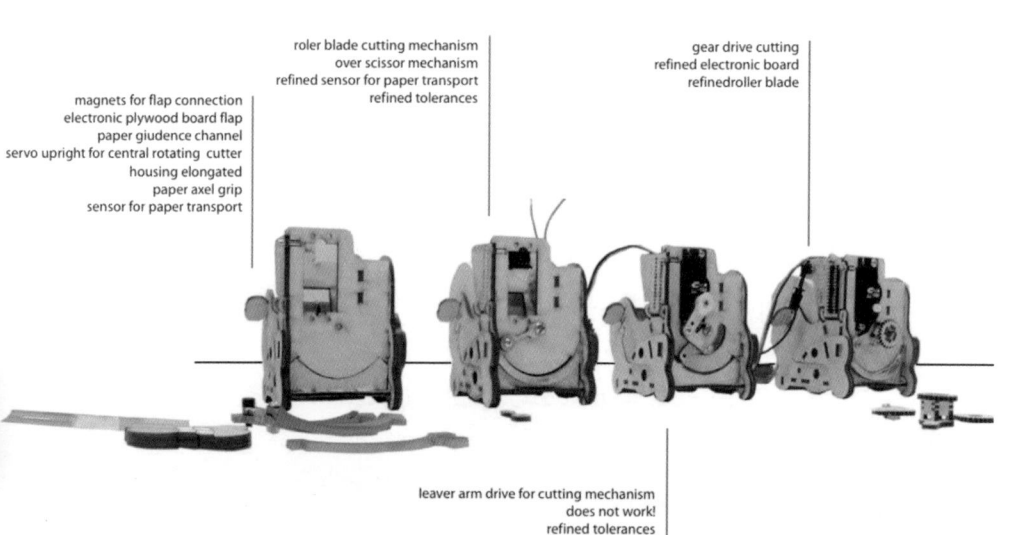

gear box
all plywood
friction fit
150:1 ratio
offset tolerance 0.007 inch

basic dimensions of paper roll
flap to reload paper
smaller motor,
quiter
overall form follows the gear shape

servo for cutting mechanism
bigger and cheaper motor
first working paper transport

motorized model
acrylic plywood combination
wooden axle
noisy

aluminium axle
teethed gears for paper transport
rj 45 connector above center of mass

roler blade cutting mechanism
over scissor mechanism
refined sensor for paper transport
refined tolerances

gear drive cutting
refined electronic board
refinedroller blade

magnets for flap connection
electronic plywood board flap
paper giudence channel
servo upright for central rotating cutter
housing elongated
paper axel grip
sensor for paper transport

leaver arm drive for cutting mechanism
does not work!
refined tolerances

Peter Schmitt
Master in Media Arts & Sciences

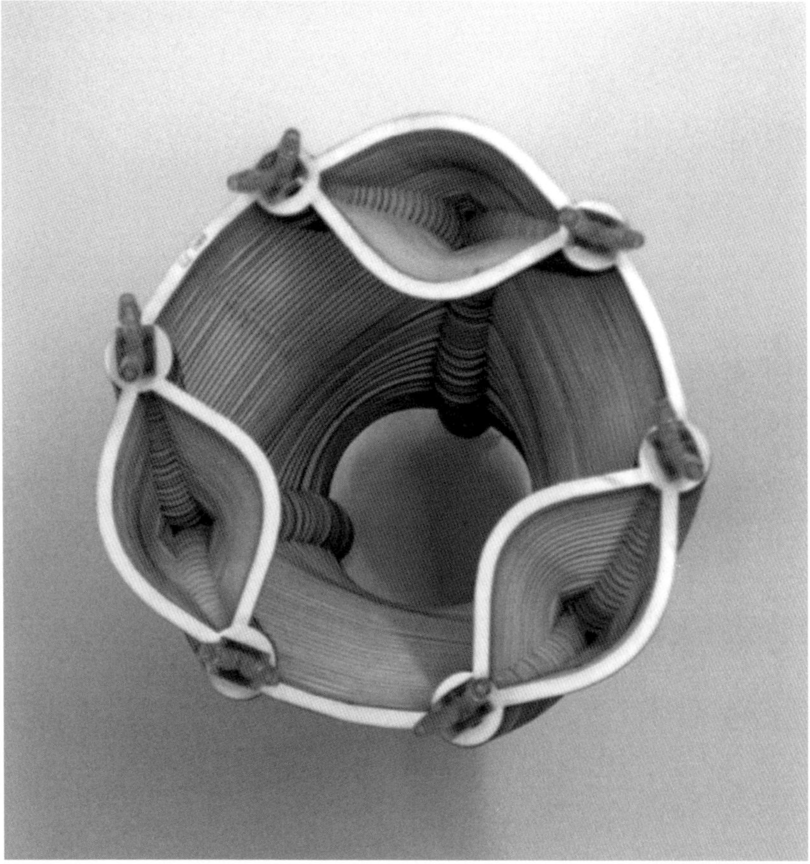

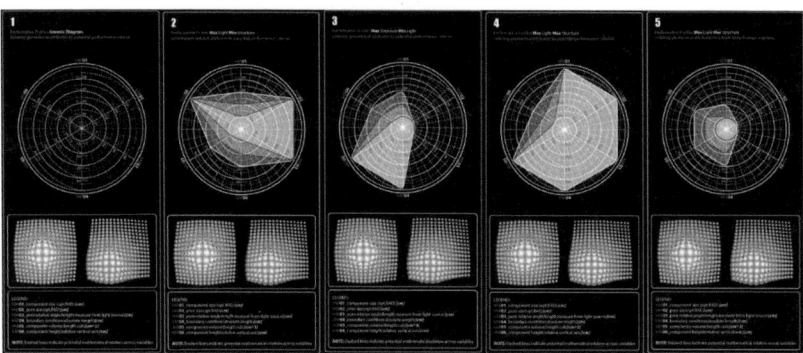

Neri Oxman
Computation PhD

123

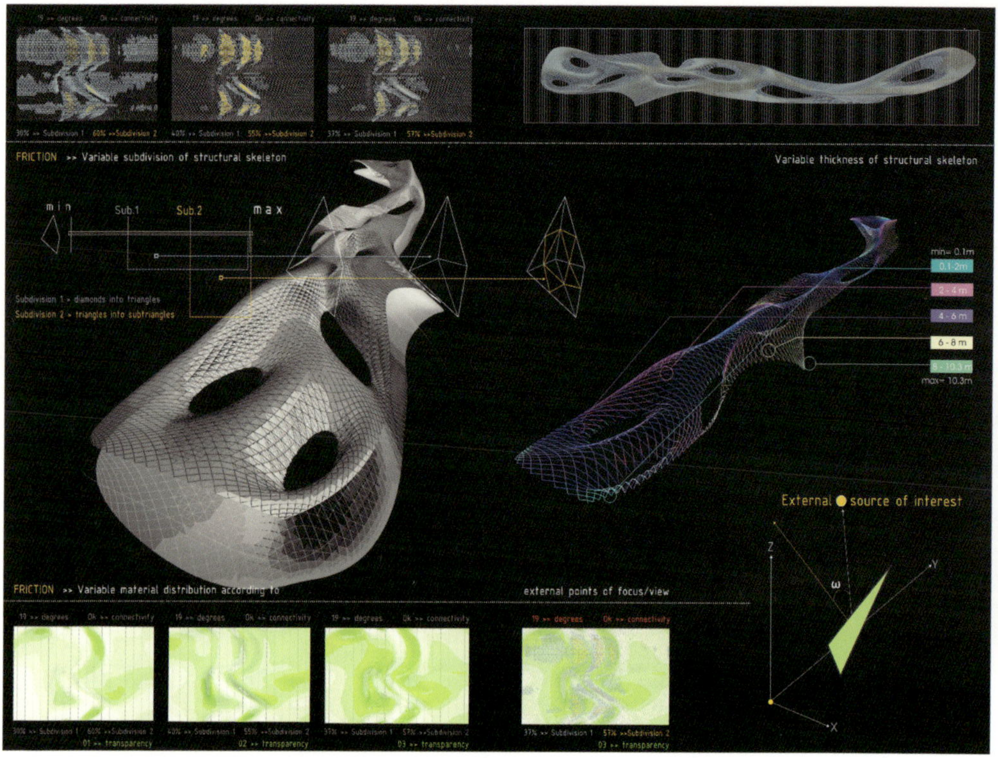

FRICTION >> Variable subdivision of structural skeleton

Variable thickness of structural skeleton

min Sub.1 Sub.2 max

Subdivision 1 > diamonds into triangles
Subdivision 2 > triangles into subtriangles

min= 0.1m
0.1-2m
2 - 4 m
4 - 6 m
6 - 8 m
8 - 10.3 m
max= 10.3m

External source of interest

FRICTION >> Variable material distribution according to

external points of focus/view

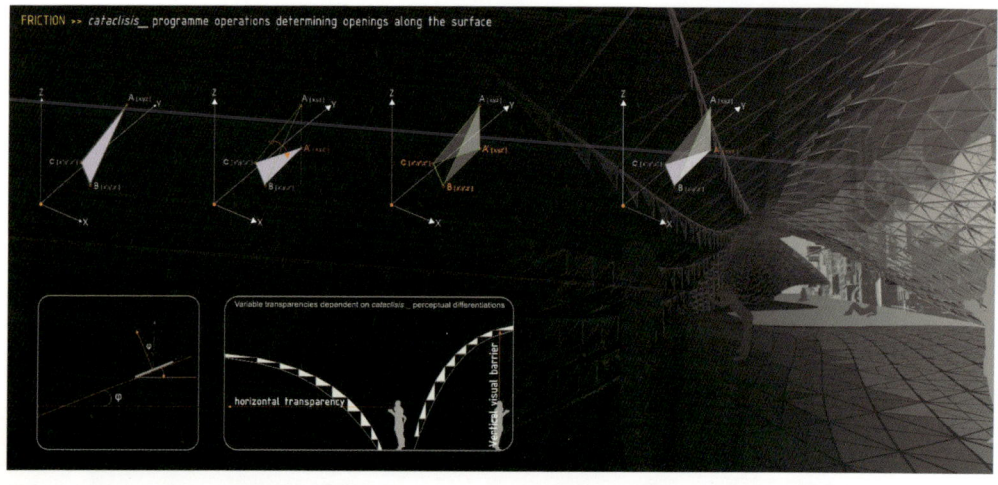

FRICTION >> *cataclisis_* programme operations determining openings along the surface

Variable transparencies dependent on cataclisis _ perceptual differentiations

_ horizontal transparency

vertical visual barrier

Alexandros Tsamis
Computation PhD

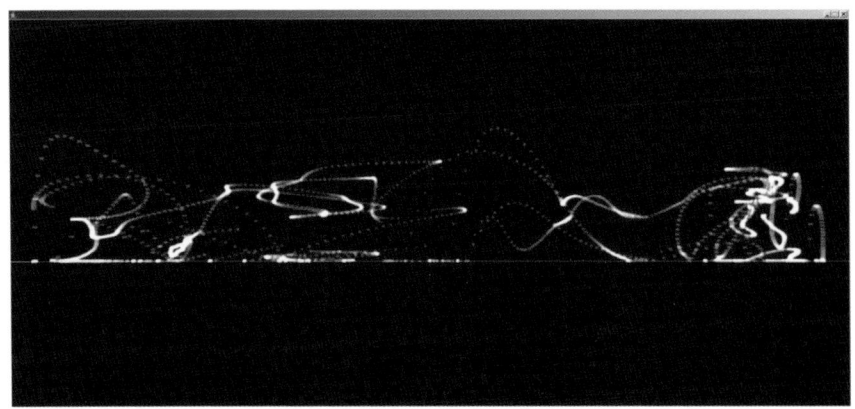

Dancer Applet
James Shen, MArch III

125

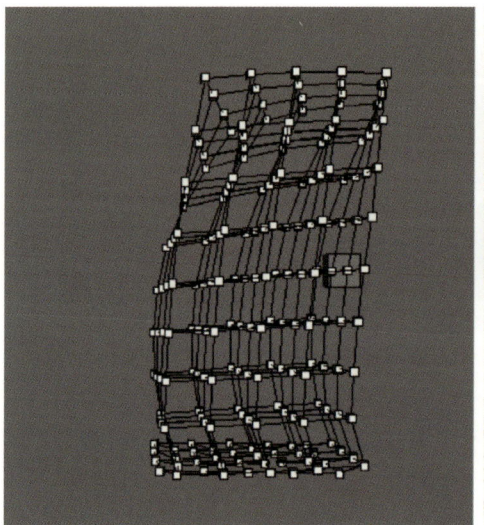
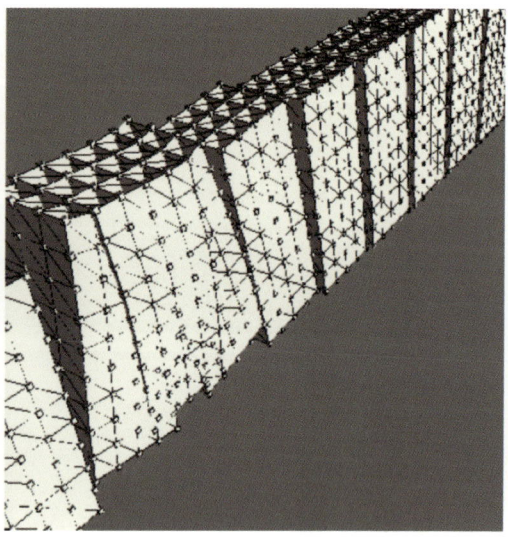

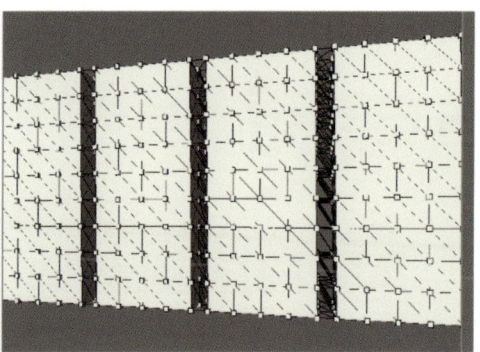
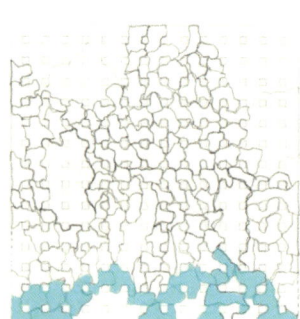

```
import processing.opengl.*;

import smeng;
import smeng.particles.*;

ParticleSystem ps;
Magnet m;
float xmag, ymag = 0;
float newXmag, newYmag = 0;

block[] myRockite;

void setup() {
  size(700, 700, OPENGL);

  ps = new ParticleSystem(this);
  ps.defaultSpringRestLength = 30;
  ps.defaultSpringStrength = 1.0;
  ps.setGravity (0,0);

  myRockite = new block (10);
  for (int i=0; i<10; i++) {
    myRockite[i] = new block(30,5,10,4, i*140, 0, 0);
    if (i>0) {
      myRockite[i-1].setNeighbor( myRockite[i]);
      myRockite[i-1].stitch();
    }
  }

  m = new Magnet (myRockite[5].citynodes[2][5][2]);
  m.strength = 0.5;
}
```

```
void draw() {
  newXmag = mouseX/float(width) * TWO_PI;
  newYmag = mouseY/float(height) * TWO_PI;

  float diff = xmag-newXmag;
  if (abs(diff) > 0.01) {
    xmag -= diff/4.0;
  }

  diff = ymag-newYmag;
  if (abs(diff) > 0.01) {
    ymag -= diff/4.0;
  }

  rotateX(-ymag);
  rotateY(-xmag);
  //noStroke();
  translate (-width/2, -height/4, 0);
  background(43, 152, 213);
  directionalLight(126, 126, 126, 0, 0, -1);
  ambientLight(102, 102, 102);
  for (int i =0; i<10; i++) {
    myRockite[i].drawblock();
  }

  fill(255,10,10,200);
  //ps.draw();
}

void mousePressed() {
  for (int i=0; i<10; i++) {
    myRockite[i].recalculate();
  }
}
```

Peter DePasquale
MArch II

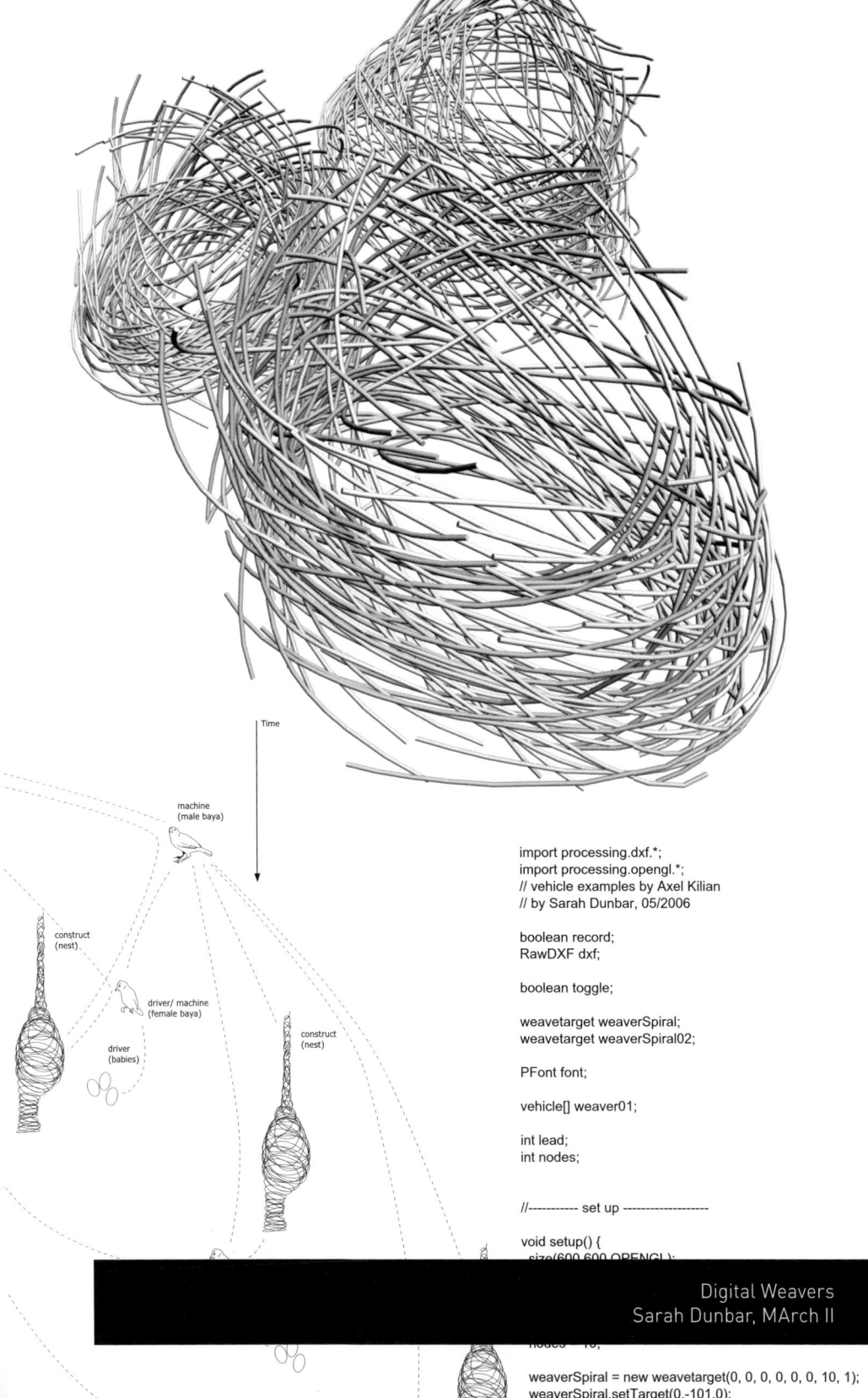

Time

machine
(male baya)

construct
(nest)

driver/ machine
(female baya)

driver
(babies)

construct
(nest)

```
import processing.dxf.*;
import processing.opengl.*;
// vehicle examples by Axel Kilian
// by Sarah Dunbar, 05/2006

boolean record;
RawDXF dxf;

boolean toggle;

weavetarget weaverSpiral;
weavetarget weaverSpiral02;

PFont font;

vehicle[] weaver01;

int lead;
int nodes;


//----------- set up -------------------

void setup() {
  size(600,600,OPENGL);
```

```
  nodes = 10;

  weaverSpiral = new weavetarget(0, 0, 0, 0, 0, 0, 10, 1);
  weaverSpiral.setTarget(0,-101,0);
```

High Performance Center for NYC

Lise Anne Couture, Instructor
Saeed Arida, TA
MArch Level III Studio 4.156
Spring 2006

"High performance" has become a ubiquitous expression that is used to characterize everything from sports equipment and apparel, vehicles and engines, hardware and software, materials and methods, stocks and bonds, to corporate culture and learning environments.

High performance is about simultaneously maximizing and minimizing. High performance is about maximizing output while minimizing resistance, maximum control with minimum risk. It involves responding to both variables and consistencies, incorporating both variation and continuity, a balance between rigidity and flexibility, harnessing opportunity while diminishing weaknesses and transforming liabilities into assets.

High performance is the optimization of redundancy in order to render it no longer redundant.

The concept of high performance is based on strategies of convergence and efficiency to increase the potential of achieving a desired outcome.

The implementation of 'high performance' apparatii offers the opportunity for improved performance and enhancement of experience.

High performance is about innovation, adaptability, integration, optimization, compliance and efficiency. It is the optimization of potential.

High performance is the pushing of limits and going to extremes.

So what is High Performance architecture and what are its effects?

The site and program for a new Museum of Sports and Athletics located along the Hudson River Park on the west side of Manhattan will be used as a vehicle for the studio's investigations this semester. It is anticipated that the different realms that will affect the architectural outcome, such as tectonics, landscape, museum culture and technology, will present competing and complimentary agendas of varying importance and shifting order. The students will establish a conceptual response and generate design parameters or a system of constraints to 'negotiate' these with the intelligence gained in Phase 1 to be used as a point of departure. The result of this 'negotiation' will be an architecture of shifting 'gradients', of simultaneous difference and continuity, of High Performance.

image by Rebecca Edson

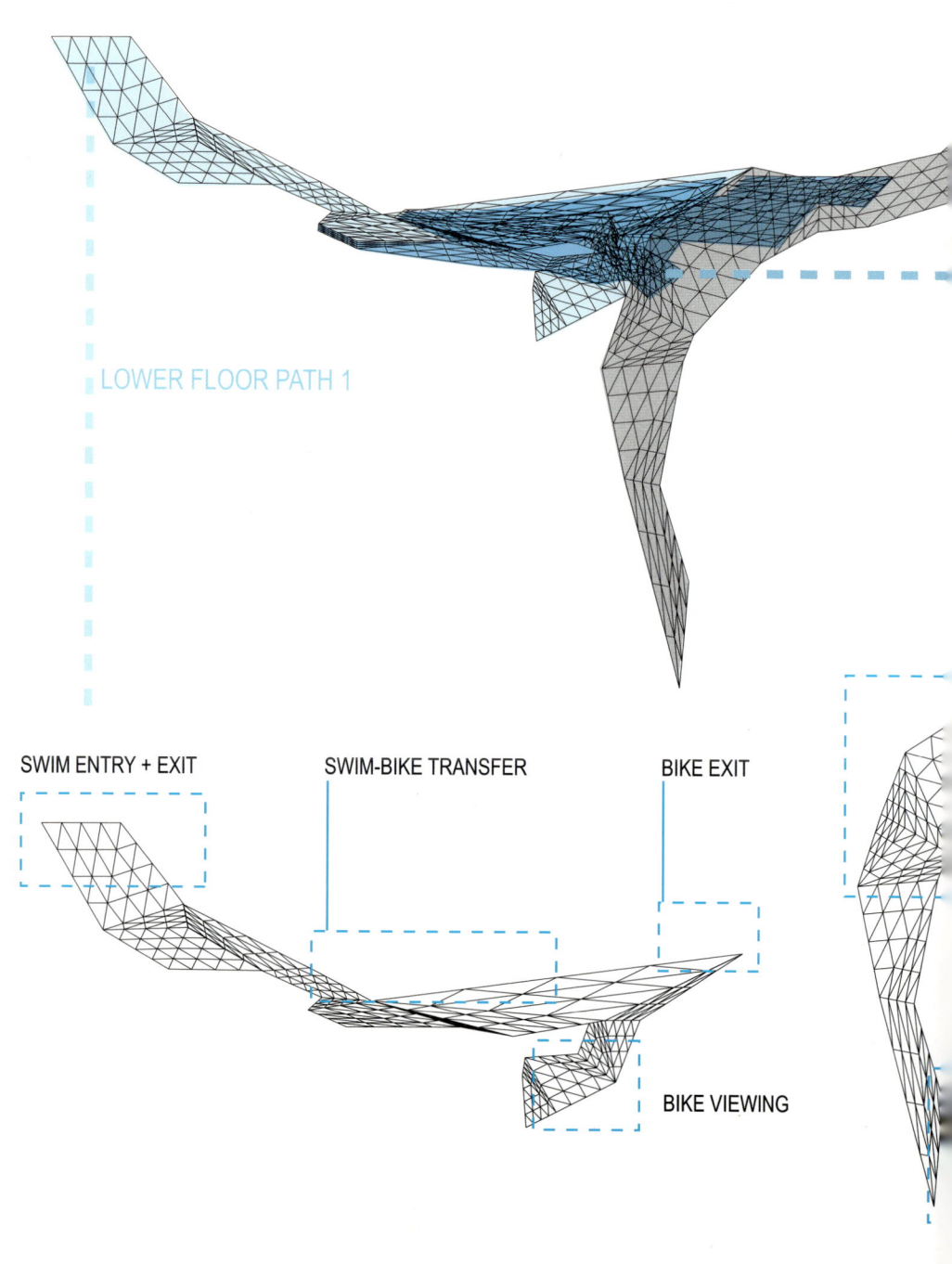

LOWER FLOOR PATH 1

SWIM ENTRY + EXIT

SWIM-BIKE TRANSFER

BIKE EXIT

BIKE VIEWING

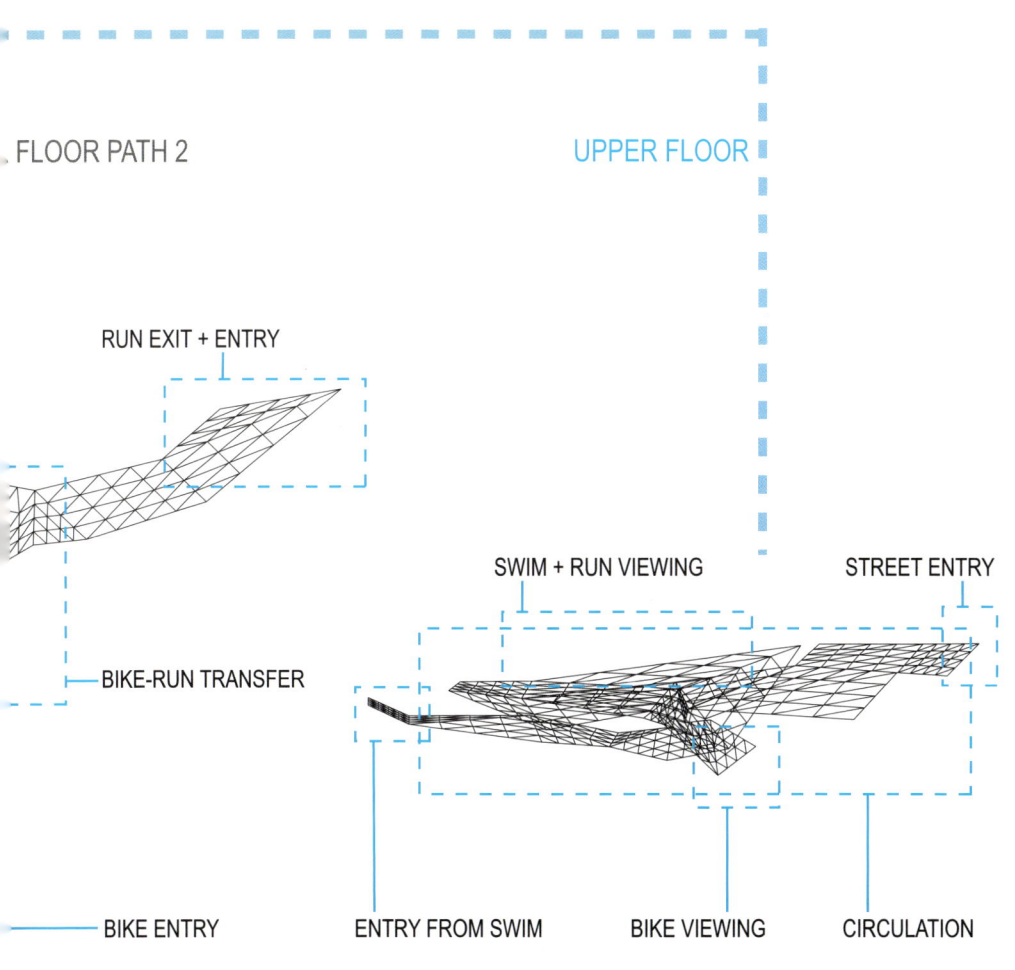

FLOOR PATH 2   UPPER FLOOR

RUN EXIT + ENTRY

SWIM + RUN VIEWING   STREET ENTRY

BIKE-RUN TRANSFER

BIKE ENTRY   ENTRY FROM SWIM   BIKE VIEWING   CIRCULATION

Rebecca Edson
MArch III

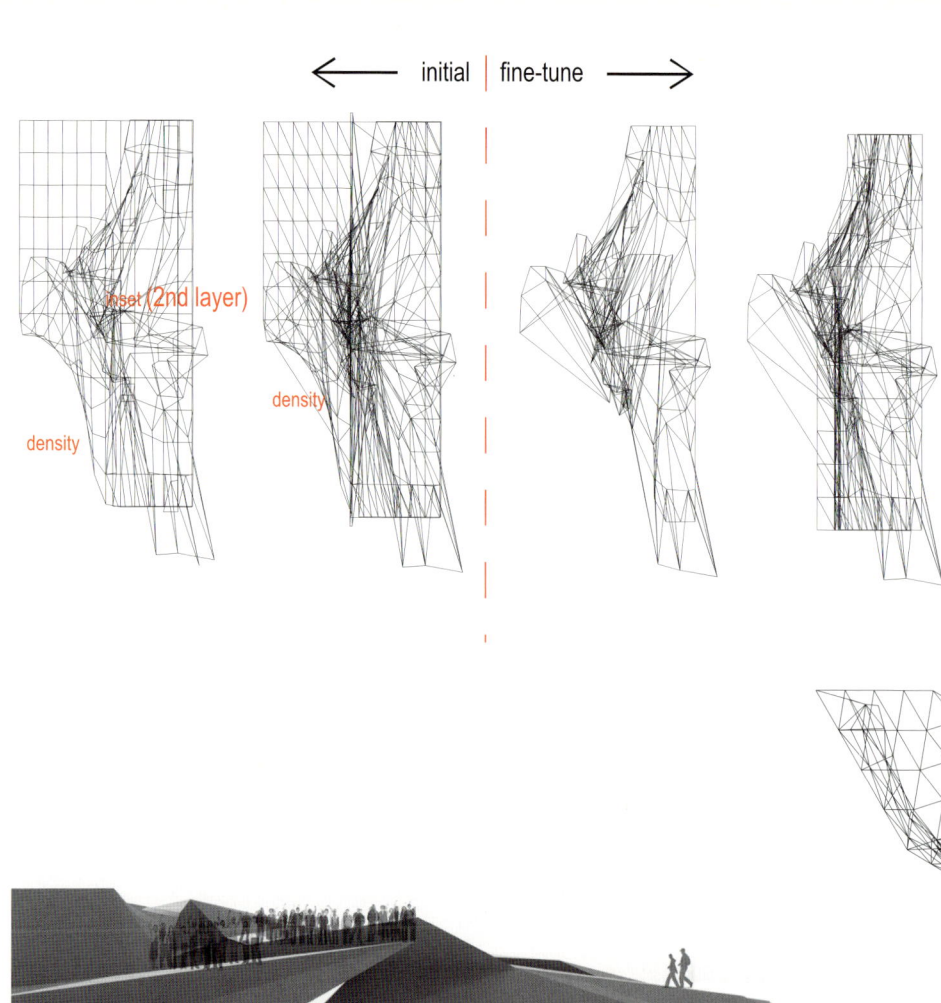

initial | fine-tune

inset (2nd layer)

density

density

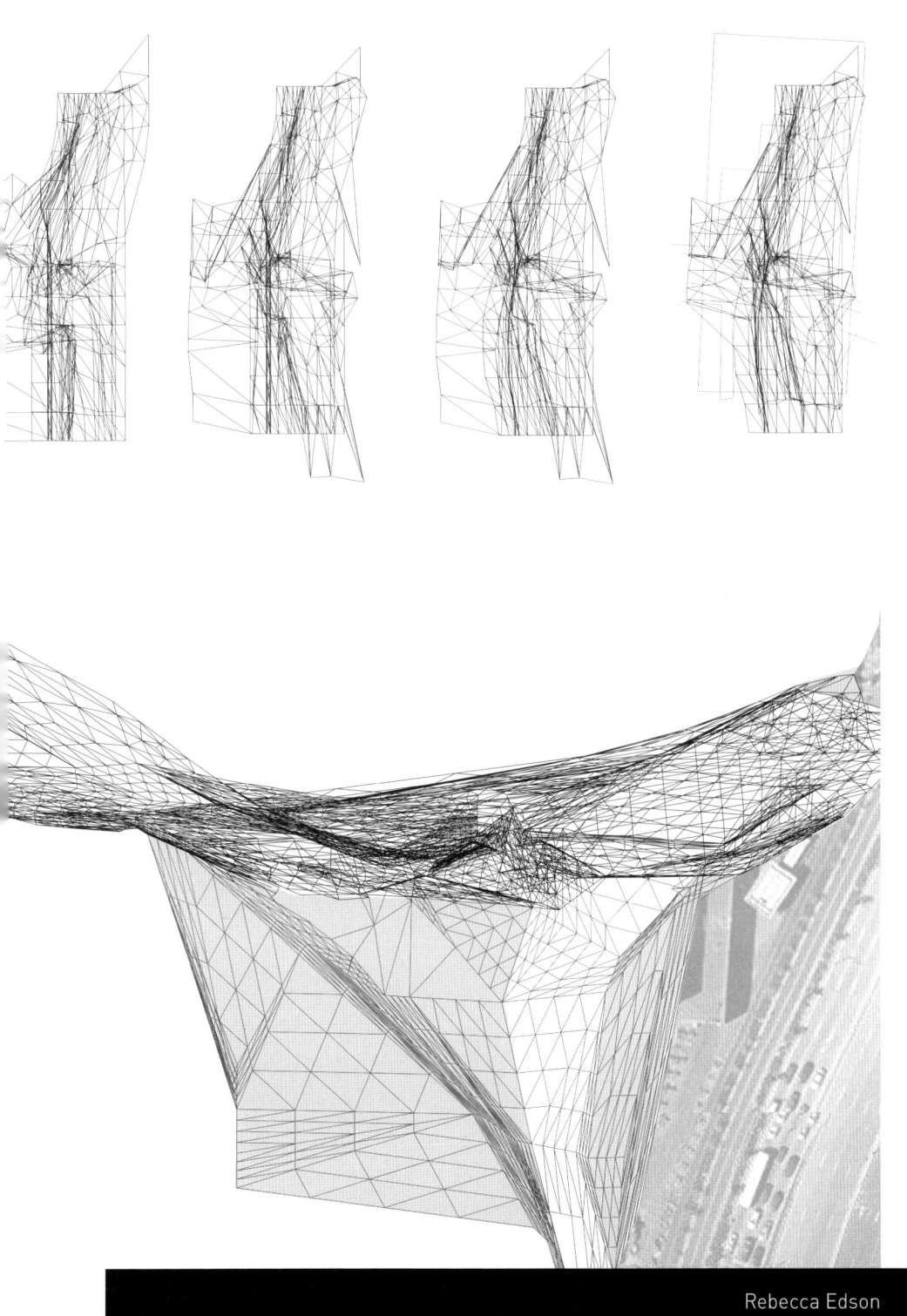

Rebecca Edson
MArch III

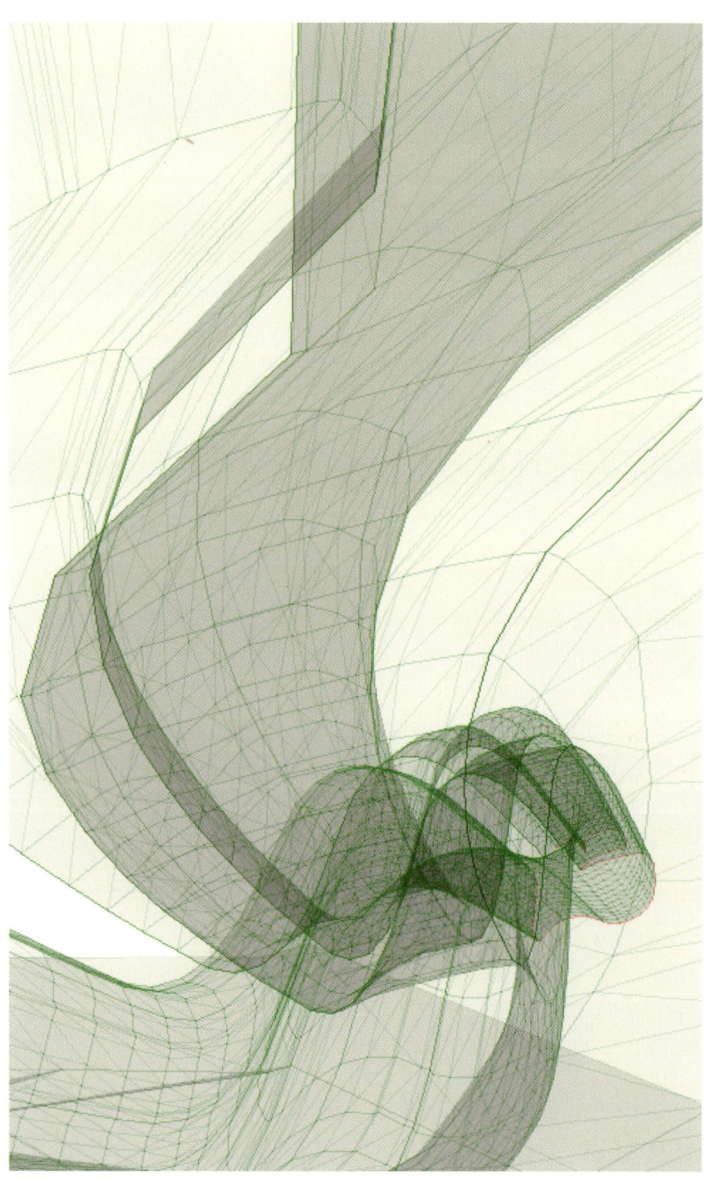

Springy Thingy

Mark Goulthorpe, Instructor
Kaustuv de Biswas, TA
John Rothenberg, James Shen,
John Snavely, Student Researchers
Workshop 4.184
Spring 2006

This workshop aimed to develop articulate 3d user-interfaces to permit real-time 3d-sketching, and then to derive 3d-printable models that would evidence the formal latency of such design processing. The work is based on several innovative software projects developed in previous design studios. The "Springy Thing' design tool developed in the workshop was created using spring-based modeling tools created by Simon Greenwold.

Spring-based modeling permits real-time 3d sketching, with points left hanging in space via a new gestural process; yet it exceeds typical hand-eye determinacy in that the point-strings are subject to continual re-adjustment, being linked in networks of dynamic force. For example, one might generate strings of pearls that describe 3d lines in space, the pearls arranged according to the speed-of-gesture; but where the strings may be plucked, or subjected to gravity, deforming under force and able to be multiplied as a set, swept into surfaces of point-cloud transformational elegance. The pearls may be subject to scripting, able to be given attributes or made responsive to 'environmental' conditions: a new alloplasticity folded into generative process.

The workshop also produced a 3d 'wand' such that one can begin to sketch in fully 3d, reintroducing bodily gesture back into design methodology.

image by Kaustuv De Biswas

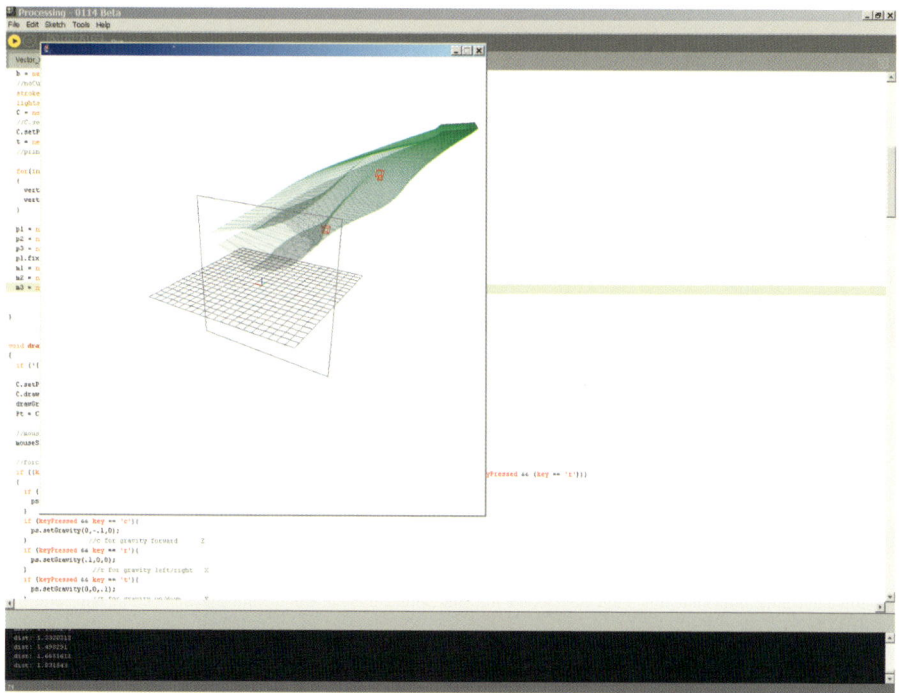

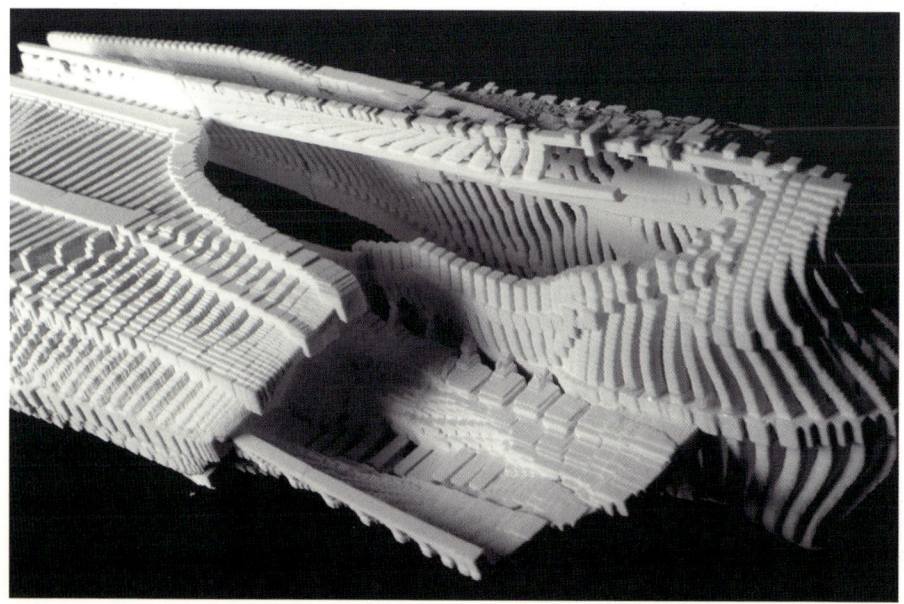

A recent iteration of the 'Springy Thingy' design tool. 3D print of earlier model.
Kaustuv De Biswas, Computation PhD, James Shen, MArch III

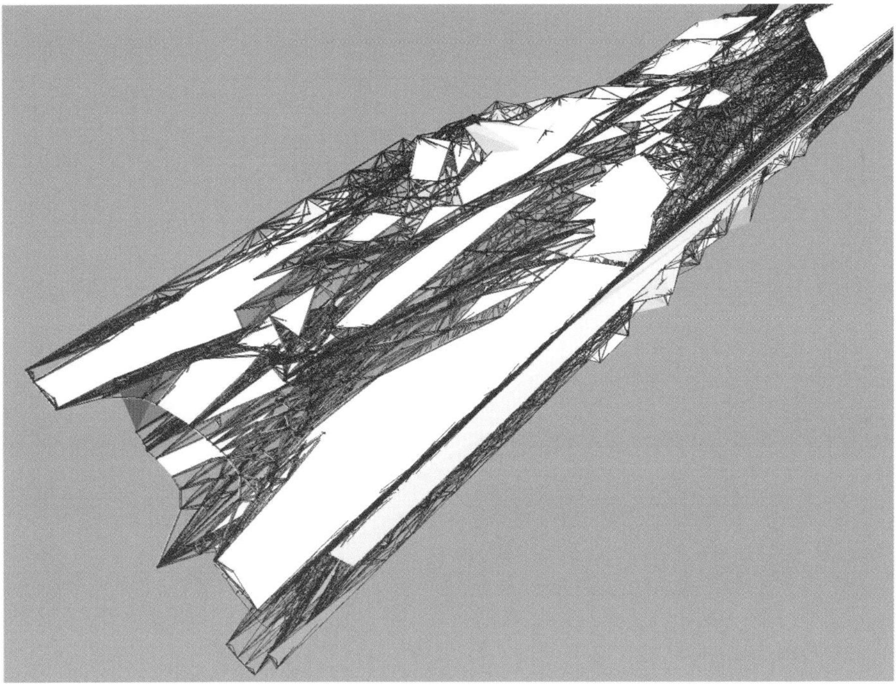

Earlier versions of 'Springy Thingy' - Kaustuv De Biswas, Computation PhD, James Shen, MArch III, John Snavely, MArch II

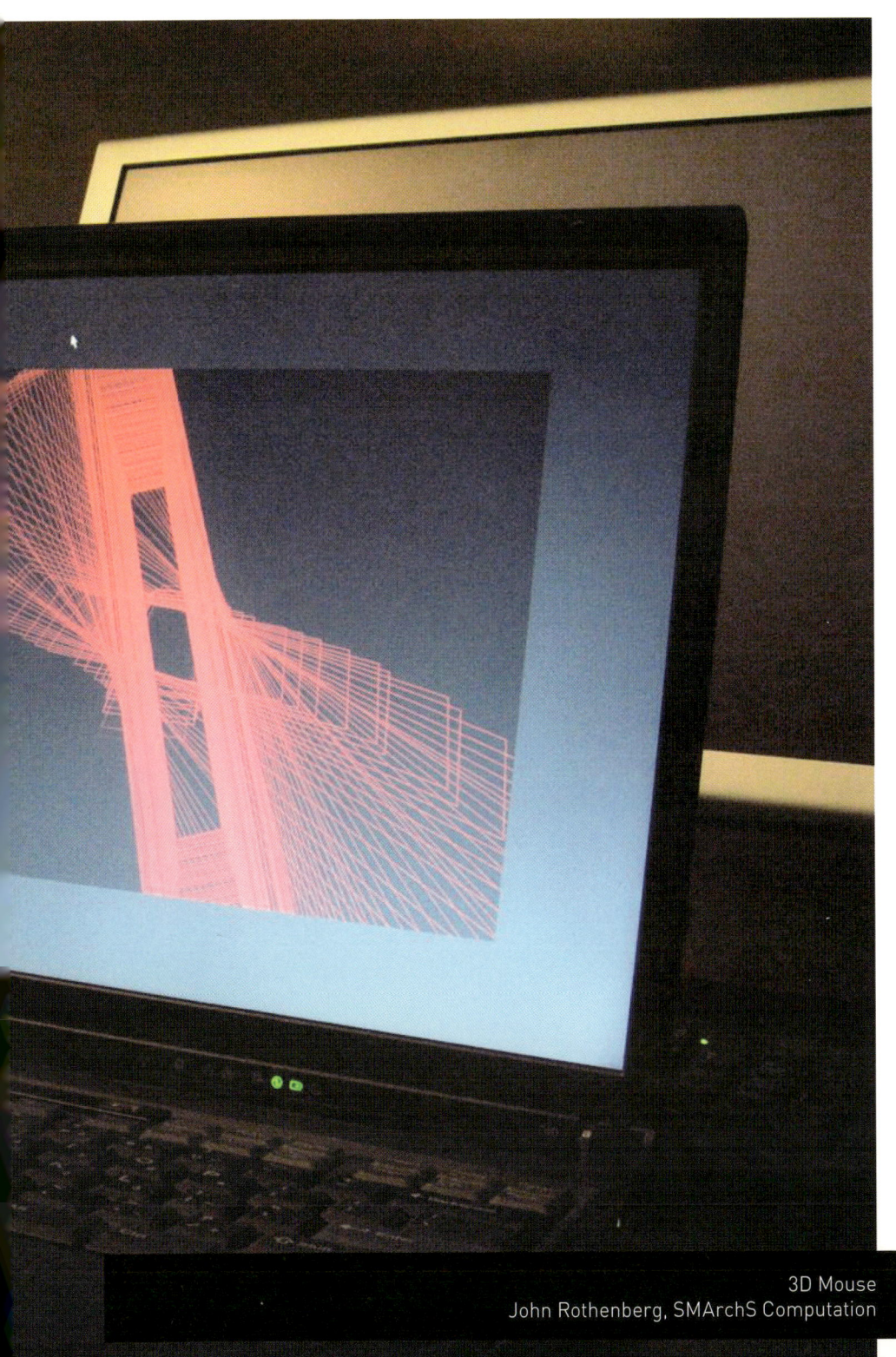

3D Mouse
John Rothenberg, SMArchS Computation

Tycho Brahe Institute

Mark Goulthorpe, Instructor
Tijana Vujosevic, TA
MArch Level II Studio 4.144
Spring 2006

By way of offering an historical context to a design
studio that looked to deploying parametric modeling
as a generative strategy, we considered building
a research institute on the Island of Hven on the
site of Tycho Brahe's famous observatory. Brahe is
one of the founding fathers of modern science, his
rigorous astronomical measurements serving to
establish empirical observation as the cornerstone
of rational scientific method. Brahe himself designed
and built hundreds of measuring instruments, many
requiring new levels of technical exactitude, but
equally requiring a hugely inventive and anticipatory
sensibility. He set out, that is, to make explicit the
hitherto implicit 'parametric' relations of the stars
and planets; and in doing so, he was able to formulate
a new cosmology that he contended would prove
wrong the models of Copernicus and Aristotle.

The students each developed a research institute via
open-ended parametric strategems, imagining what
Brahe would have done within a digital paradigm.
The projects were varied, inventive, often prescient,
the process certainly requiring a new level of
mental agility in the generative profligacy of digital
methodologies.

image from http://www.upscale.utorontotca/PHY100F/brahe.jpg

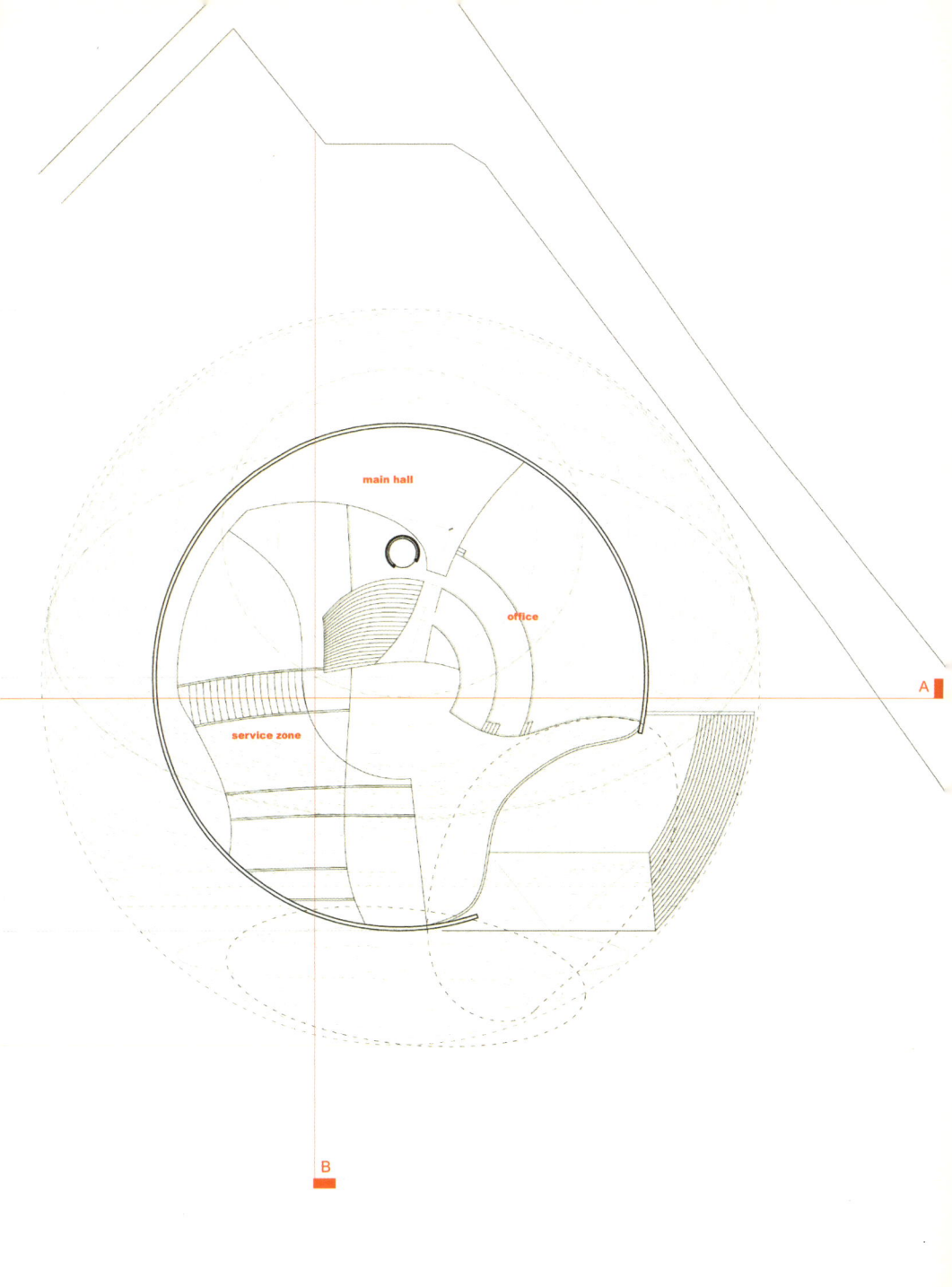

main hall

office

service zone

A

B

Young-Ju Kim
MArch II

143

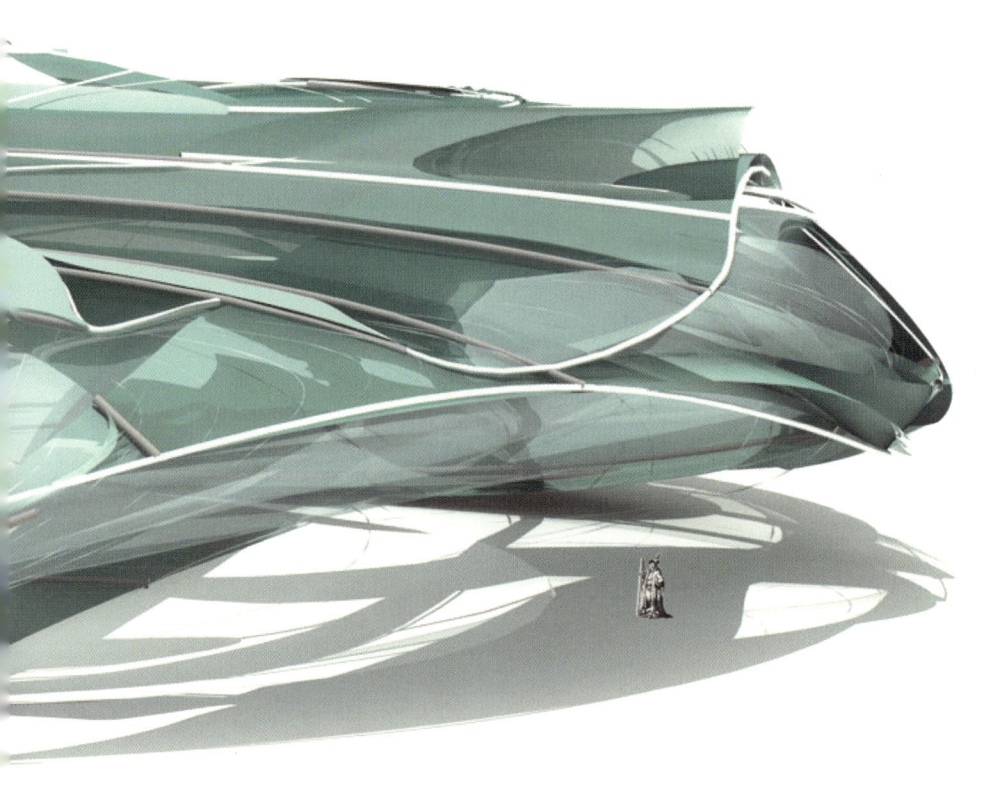

```
// ActionScript file
package {
        import flash.display.Bitmap;
        import flash.display.Sprite;
        import flash.display.BitmapData;
        import flash.geom.Matrix;
        import flash.events.MouseEvent;
        import flash.events.KeyboardEvent;
        import flash.display.TextField;
        public class ParticleApp extends Sprite {
                private const IDENTITY: Matrix = new Matrix();
                private const WIDTH: int = 1024;
                private const HEIGHT: int = 768;
                private var pattern: Pattern;
                [Embed(source='pattern.gif')] public var PImage: Class;
                private var pwin:ParticleWindow;
                private var vwin:ViewWindow;
                private var vwin2:ViewWindow;
                private var titleText: TextField;
                private var controlsText: TextField;

                public function ParticleApp(){
                        stage.scaleMode = 'noScale';
                        stage.align = StageAlign.TOP_LEFT;
                        //-- create background
                        var bgLib: Bitmap = new PImage();
                        var bgBmp: BitmapData = new BitmapData( bgLib.width, bgLib.height, false, 0 );
                        bgBmp.draw( bgLib, IDENTITY );
                        pattern = new Pattern( WIDTH, HEIGHT, bgBmp );
                        pattern.drawUnify();
                        addChild( new Bitmap( pattern ) );

                        pwin = new ParticleWindow();
                        pwin.x = 150;
                        pwin.y = 10;
                        stage.addEventListener(KeyboardEvent.KEY_DOWN, pwin.keyDownHandler);

                        addChild(pwin);
```

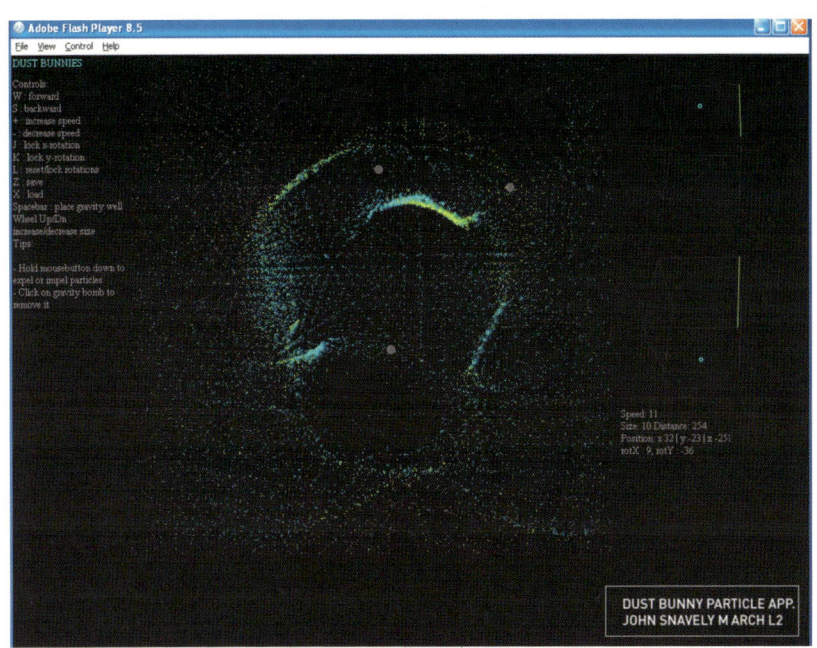

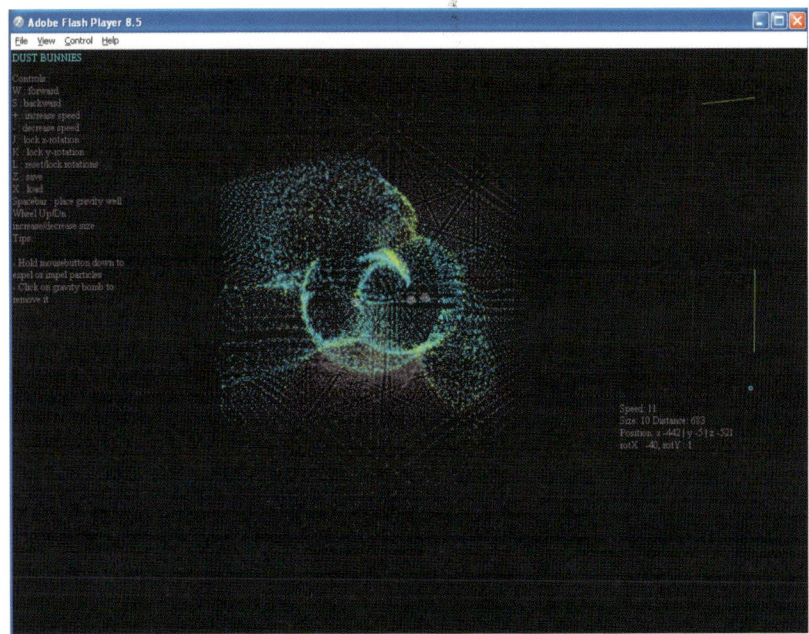

Dustbunnies
John Snavely, MArch II

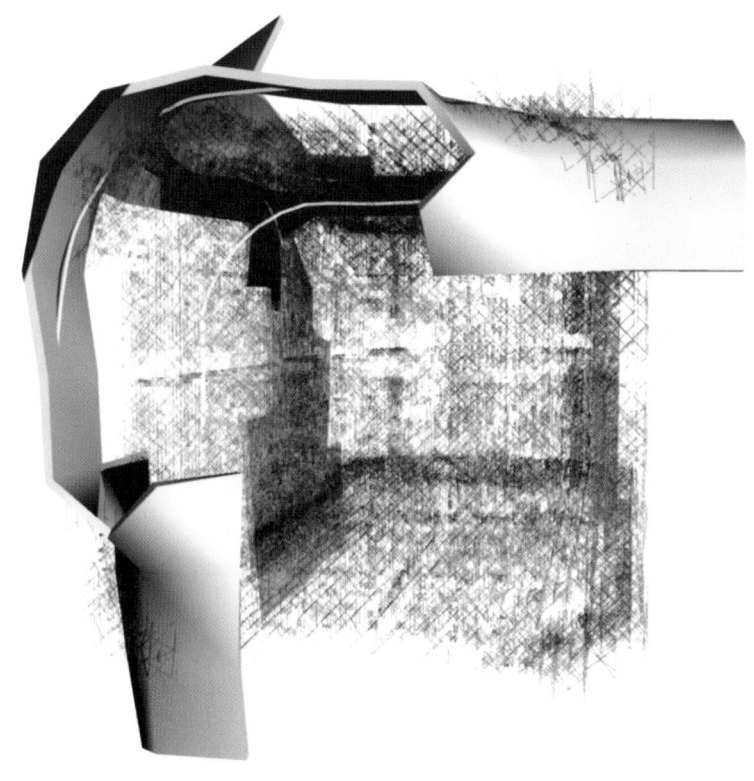

Dustbunnies
John Snavely, MArch II

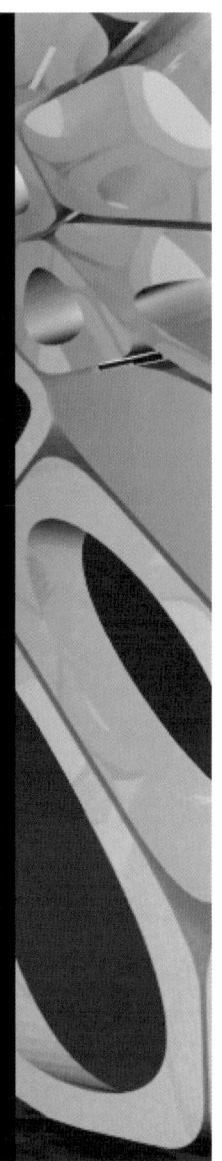

Sinthome Sculpture Workshop

Mark Goulthorpe, Instructor (Architecture)
Barbara Cutler, TA/ Instructor (Computer Science)
Ove Arup & Partners: Group IV London, Structural
Engineers
Jeff Anderson, Dennis Michaud, John Rothenburg,
Matt Trimble, Emily Whiting, Student Researchers
Workshop 4.183
Spring 2006

The Sinthome workshop looked to creating a
sculpture for Art Omi Sculpture Park in upstate
New York that would allow reflection on the base
condition of the plastic arts – what Joseph Beuys
called 'die Plastik' – at the threshold of a digital
era. At one level, this involved gathering a multi-
disciplinary team to develop a series of generative
digital techniques, linking parametric, programmatic
and algorithmic methodologies into a seamless
design-to-build CAD-CAM protocol. At another
level, it looked to offer a provocative critical context
to such generative techniques through exploration
of Jaques Lacan's 'Sinthome' seminar, where he
interrogates the base subjective drive of James Joyce
in his deployment of auto-poetic writing techniques.
At issue is not merely a radically revised design-
build logic as digital systems are allowed to develop
full generative profligacy, where even the structure
'grows' automatically in response to any given formal
iteration; but rather the locus of subjectivity within
such hyper-mechanistic automatic processing at the
threshold of a new man-machine symbiosis – the
digital.

rendering by Matthew Trimble

Rendering of Sinthome Sculpture
Matthew Trimble, MArch II

Design Computing of Complex-Curved Geometry using Digital Fabrication Methods

Kenfield Griffith
SMArchS Thesis
Lawrence Sass, Advisor
Terry Knight and Fernando Domeyko, Readers
Spring 2006

The production of design information for digital fabrication is presented in this thesis. This thesis outlines the research of generating information for physical construction as architectural models of complex curved walls built from unique units. A series of computer programs and physical models as examples of orthogonal, non-orthogonal, and complex curved walls as designs were developed. The wall examples here are built of non-uniform, interlocking units using an integral connection approach. This is an exploration of design tools that construct complex curved structures in CAD for fabrication with a 3D printer. The thesis explores the evaluation processes used by architects when evaluating digitally fabricated desktop models. The research involved in this thesis takes the direction of investigating a new methodology for solving a modern and aesthetic approach to architecture. The research conducted investigates design as a way for synthesizing a grammatical (Stiny, 1977) approach as the systematic engine that is used to solve less systematic, curved, non-uniform form (Smithers, 1989).

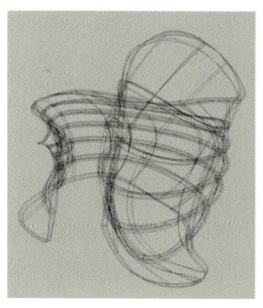
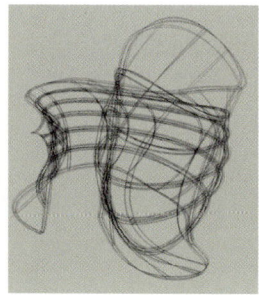

Design Computing of Complex-Curved Geometry using Digital Fabrication
Methods, Kenfield Griffith SMArchS Computation

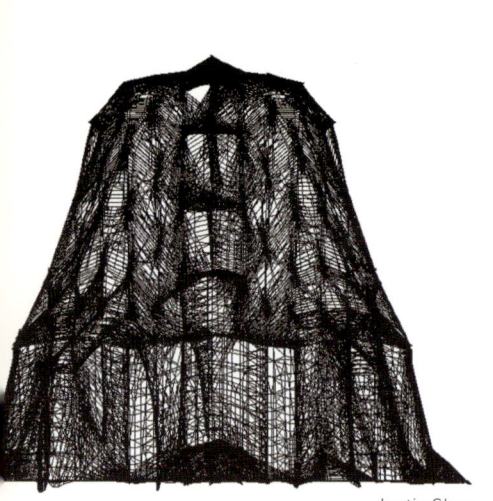

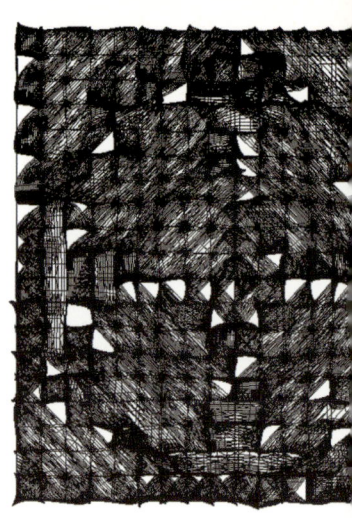

Justin Shea

Coryn Kempster

Design Explorers (Part II)
Axel Kilian, Instructor
Workshop 4.593
Fall 2006

A second installation of the design explorer workshop revisited the idea of a design explorer following the process further in detail. A design explorer is a construct for externalizing design intention. This workshop investigated the design process as an exploration with distinct stages. The exploration was modeled through iterative computational and physical representations. The goal of the workshop is to develop alternatives to the use of geometry as literal form. We will investigate other criteria as drivers for design concept and form in architecture. Depending on the design problem these might be performative, programmatic or conceptual in nature.

Jeffrey Anderson

Cellular Automata
Behavior types
Periodic
Rule 58

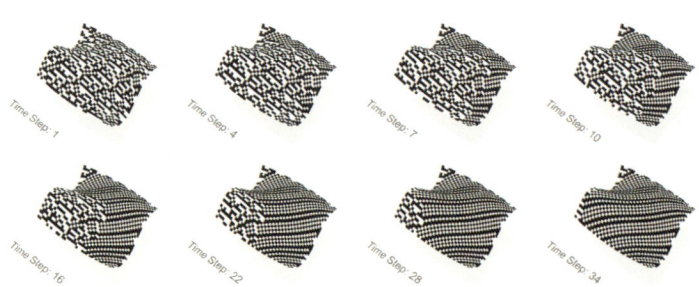

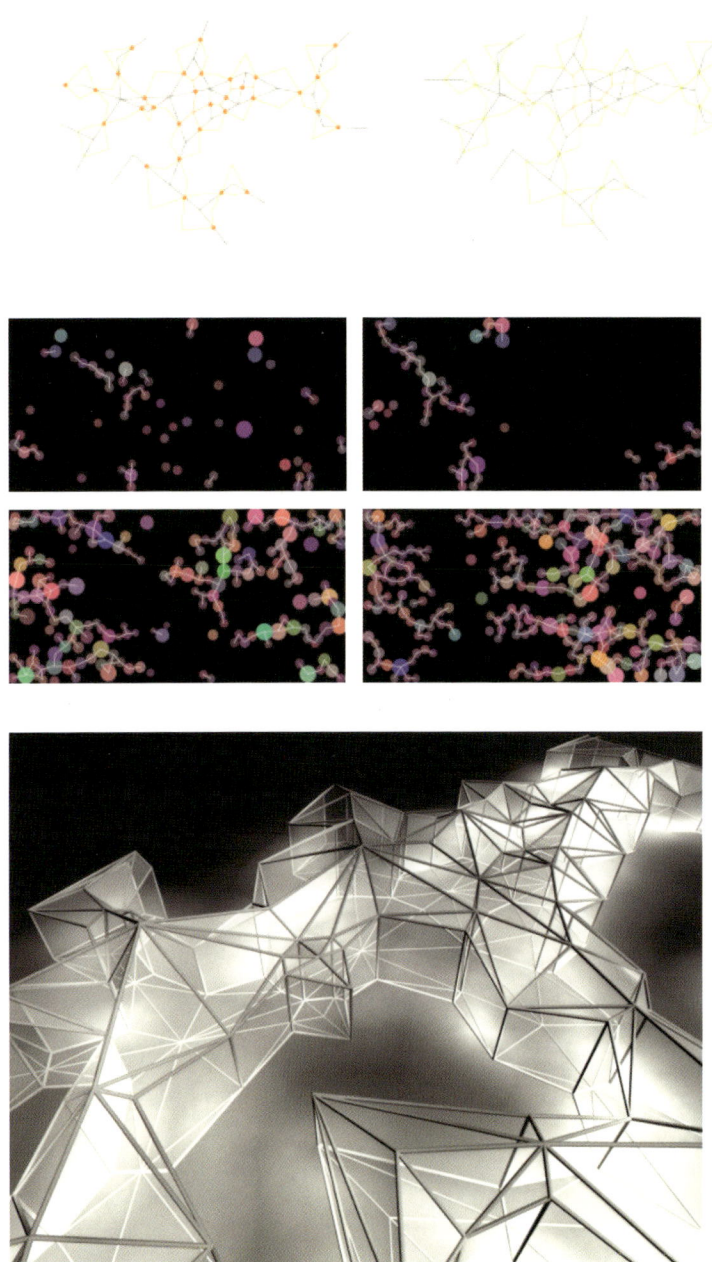

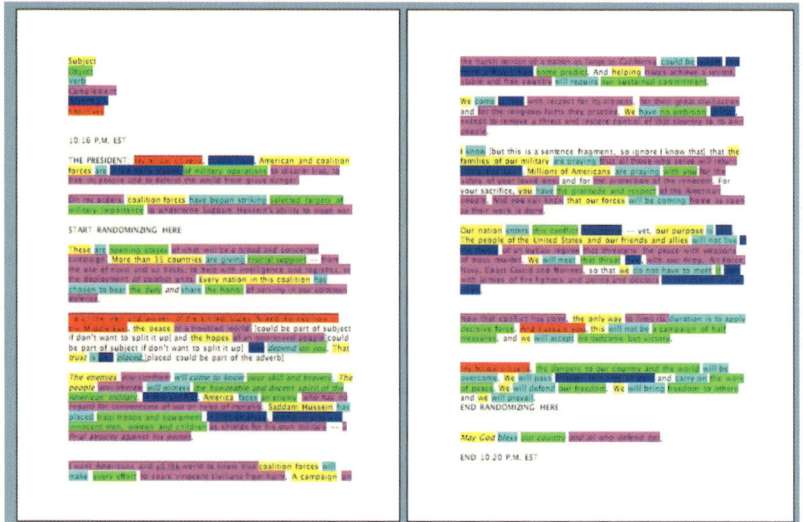

Speech broken down into clause elements

Bushyball Project
Coryn Kempster, MArch III

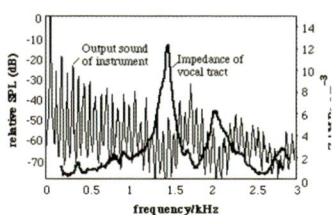

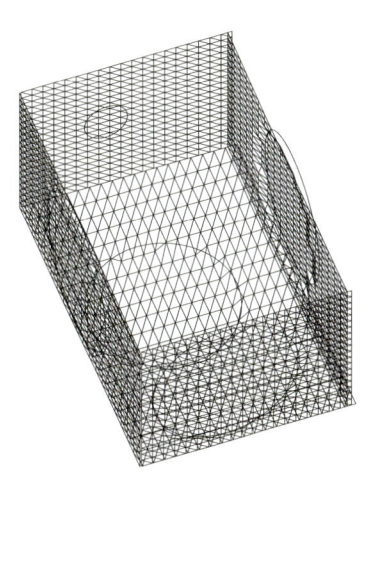

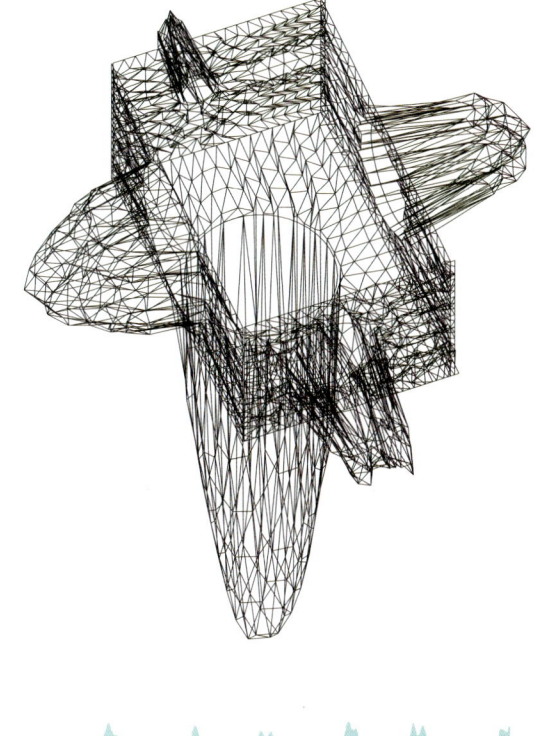

CONTAINED : UNCONTAINED

LEFT: Sample of final model during segment of minimal sound fluctuation.
Blue line below container describes sound spectrum.

RIGHT: Sampled at maximum sound fluctuation. Each wall of the container is corresponding
with a particular frequency which is controlled by musical input.

Contained/ Uncontained
Justin Shea, MArch III

FABRIC

The fabric vs. monument binary was publicly debated at MIT during an event called "Fightclub," wherein Yung Ho Chang defended the notion of "fabric," attacking the use of monumentality, while his opponent, Alexander D'Hooghe took the exact opposite position. Sanford Kwinter refereed the debate. What follows are some highlights from the transcripts of the debate.

Chang: "We [in Beijing] started to build monuments right in the center of the city, in the middle of Tiananmen Square... This is the new Beijing: a city of objects. ...monuments work very closely with roads for automobiles, which also function to cut the city off from itself."

D'Hooghe: "...I would like to posit that the idealization of fabric is nothing else than the outcome of a belief system which is fundamentally totalitarian. Essentially, the notion of fabric is the lack of boundaries. So fabric, by its very definition, can expand and continue forever. I wouldn't want to live in a city which is dominated by a single system that keeps expanding forever. Second, fabric can only be complete by expunging that which does not conform to it. In that sense it installs a kind of homogeneity that tries to include and imprison everything that is different and succeeds in imposing a tyranny of the majority. Finally, fabric is based on a narrative of loss, on an idea that at some point in history there was a more harmonious unified society, hence the word 'fabric.' One of the great emancipations of modern time is that we no longer have to be unified. It is liberating to be fragmented, with many pieces each proclaiming their identity and pride, these would be monuments rather than fabric.

MONUMENT

Chang: "The problem with monuments is that they internalize urban life and kill it. I don't think nostalgia is the issue. I see fabric having a possible new life. The point is to weave public and not so public spaces within a certain fabric, to see how interior and exterior space starts to be organized in a fabric-like manner. In a city of monuments, leftover space is just residual. In a fabric city, surrounding spaces are organized to become part of urban life, which is not a simple mimicry of the old fabric of Beijing... we see how urban life might unfold in the fabric and generate a new fabric to accommodate that life."

D'Hooghe: What I resent is the right wing's ability to hijack monumentality to a right wing discourse. Is it not possible to use the monumental to propagate a different ideal, pluralism or pluralist liberalism? Can we build an equally strong symbolic form as a counter project?

Kwinter: It is very clear that any discussion you guys have will narrow itself down to politics. What one thinks when Alexander speaks about monuments is the sublime... something larger than what can be contained in emotions. That is why what we see as classically monumental spaces were always put at the service of demagoguery...Yung Ho is probably right about this, that the monument operates through symbolism and the propagation of meaning often associated with despotic control, versus what you talk about as the tyranny of the masses that sounded so much like Democracy." (continued)...

A full transcript of the debate has been published in Thresholds 33 'Formalism'.

FABRIC

China in London
James Shen and Jennifer Tran, MArch Entrants
London Biennale

Beijing Studio
Dennis Frenchman and Jan Wampler, Instructors
Workshop 4.166

Courtyard Housing at Bahia Balandra
Rick Joy, Instructor
Studio 4.155

China in London

London Biennale / Independent Project
James Shen and Jennifer Tran
Alexander D'Hooghe, Mark Jarzombek [Metabolism
Workshop with Yung Ho Chang], Advisors
Fall 2006

2004
Mayor Livingstone announces plans for a new
Chinatown in London's Thames Gateway: "We want
London to be the Chinese economy's gateway into
Europe."

The Government promises 120,000 new homes by
2016 to ease the housing crisis in the city's South-
East.

2007
The Housing Shortage is compounded by skyrocketing
oil prices. Automobiles become luxuries. The Tube
operates beyond capacity, The Olympics are coming.

2008
The city builds.
Public transportation and production of habitable
square footage become monumental enterprises.

2009
The newly formed Socialist Chinese-British City
Corp.'s mantra: "We bring China(town) to you!"

Made in China-Raised in China units, prepackaged
with Chinese, are transported along the Thames to
Canary Wharf: an instant city of Imports skilled in
Olympic-sized construction.

2014
New Chinatown fills London's roads, sidewalks,
backyards, and crevices. Streets are eradicated. The
interior takes over.
Public property remains public. Private property
becomes public.

Welcome to London.

39°N 116°E

TUNG HO CHANG ATELIER FEICHANG JIANZHU

China Limited
Location

Jennifer Tran, MArch Level II and James Shen, MArch Level III

Beijing Workshop

Yung Ho Chang, Dennis Frenchman, Zhang Jie,
Wu Liangyong and Jan Wampler, Instructors
Workshop 4.166/ 11.307
Summer 2006

For five weeks during the summer, MIT and Tsinghua University jointly offers an Urban Design Studio in China's capital city. This is an outstanding opportunity for American and Chinese students to learn urban design and to jointly consider the issues of development and urban form in the context of China's rapid modernization.

The studio centers on preparing designs for an urban district in Beijing, including housing and shopping, and includes lectures on Chinese architecture, planning theory, and urbanism. The participants take bicycle and walking trips to the project site, historic monuments and districts in Beijing and its vicinity. The Workshop is interspersed with short study tours of new and traditional Chinese cities.

Image by Marissa Cheng, Liz Nguyen, Jiang Yang, Liu Peng and Neeraj Bhatia

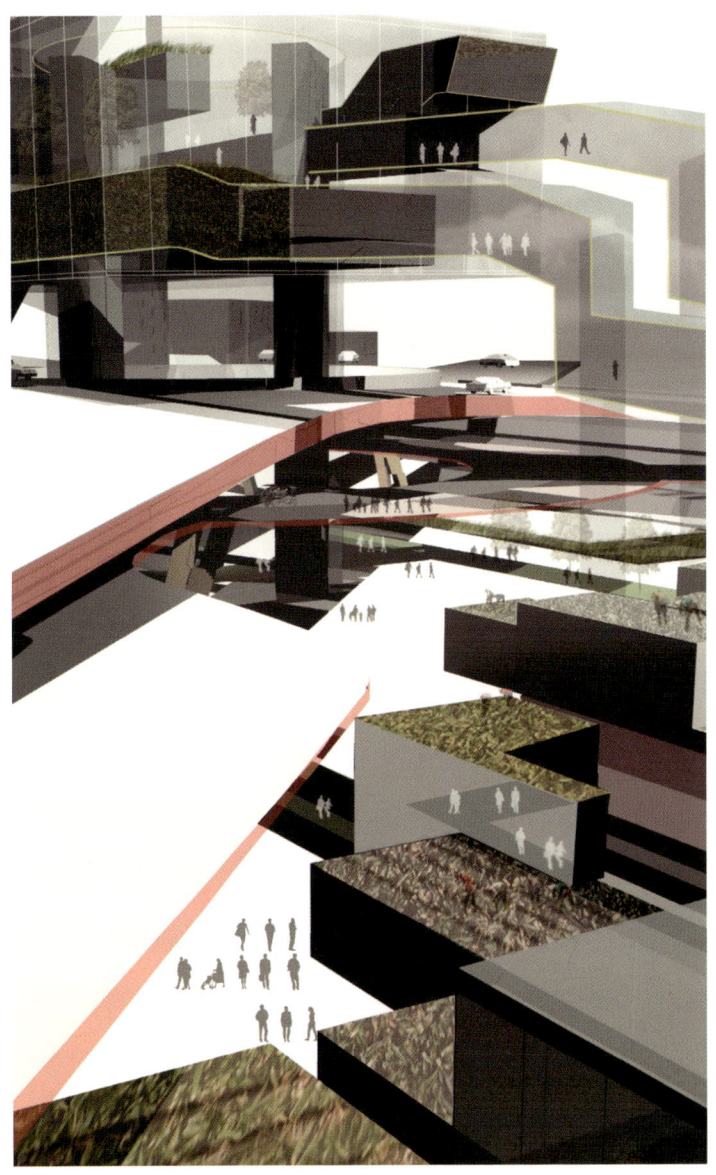

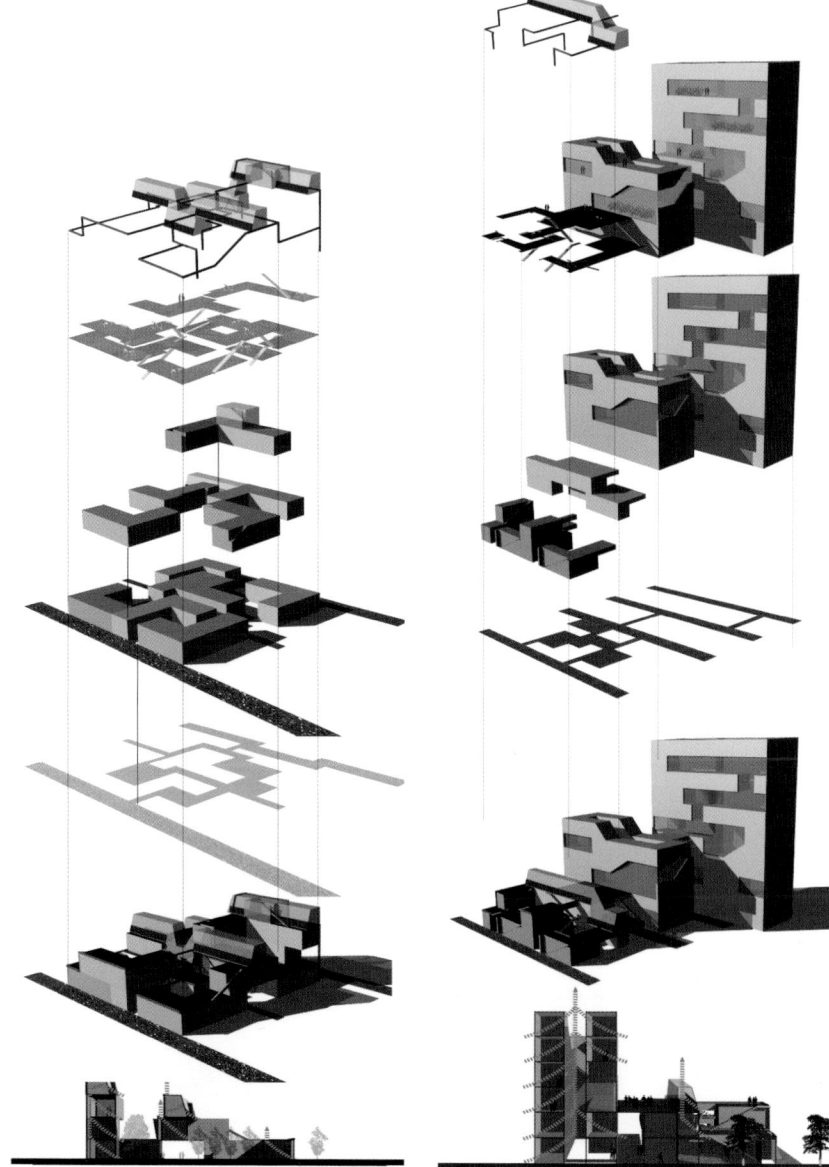

Marissa Cheng, MCP, Liz Nguyen, MArch III, Jiang Yang and Liu Peng, Tsinghua University, and Neeraj Bhatia, SMArchS Urbanism

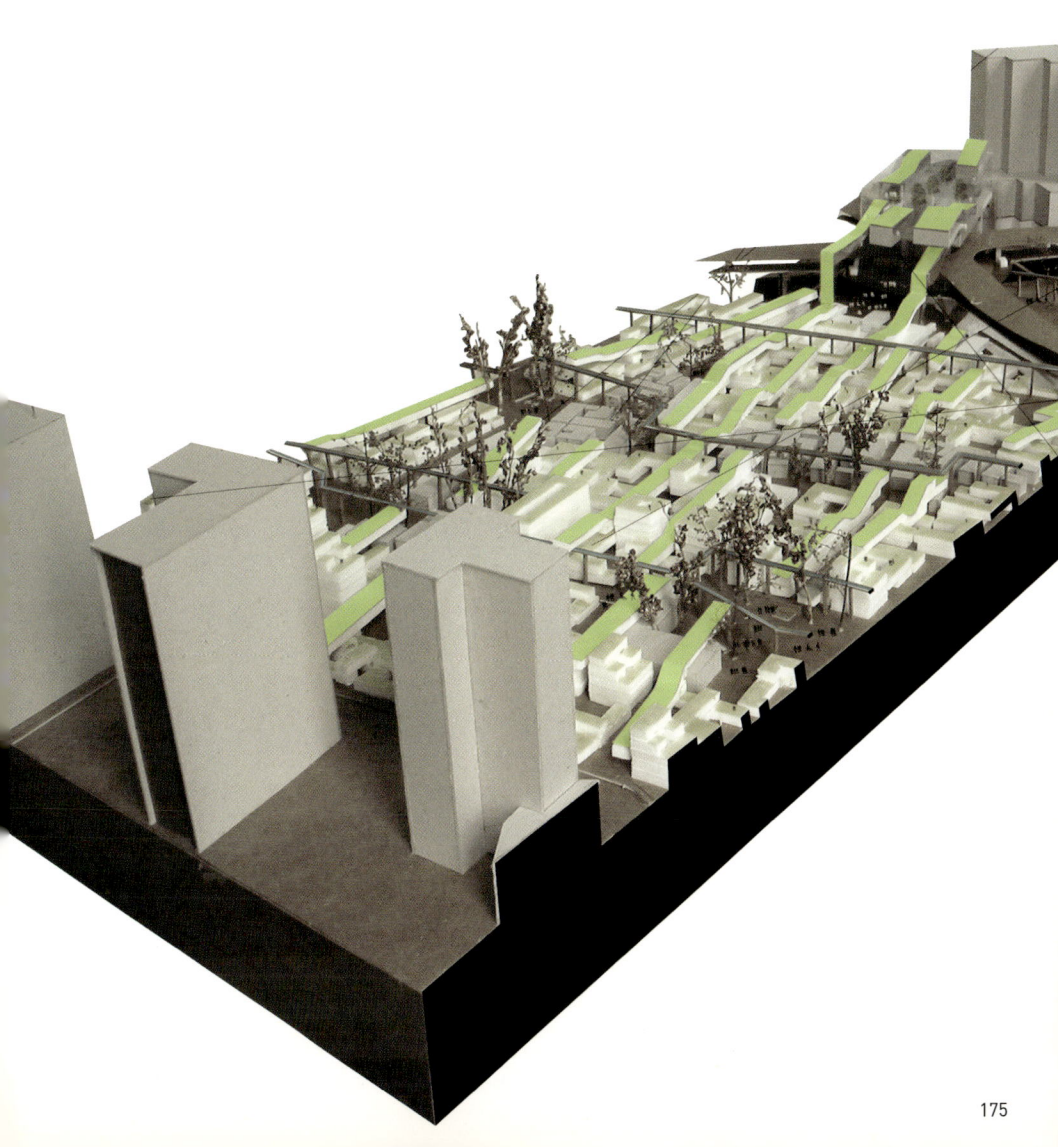

Courtyard Housing at Bahia Balandra

Rick Joy, Instructor
MArch Level III Studio 4.155
Fall 2006

Rick Joy's masterplan for a new resort development, Bahia Balandra, just to the north of La Paz on the Sea of Cortez in Baja, Mexico serves as the basis for the studio. The proposal involves the condensing of the resort into a small town, ala St. Tropez or Cinquaterra, in order to preserve the vast remaining acreages as a wilderness. When this master planning is completed, many architects will be invited to design the buildings.

The goal of the studio is to take on the design of various urban housing typologies in such a context, using the parameters of the master plan as the working tools for individual and collective explorations. It proposes investigating architecture within a specific urban setting using customary methods of programming, case study research, schematic design and design development, while simultaneously testing the efficacy of some alternative and more ephemeral processes, such as the creation of narrative frameworks examining the psychological and social implications of design. As the studio progresses, the scenario-based investigations will be used to unearth human relationships in architecture that exist outside the standard client-based model.

model by Daniel Bonham

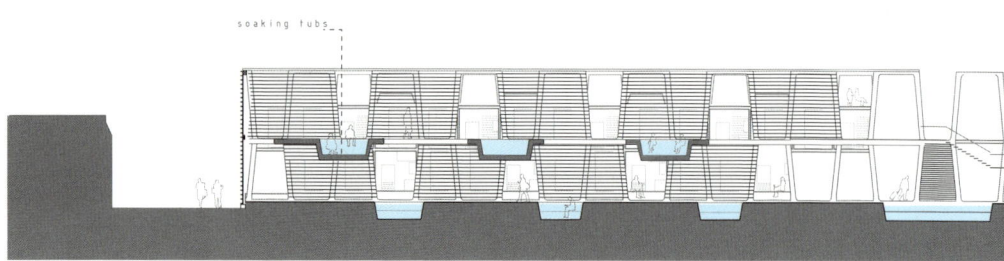

transverse section

cross section

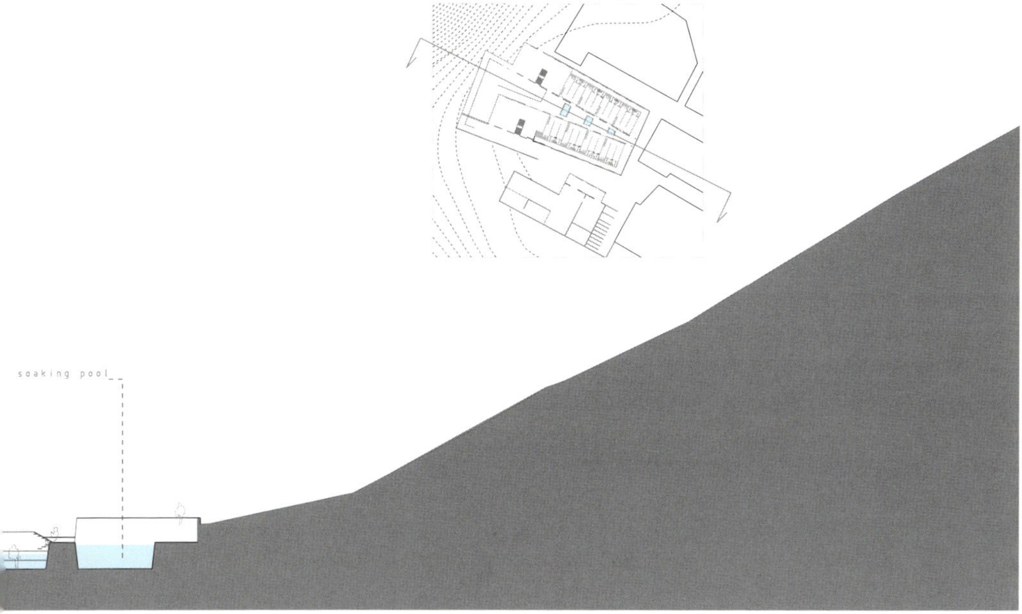

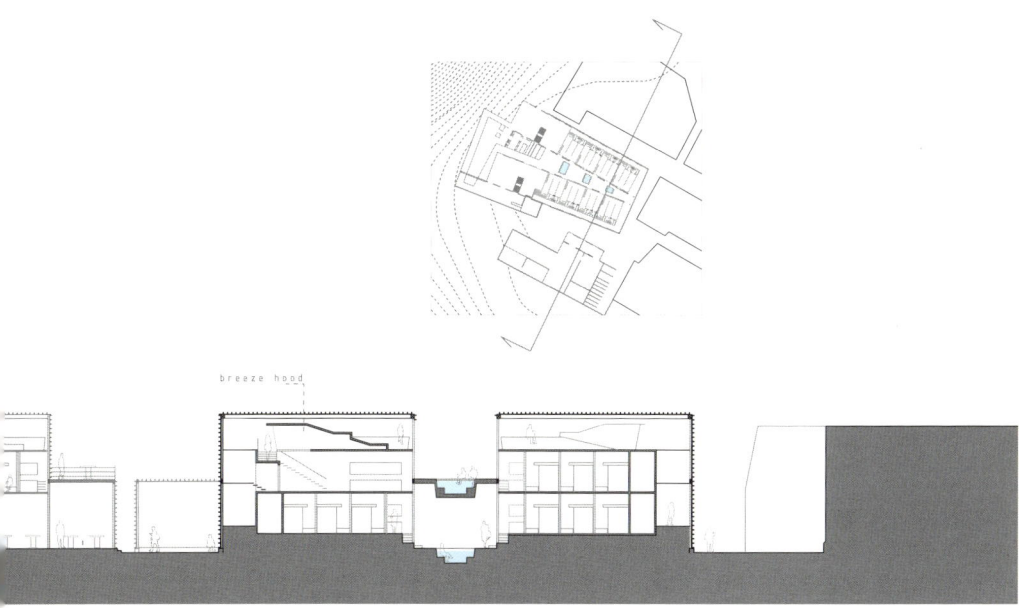

soaking pool

breeze hood

Daniel Bonham
MArch III

taqueria

soaking pool

Daniel Bonham
MArch III

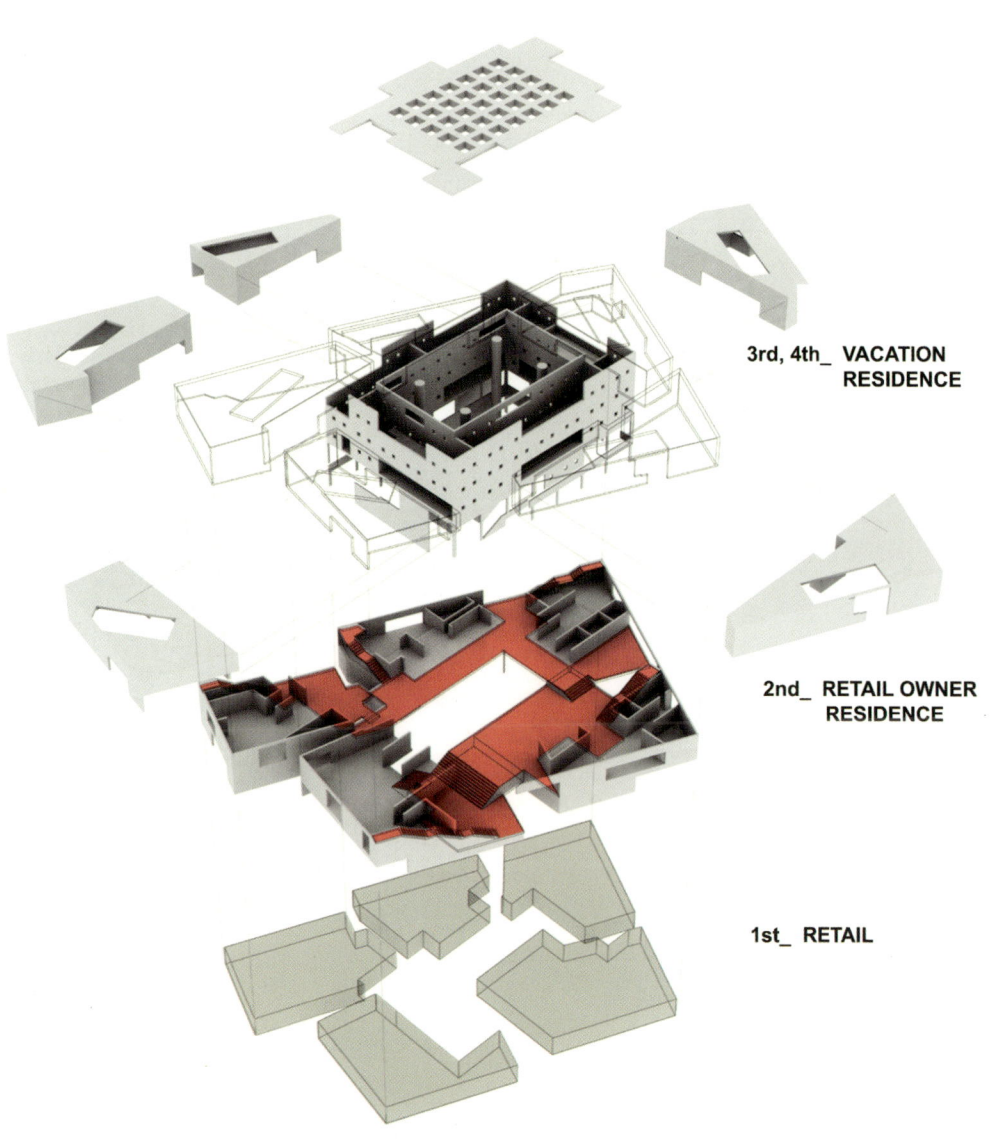

3rd, 4th_ **VACATION RESIDENCE**

2nd_ **RETAIL OWNER RESIDENCE**

1st_ **RETAIL**

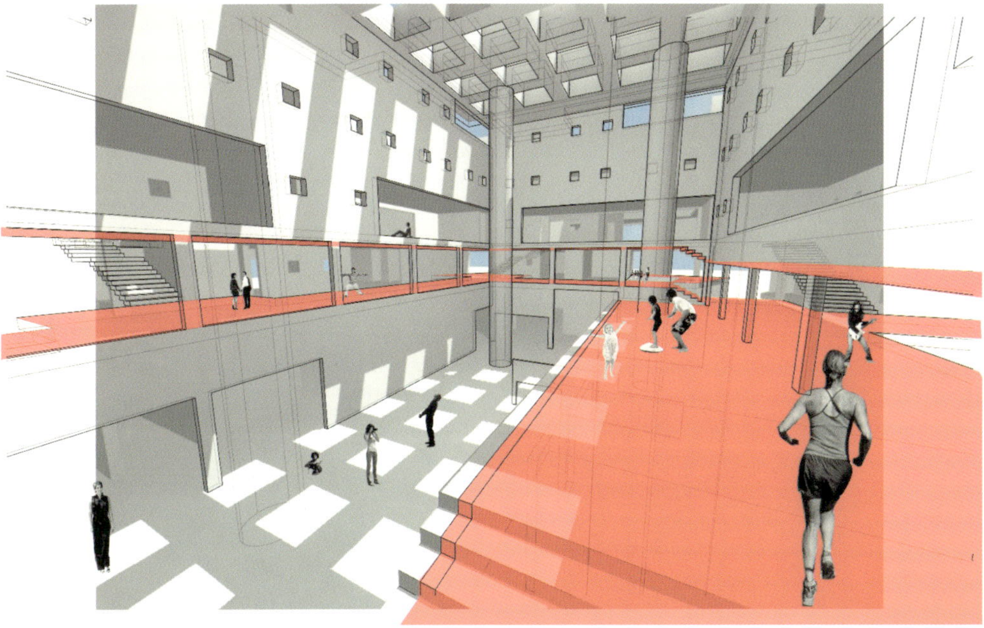

Young-Ju Kim
MArch III

183

183

MONUMENT

Towards a New Monumentality in Passaic New Jersey
Alexander D'Hooghe, Instructor
Urban Design/ MArch Level III Studio 11.332 J/ 4.163 J

Community Aquatic Center
Shun Kanda, Instructor
MArch Level II Studio 4.144

Megaport:
Architecture in Infrastructural Environments
Saud Sharaf
MArch Thesis

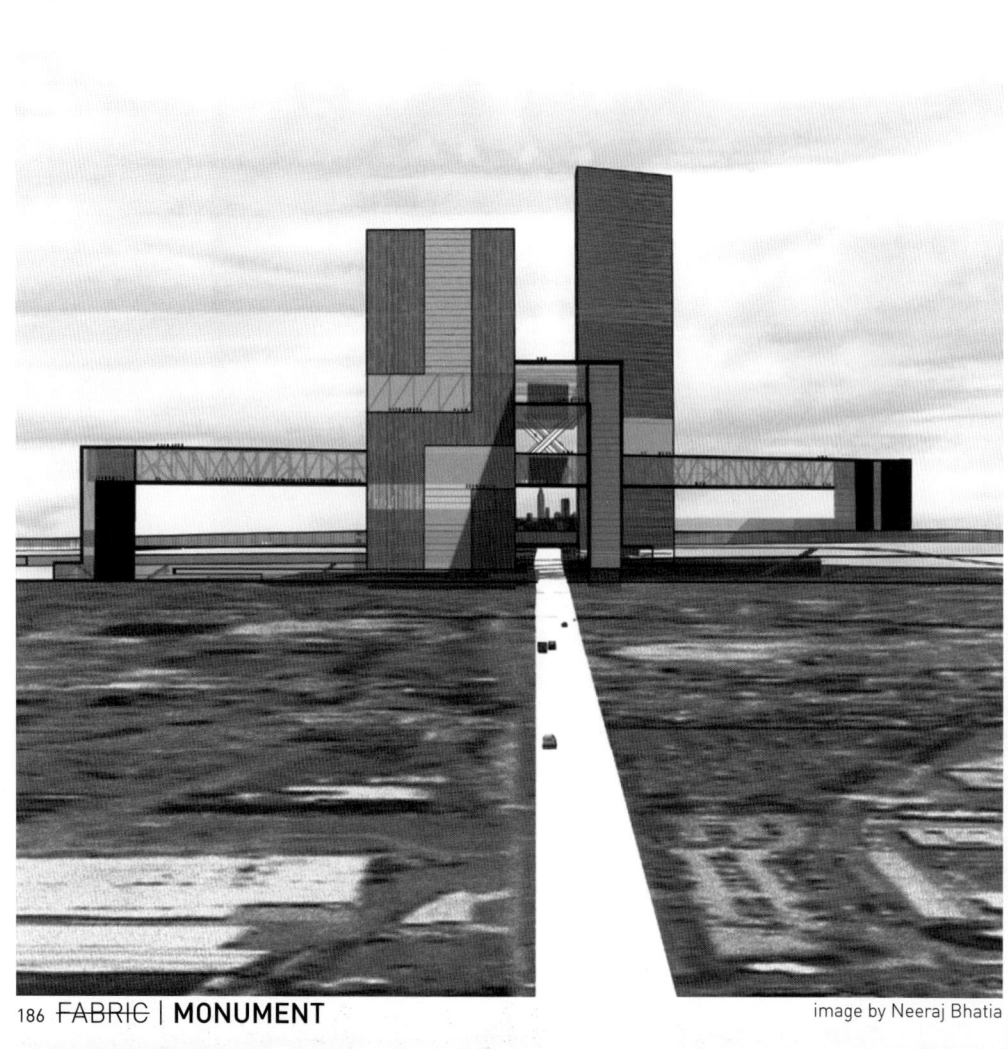

image by Neeraj Bhatia

Towards a New Monumentality in Passaic, New Jersey

Alexander D'Hooghe, Instructor
Nadya Nilina, TA
Urban Design/ MArch Level III Studio 11.332 J/ 4.163 J
Spring 2006

This studio investigates how architecture can still contribute to the civicness and legibility of the territories of sprawl, under the assumption that in the next decade, America will witness a return of the State in policies influencing urban development. Recent evolutions in urban design seem to suggest an abandonment of architecture's tools in favor of landscape and infrastructure design. The studio is a design research project to determine, one last time, what architecture can still do in terms of contributing a larger territorial civic structure to the 'grey goo' of sprawl.

The studio operates in New Jersey's Passaic County. Not only is this area emblematic for many areas surrounding American cities, this location also allows us to build an answer to Robert Smithson's seminal 1967 article 'Tour of the Monuments of Passaic, NJ'

Finally, the studio, in order to innovate, will assume a fundamental change in the parameters of the urban project: instead of continuing privatization, we will assume a return of the state: a renewed role of government in the sponsoring of housing, infrastructure and civic projects as ways to create employment and economic growth for the impoverished population of Passaic.

Enrollment is limited to 12. The constituency of the work is our peers across the world: the purpose is to contribute to the disciplinary discourse about architecture's role in urbanism and planning. For that reason, publication of the work is of prime importance.

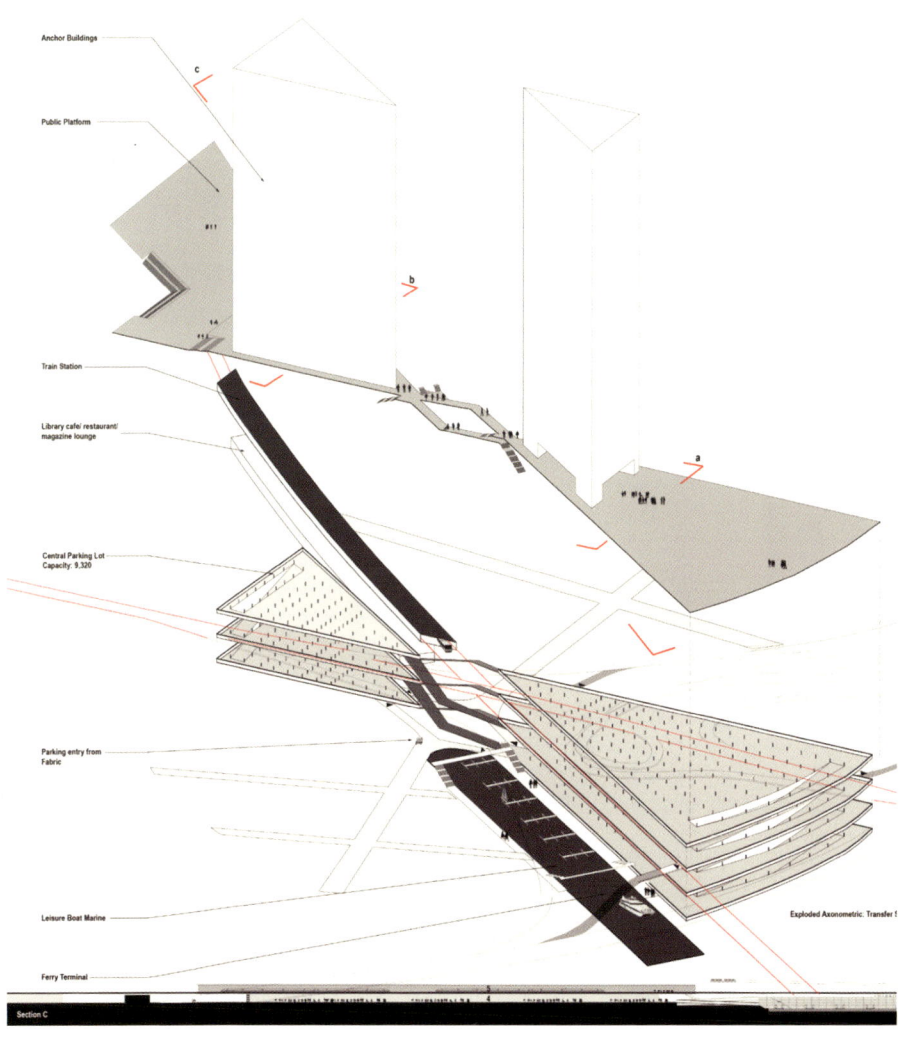

Anchor Buildings

c

Public Platform

b

Train Station

Library cafe/ restaurant/
magazine lounge

a

Central Parking Lot
Capacity: 9,320

Parking entry from
Fabric

Leisure Boat Marine

Exploded Axonometric: Transfer S

Ferry Terminal

Section C

Neeraj Bhatia
SMArchS Urbanism

Infrastructural Hills of Passaic
Elevated Traffic Circle

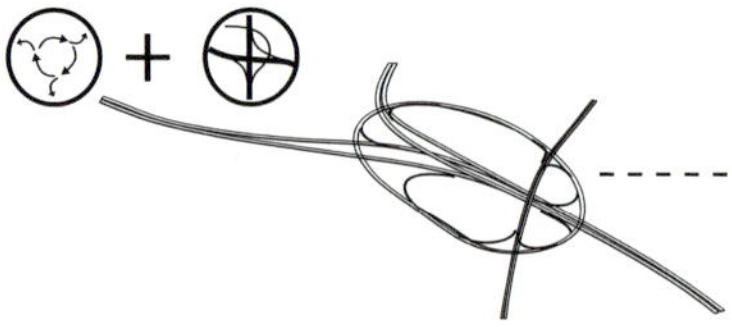

New Chinatown of Passaic

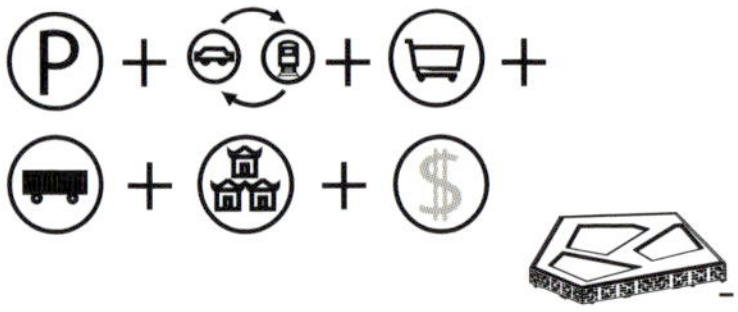

Big Box Rail

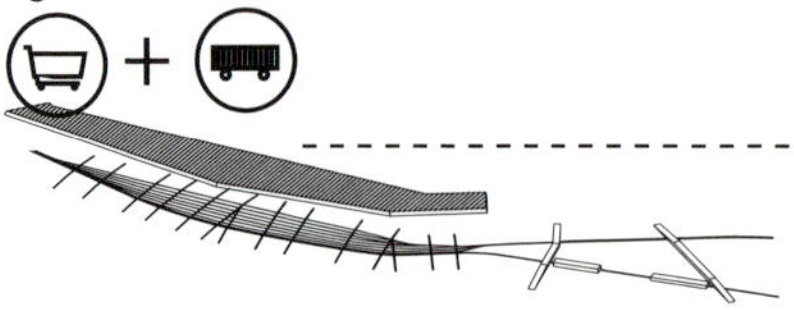

Public Tarmac

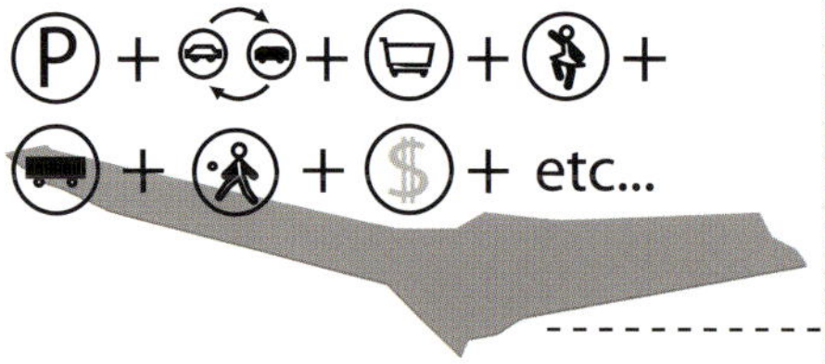

etc...

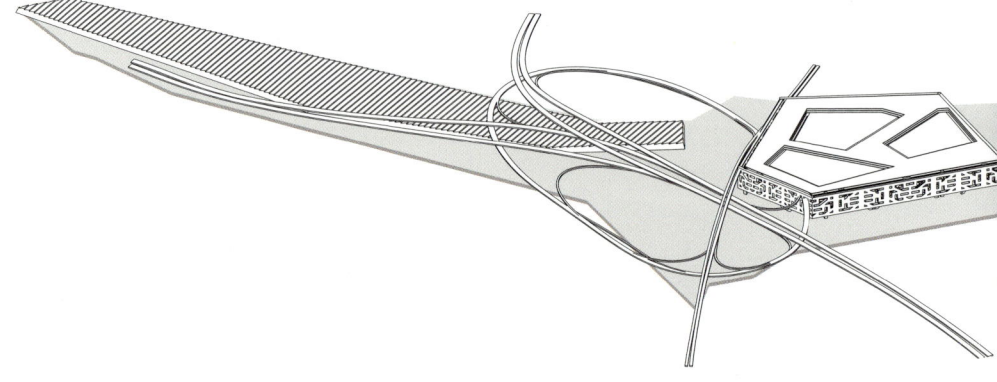

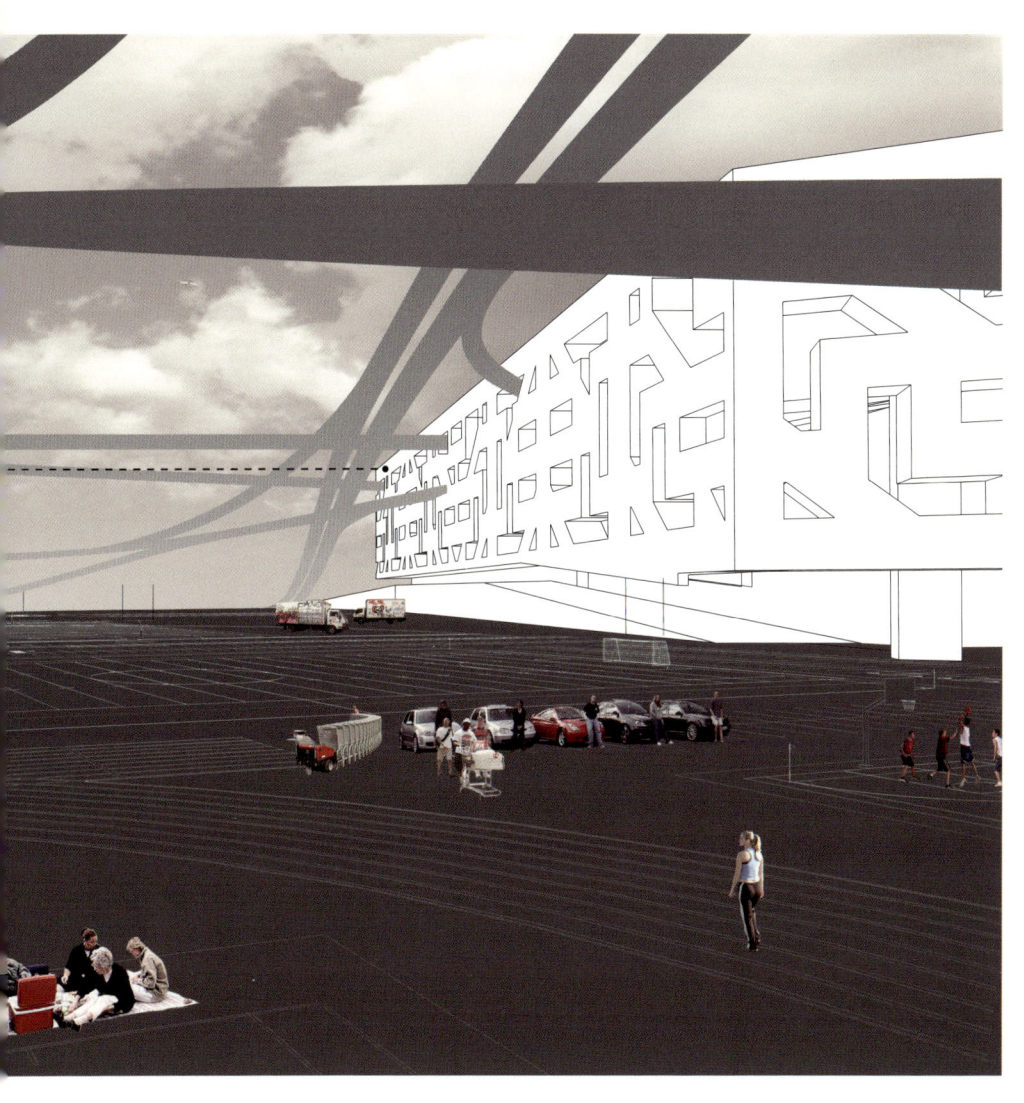

James Shen
MArch III

Community Aquatic Center

Shun Kanda, Instructor
Edward Rice, TA
MArch Level II Studio 4.144
Spring 2006

This studio undertook as its project a Community Aquatic Center at Magazine Beach alongside the Charles River bank in Cambrige. The facility, adjacent to an existing MDC Bathhouse, is to provide a year-round family recreation amenity in this urban context.

The studio explored notion of a place for public community bathing, recreation and physical fitness for all ages year-round and the use of waterfront sites as a land/water interface and appropriate architectural intervention. The deployment of steel construction was required as a structural and tectonic language.

Studio consultants included Ed Allen on steel construction, John Fernandez on materials & building technology, Carl Rosenberg on acoustics, and Maryline Andersen on Daylighting.

image by Peter DePasquale

197

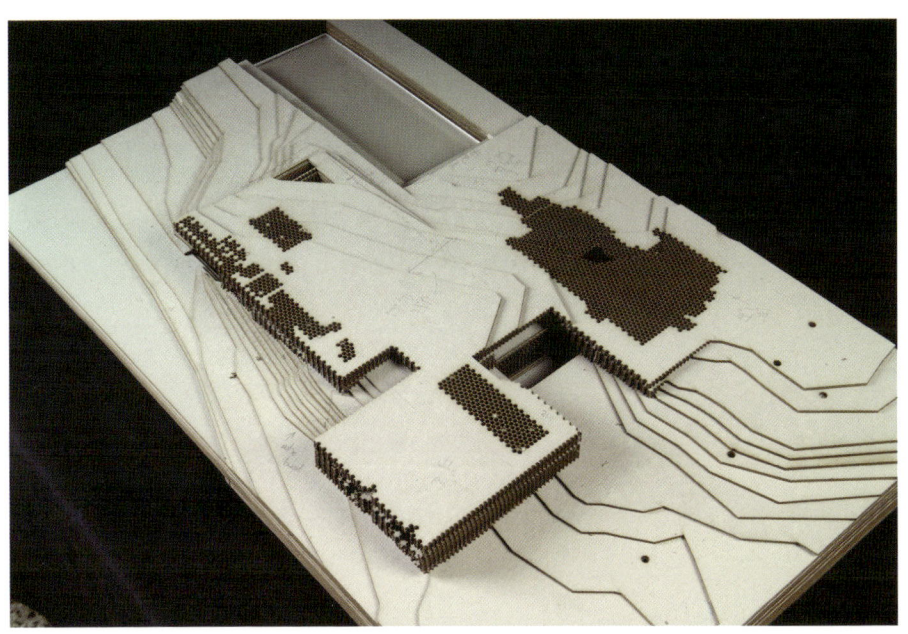

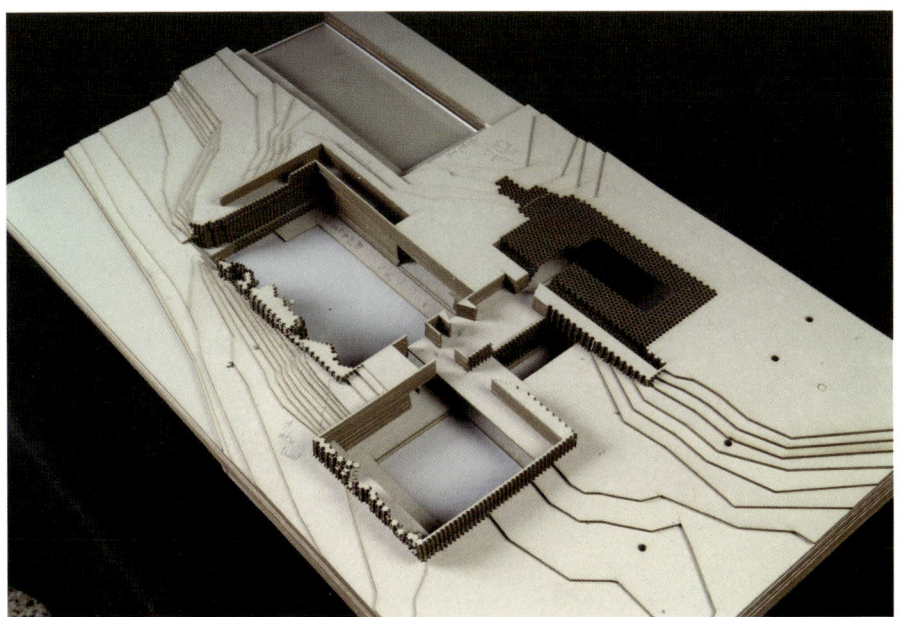

Peter DePasquale
MArch II

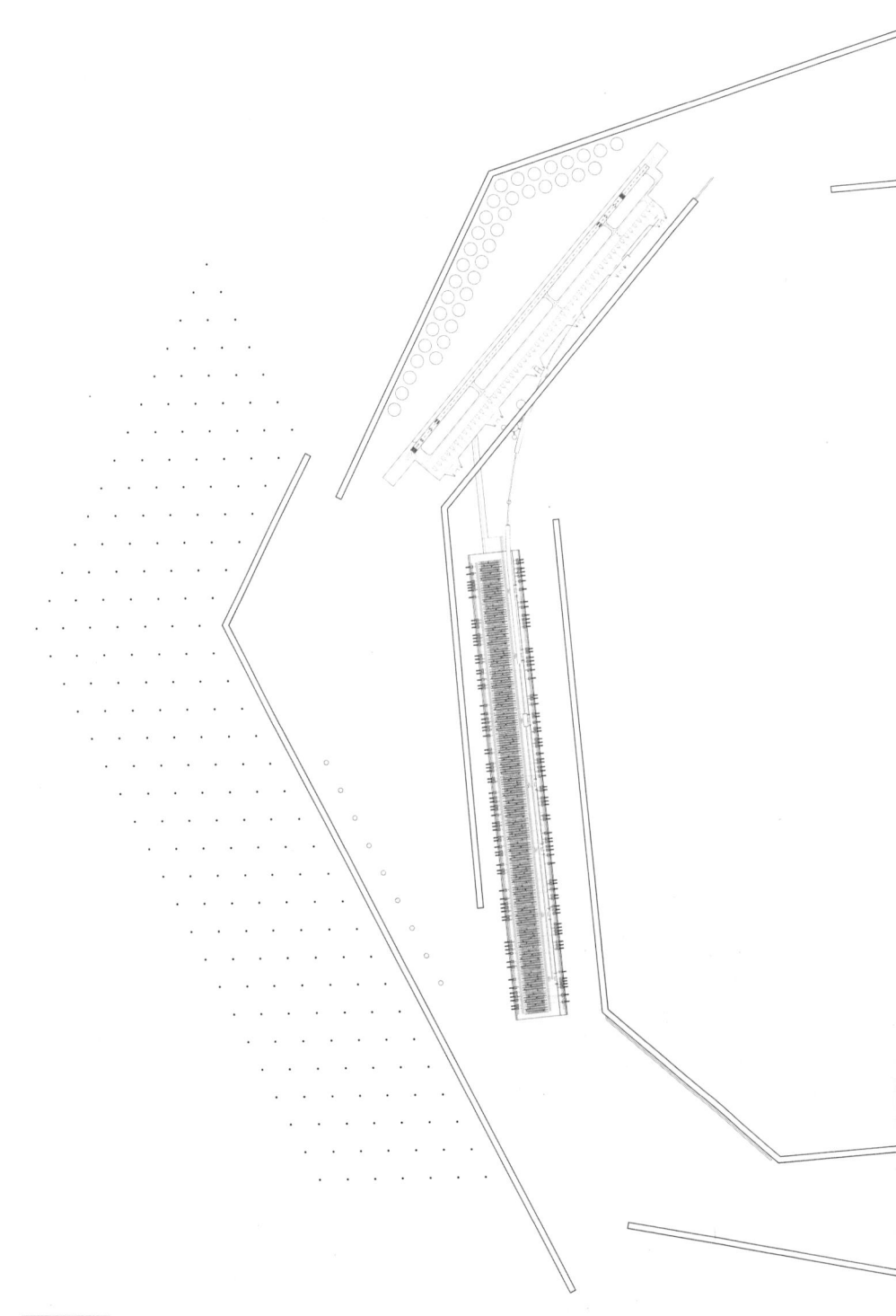

MEGAPORT: Architecture in Infrastructural Environments

Saud Sharaf
MArch Thesis
Alexander D'Hooghe, Advisor
Julian Beinart, Arindam Dutta and
Nasser Rabbat, Readers
Fall 2006

Site: Arabian Sea, major region for container shipping bulk breaking.

World trade is growing at a rate twice the world's economy. The assembly and customization of traded goods are increasingly decentralized around the globe. The frequency of their transportation and exchange is increasing. The phenomenon is of container freights, specifically transshipment. Transshipment ports are no portals to cities, but are increasingly becoming autonomous global entities. The ports are mere switchboards, an exchange mechanism between ships. Transshipment is the fastest growing shipping market. Ships are getting bigger. Ports are expanding and dredging deeper, as they struggle today with overcapacity. New terminals are built, as economies of scale reach saturation in existing ports. The form of the global infrastructure is changing. In response, a new infrastructural move is necessary: a Megaport for transshipment. The Megaport is a transshipment port solely for ultra large containerships. It affords an economy for such transoceanic ships to remain in sea, and for local ports to be served through feeder ships. The Megaport is self-sufficient, autonomous and offshore. In this colony of globalization, an infrastructural architecture is absolutely necessary.

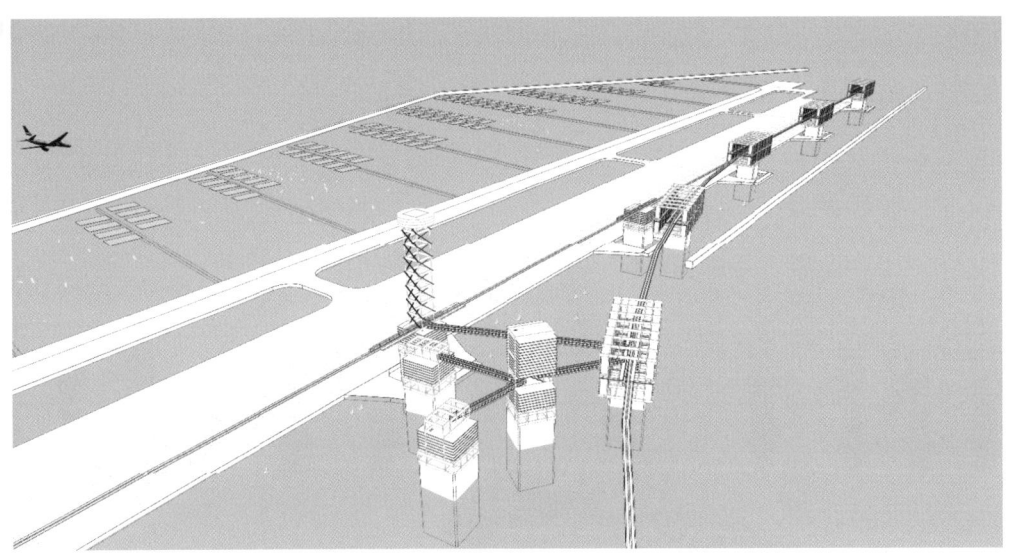

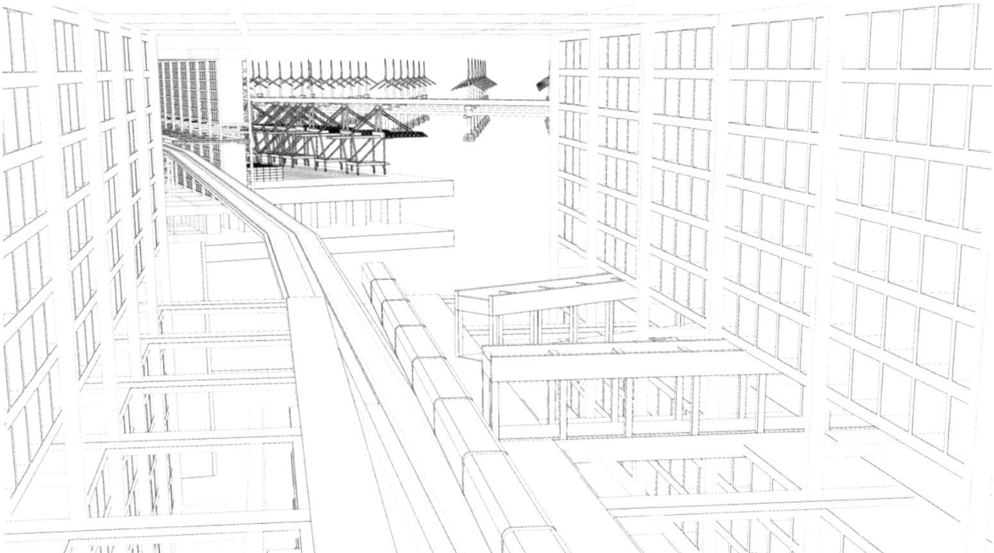

MEGAPORT: Architecture in Infrastructural Environments
Saud Sharaf, MArch Thesis

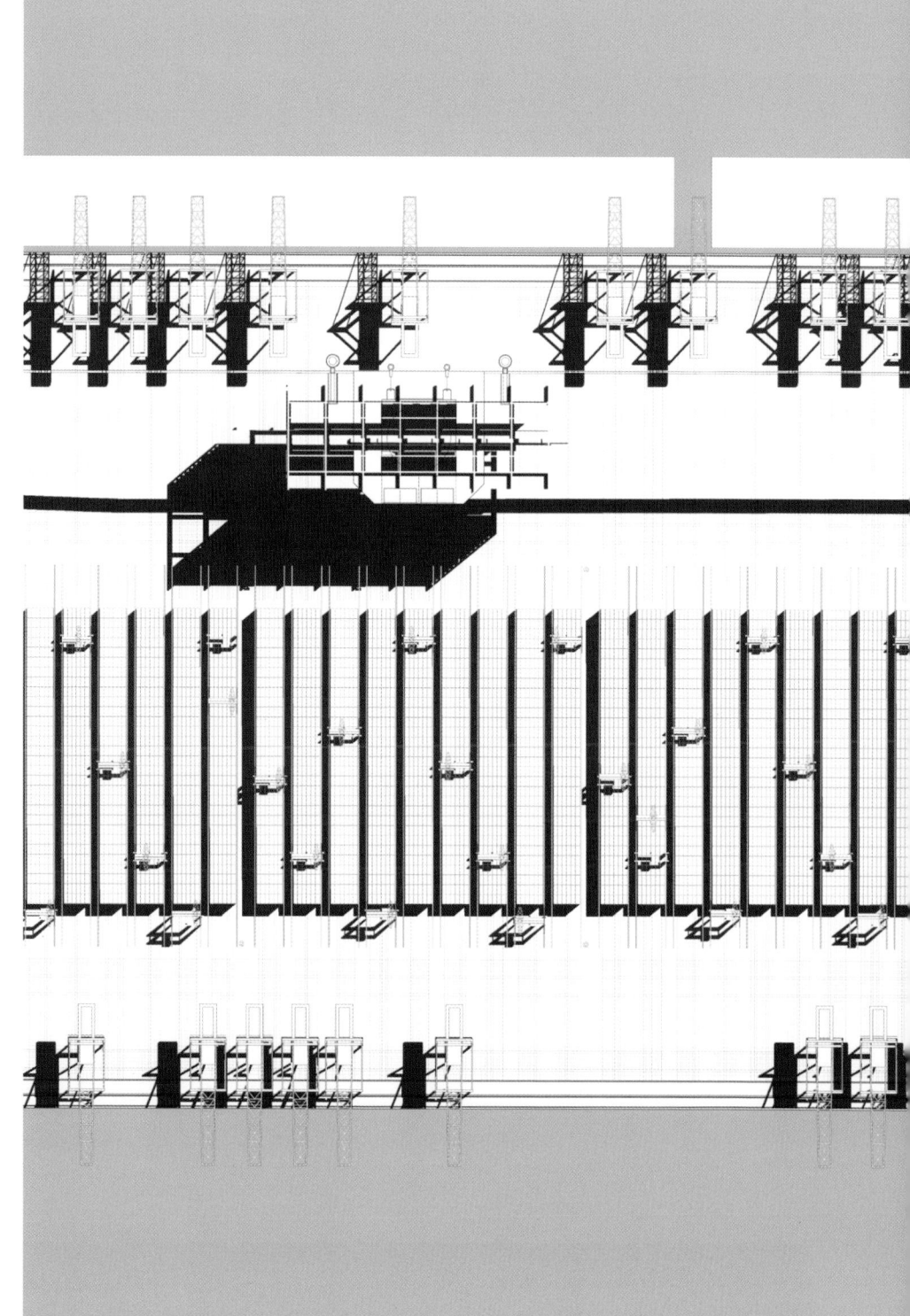

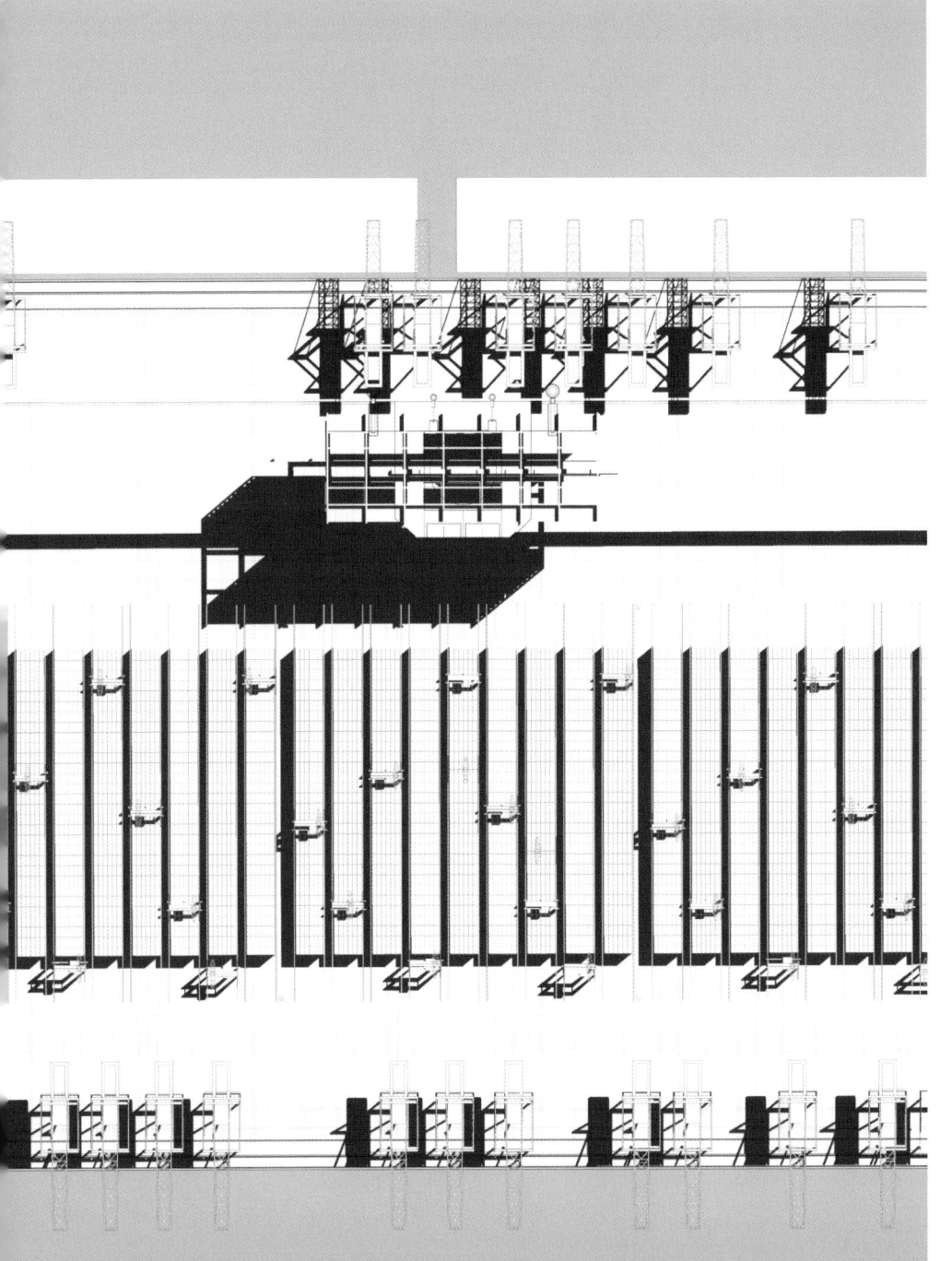

MEGAPORT: Architecture in Infrastructural Environments
Saud Sharaf, MArch Thesis

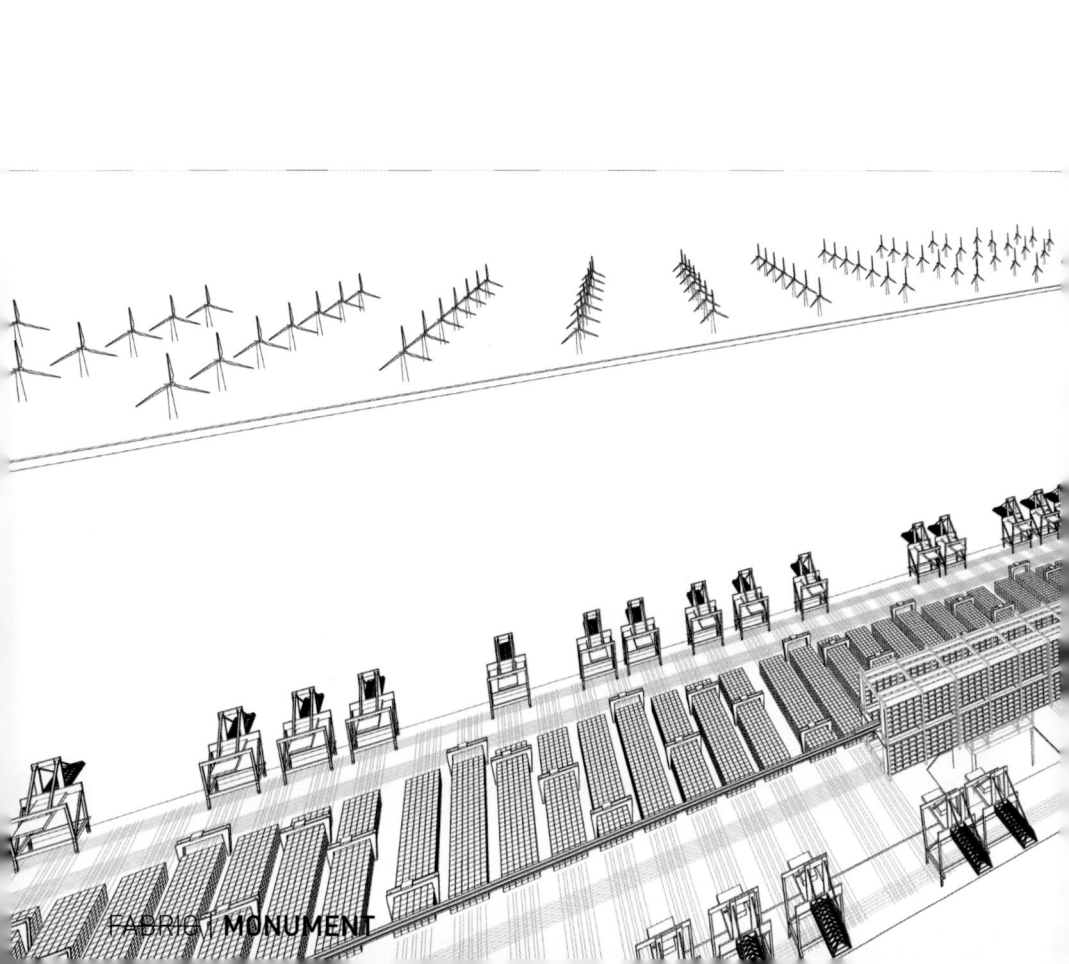

FABRICA MONUMENT

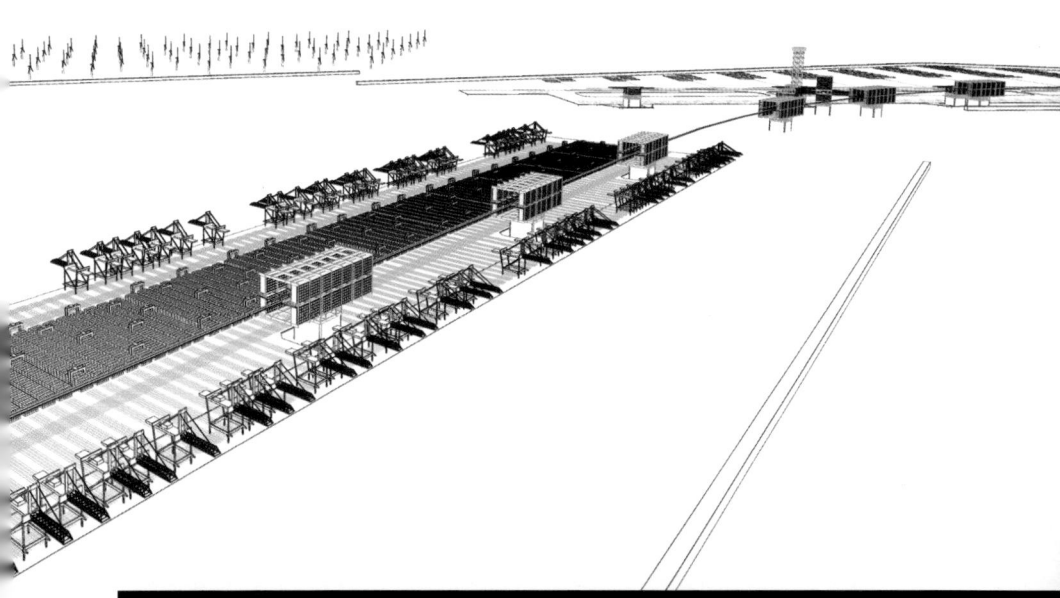

MEGAPORT: Architecture in Infrastructural Environments
Saud Sharaf, MArch Thesis

RECONCILIATION

The massive global uprooting going on since the 18th century is leaving increasing numbers of people culturally displaced, conscious of the fact that an organic, reconciled existence – the promise of harmonious life – is beyond reach. Just as technology alienates one from nature; globalization destroys the myth of homogeneous, static communities. The consciousness of loss, while coupled with the promise of potential emancipation from the shackles of history, dogma and convention, nevertheless inflicts a deep and lasting trauma. This is the trauma of modernity, endlessly described from Simmel in the 19th century, up until the revolt literature of the 1960s, and cyberpunk in the 1980s.

The trauma elicits, among others, two very different reactions. The first engages in a hopeful operation of overcoming the trauma of modernity: restoring, through images and action, the possibility of a sustainable society. Political movements from anti-globalization to the green movement, contain this belief system. In urban planning, this approach finds an apt expression in community-building operations and bottom-up initiatives.

In architecture, on the one hand, the primary expression of this belief system is aesthetic: the quest for reconciliation leads in some cases to a neo-organicist aesthetic. This agenda is based on the hypothesis that the exploration of advanced technologies and innovative use of materials may provide a means for the creation of new forms which reconcile contemporary culture and local identity. In urban design, on the other hand, such a belief system leads to the

TRAUMA

re-introduction of older patterns of urbanization, that have a
more old-worldish, organic overtone.

The other reaction is to actively address the trauma in
full awareness that we are dealing with a structural fact
of modern society, without any illusions about a return to
wholeness.

Modernity as a positive project invites a full embrace of the
emancipating potentials of trauma. Modernity's capacity to
emancipate – from history, dogma, oppression, myth – is
indeed the central parti of the other road. Trauma is just a
part of that path. Mobility, freedom of movement, dazzling
technology, an excitement of the modern – where 'all that is
solid melts into air' – here becomes a working hypothesis.

Both terms invoke a narrative of loss: something is broken;
reconciliation regrets the loss and works to make things
whole again; trauma accepts that the breaking of the moulds
creates as of yet unimaginable freedoms, which are more
important than the harmony that appears lost.

RECONCILIATION

Generative Opponents:
A New Architecture for Native Soil
Axel Paredes
MArch Thesis

'Coming Together'
Housing in New Orleans
Jan Wampler, Instructor
MArch Level II Studio 4.143

A Transformation of Shanghai's Urban Fabric
Christine Caine
MArch Thesis

Personal Geographies: Life and Culture in
Mexico City
Simi Hoque, Instructor
Undergraduate/ MArch Level II Studio 4.131

Japan Workshop: Continuity and Transformation
Shun Kanda, Instructor
Workshop 4.183

São Paolo Urban Design Studio
Julian Beinart and John de Monchaux, Instructors
MArch Level III, SMArchS, MCP Studio 4.163J/ 11/332J

Generative Opponents: A New Architecture for Native Soil

Axel Paredes
MArch Thesis
Yung Ho Chang, Advisor
John Fernandez, Axel Kilian, Readers
Fall 2006

A design of an Ecological Visitor Center for the Central American country of Guatemala was carried out based on a series of explorations with analogue and digital design techniques. The architecture of the project explores a possible use in the utilization of locally available materials in design, both natural and industrial, suggesting innovative architectural possibilities beyond the handcrafted vernacular language of conventional practice and the synthetic perfection of contemporary digital design. Using bamboo as the main construction material, the building was designed from a series of studies that were developed to solve the building's complex geometry with locally available methods. The proposal for this Ecological Visitor Center in the ravines that form part of the city's urban fabric provides a solution for new types of public spaces and parks for Guatemala City, while it raises the awareness of these natural corridors in this sprawling city. New solutions for their sensitive use need to be proposed by re-thinking these corridors beyond "obstacles" for urban development or enclosed out-of-bounds areas. Instead, these ravines have the potential to become natural urban lungs for public access and sensitive recreation. Nature does not end with technology. Instead, their generative potential is enhanced by the constant feedback between analogue and digital tools, natural and synthetic materials and hand-craft and automated methods.

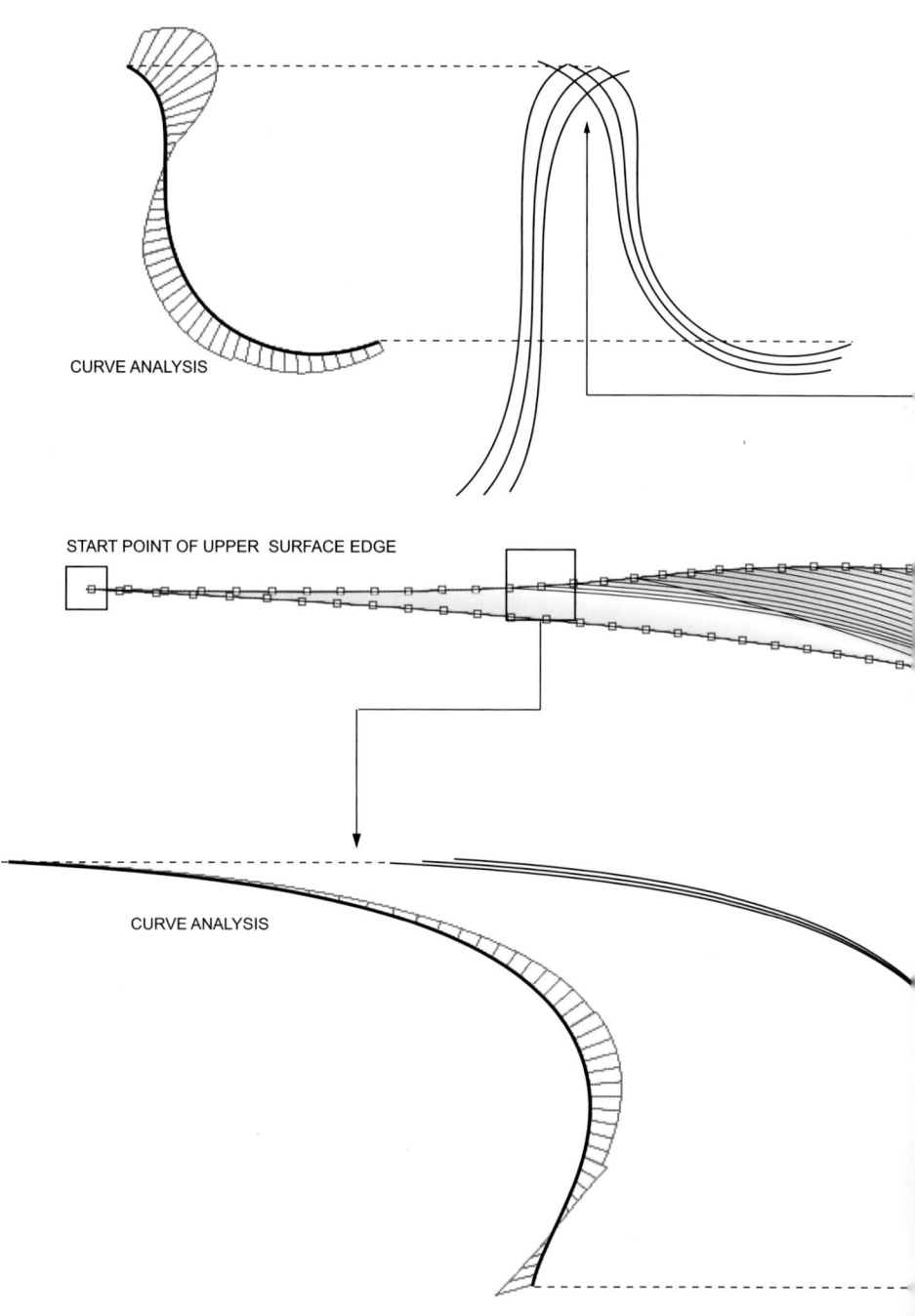

CURVE ANALYSIS

START POINT OF UPPER SURFACE EDGE

CURVE ANALYSIS

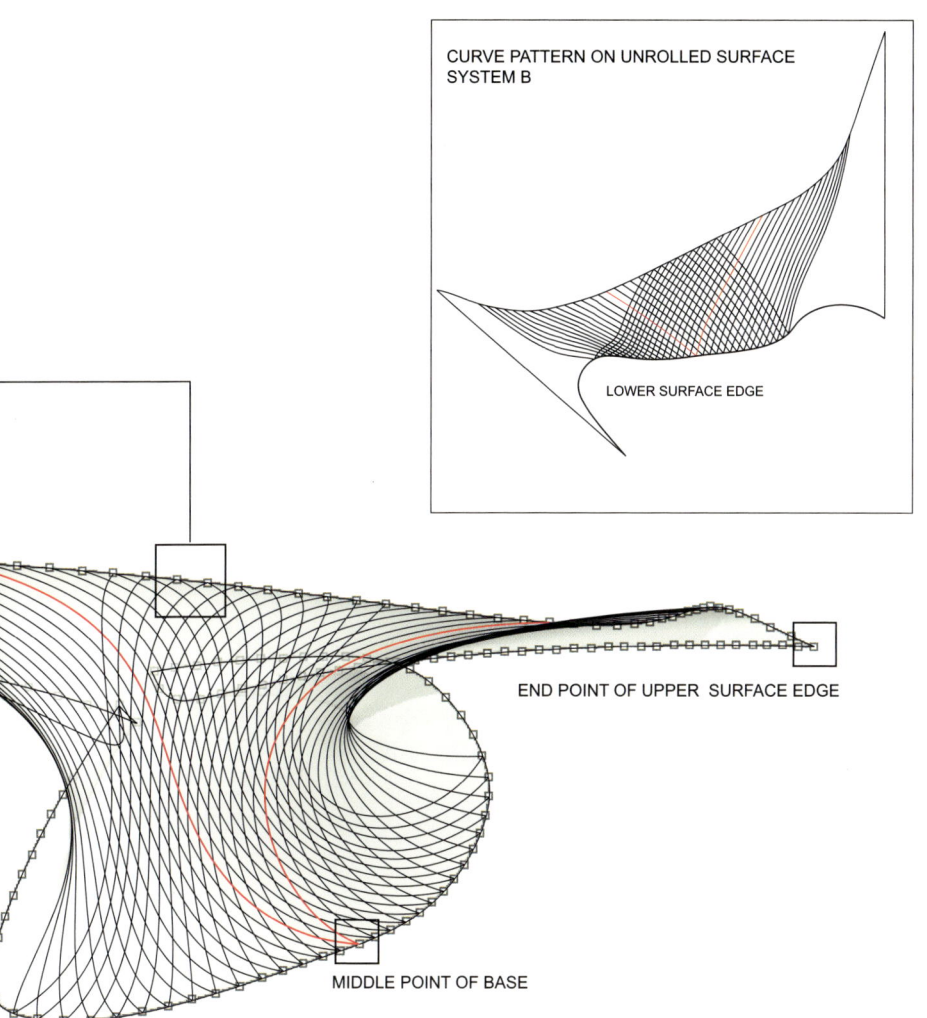

CURVE PATTERN ON UNROLLED SURFACE
SYSTEM B

LOWER SURFACE EDGE

END POINT OF UPPER SURFACE EDGE

MIDDLE POINT OF BASE

Generative Opponents: A New Architecture for Native Soil
Axel Paredes, MArch Thesis

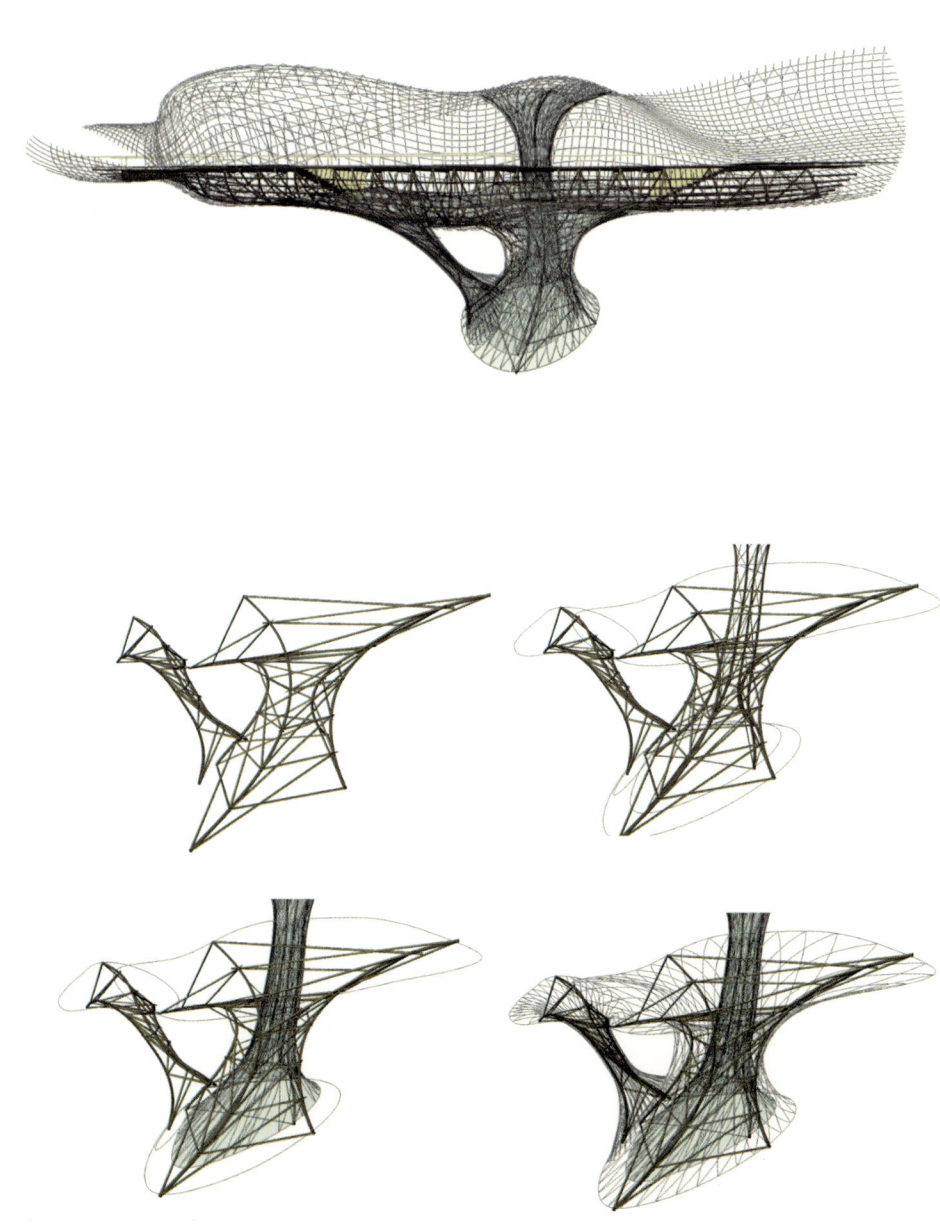

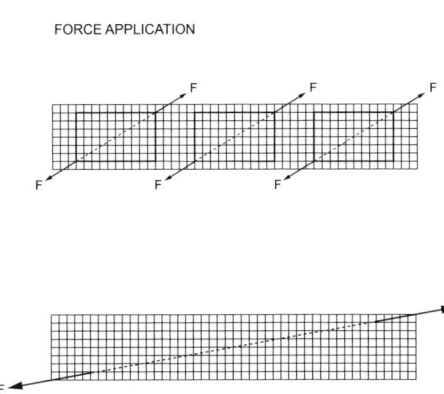

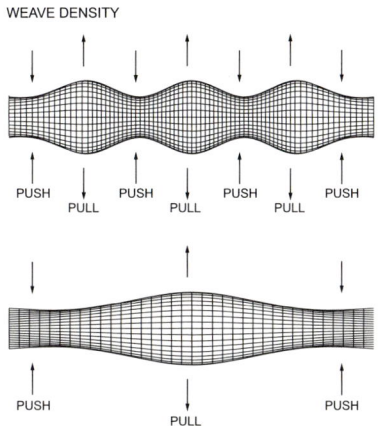

Generative Opponents: A New Architecture for Native Soil
Axel Paredes, MArch Thesis

Generative Opponents: A New Architecture for Native Soil
Axel Paredes, MArch Thesis

'Coming Together'
Housing in New Orleans

Jan Wampler, Instructor
Saba Ghole, TA
MArch Level II Studio 4.144
Spring 2006

Since it is unclear how and where New Orleans will be
rebuilt, the site chosen for this project is next to the
French Quarter and was not flooded during Hurricane
Katrina. Here, we will look for clues from the old
city to design new housing without imitating the old.
Special emphasis will be place on designing around
"three dimensional courtyards" for both community
use and natural ventilation.

The objectives of the project are as follows:
1. To design dense housing, community, educational
and commercial facilities in 4 to 6 story buildings.
2. To explore the "space between" buildings as a way
of providing places of "coming together".
3. To design at three scales - dwelling, cluster and
overall.
4. To design dwellings that residents may assist in
building and therefore gain skills
for employment as well as a connection to their
housing.

During the semester we will work with an NGO group
called "The Urban Conservancy" that is helping
rebuild New Orleans using local labor. We will
invite community, city and NGO groups to our final
review and organize the studio designs into a small
publication to send to the city of New Orleans. As
architects we can new-build, not just rebuild.

drawing by Patrick Rhodes-Vivour

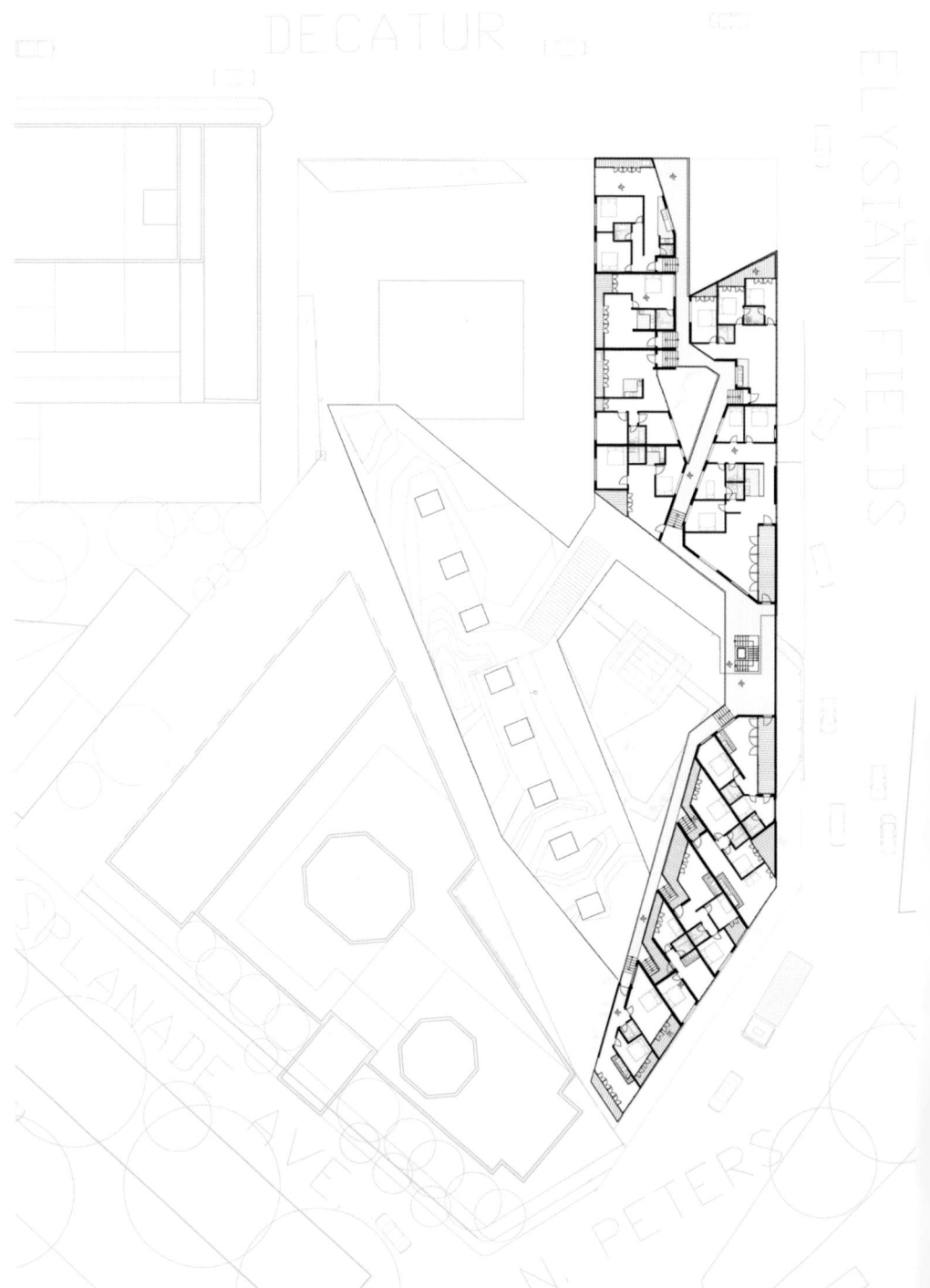

DECATUR

ELYSIAN FIELDS

ESPLANADE AVE

N. PETERS

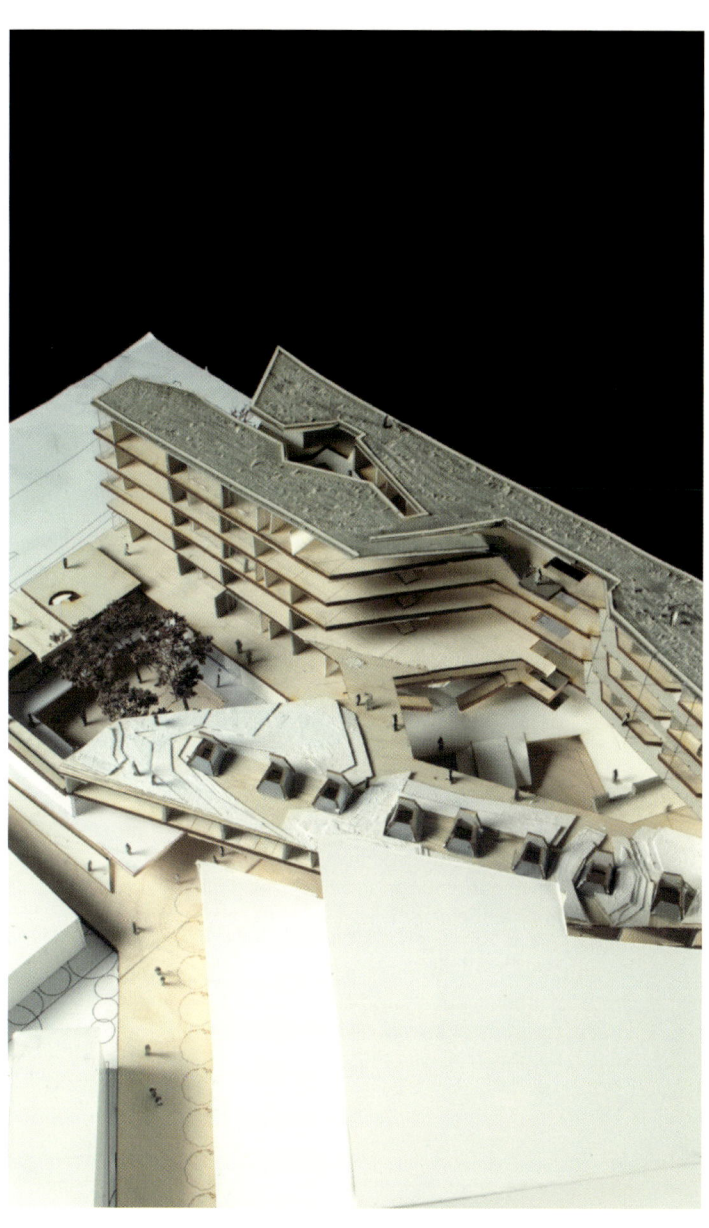

A Transformation of Shanghai's Urban Fabric

Christine Caine
SMArchS Thesis
Yung Ho Chang, Advisor
Julian Beinart, Reader
Spring 2006

Due to rapid development of the city, Shanghai has become characterized by drastic juxtapositions of building typologies and urban forms. Entire sections of the urban center are being replaced with large scale developments while the city overall expands into the periphery, replacing farmland with gated superblock developments. The city may be said to be losing identity as large sections of traditional urban fabric are being replaced. It is presented in this Thesis, that preservation of this identity is feasible by the implementation of a plan for the transformation of urban fabric. This thesis investigates a methodology by which an appropriate stepped transformation of urban form arises out of the intense analysis and comparison of traditional and new development samples. The first part of this thesis is titled Context and traces the numerous levels of juxtaposition within the urban environemnt of Shanghai, based on observations during site visit and research conducted in the Fall of 2005 with the MIT research seminar, Sustainable Development in Shanghai. Elaborating on these observations and clarifying the distinct characteristics of each side being juxtaposed, the next section of this thesis is titled Analysis.

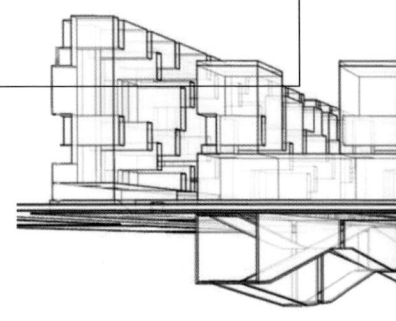

This analysis takes each sample set and extracts the essential components in order to form a resource data set, refereed to as the "kit of parts". The final section is titled Transformation and proposes a fabric that intends to preserve Shanghai's urban identity. Believing that factors of identity are embedded in the basic Lilong urban structure, an average model, representative of the Lilong form is used as the starting point for the transformation that follows. The fabric is arrived at by a designed transformation process of steps onto this initial average model, informed by the introduction of pieces from the kit of parts for both old and new developments. It is proposed that the final outcome of this transformation is inevitably tied to traditional urbanity while addressing modern standards of living as it's foundation is the average model of Lilong neighborhood and it's transformation is partially guided by elements of superblock development within the kit of parts.

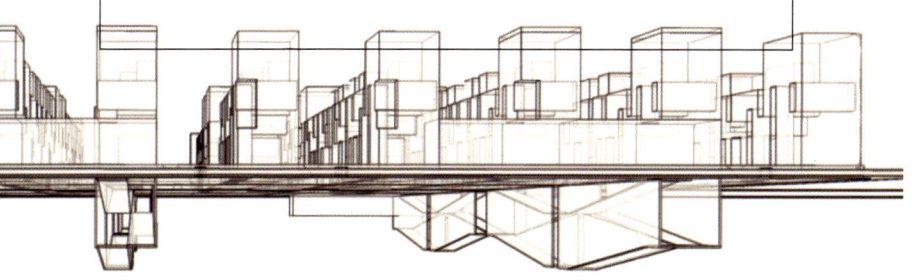

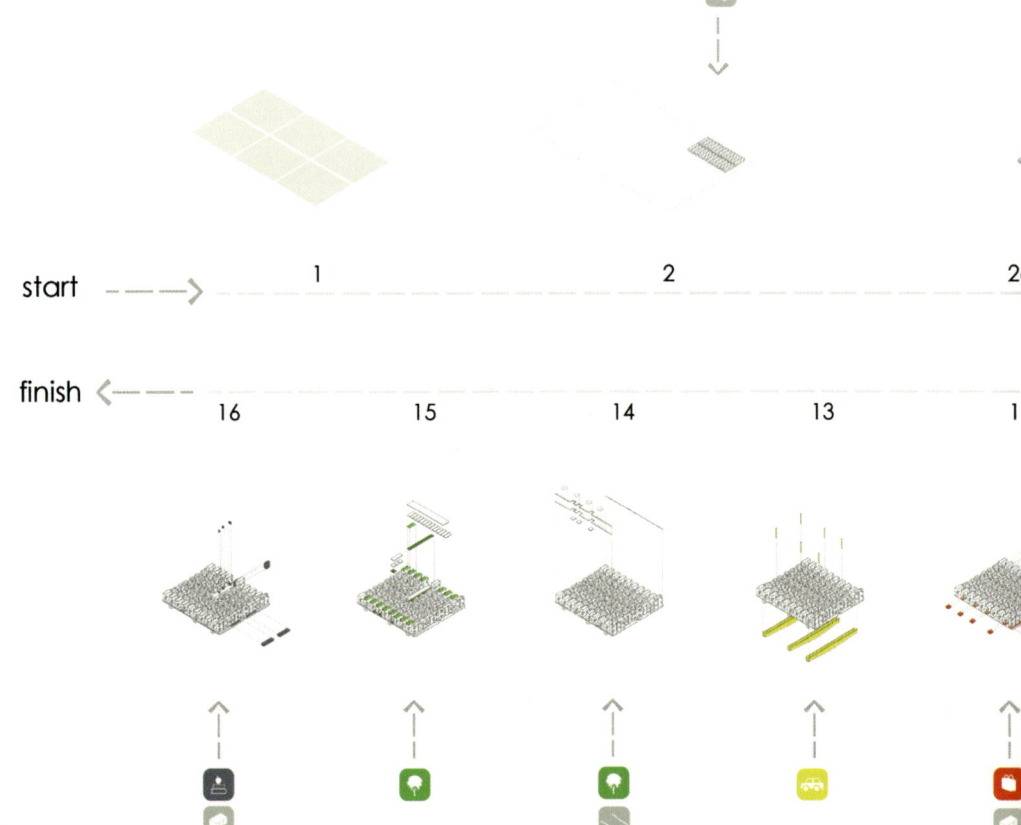

start - - - ->   1   2   2

finish <- - - -
16   15   14   13   1

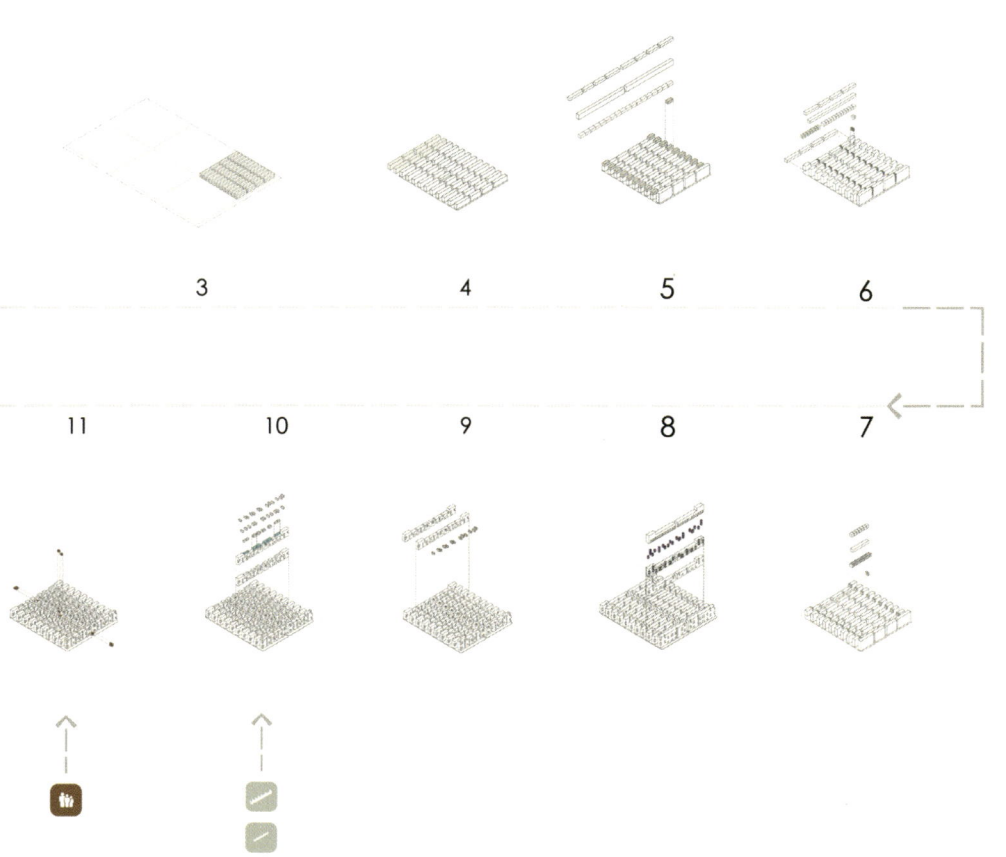

3 4 5 6

11 10 9 8 7

A Transformation of Shanghai's Urban Fabric
Christine Caine, SMArchS Thesis

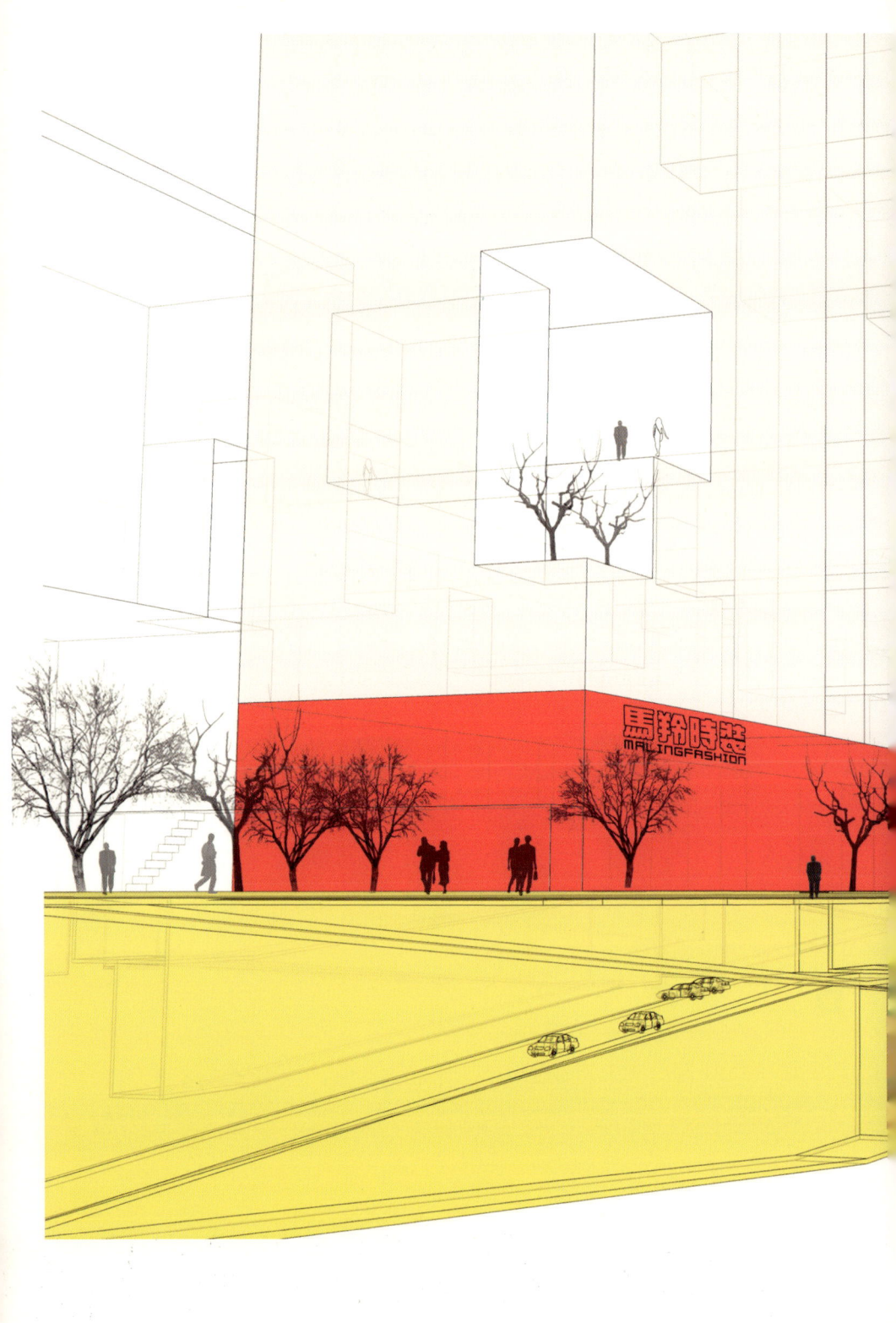

A Transformation of Shanghai's Urban Fabric
Christine Caine, SMArchS Thesis

Personal Geographies:
Life and Culture in Mexico City

Simi Hoque, Instructor
Christoforos Romanos, TA
Undergraduate/MArch Level II Studio 4.131
Fall 2006

This is a vertical studio premised on understanding how our personal geographies bear on design. We will confront the forces of our history, culture, and tradition by putting them in tension with another history, culture and tradition. The goal is to develop a framework, a thesis, and an argument for who we are and how we hope to live.

We will be working on designing a mid-scale urban housing intervention of 25-50 dwelling units in the Metropolitan Zone of Mexico City (ZMCM). With more than 18 million inhabitants and 80% of its area developed without the professional intervention of architects, city planners or public agencies, Mexico City
presents an interesting condition for architects. It is the second most populated city in the world. Many of Mexico's urban poor live in overcrowded and substandard rental dwellings, and twenty nine percent of Mexico City's total urbanized area currently has illegal land tenure status. Its overwhelming statistics, teeming population, and absence of coordinated urban planning create a series of challenges and opportunities for us to negotiate, engage, and establish a dialogue with the city and its inhabitants.

image by Kevin Moore

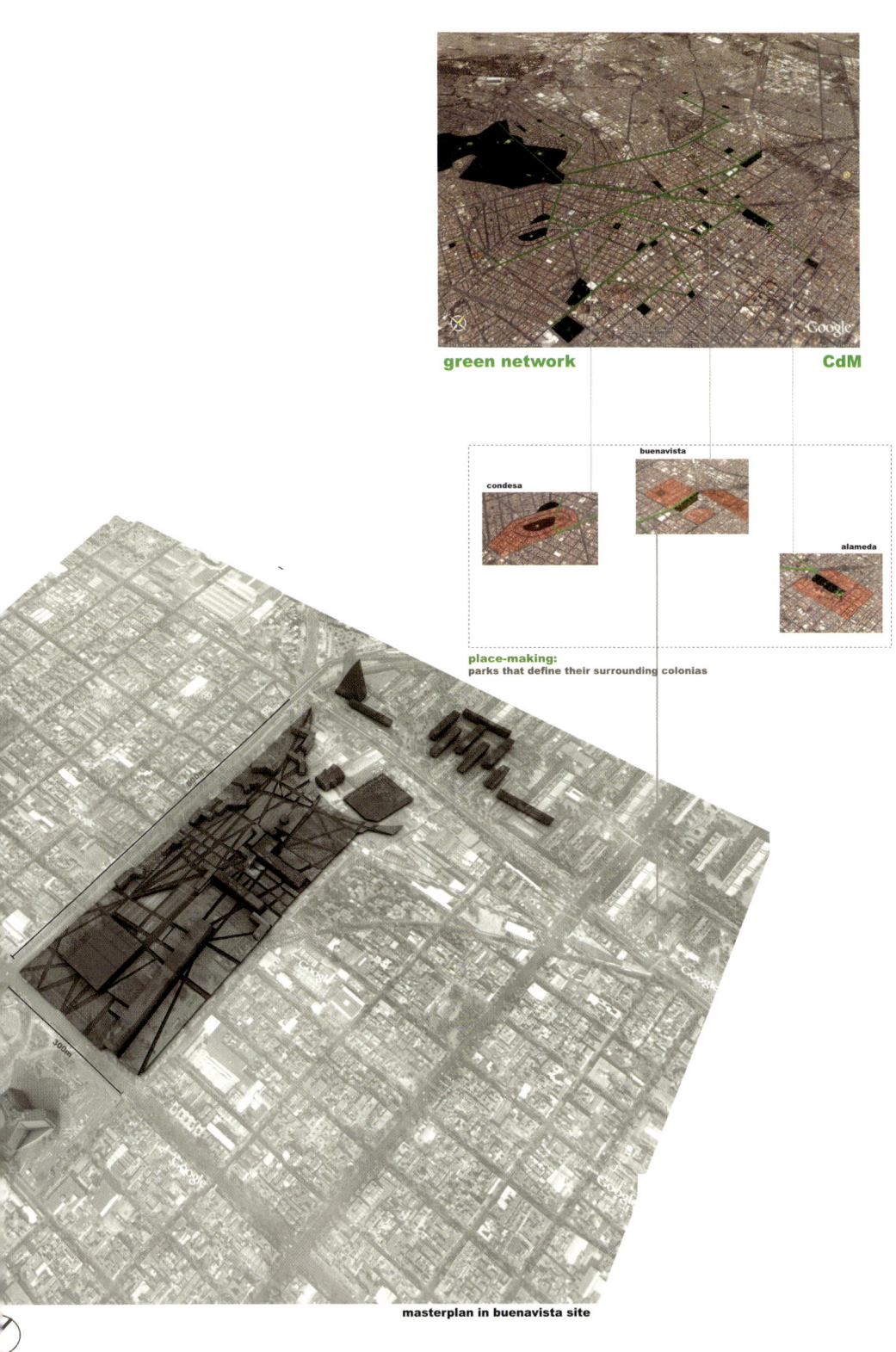

green network **CdM**

buenavista

condesa

alameda

place-making:
parks that define their surrounding colonias

masterplan in buenavista site

231

Japan Workshop:
Continuity and Transformation

Shun Kanda, Instructor
Wokrshop 4.183
Summer 2006

This annual summer workshop engages graduate students in a series of design charrettes on the theme of "Continuity/Transformation in Architecture & Community Form" within a specific site and project context. As in the past, our students live and work both in an urban context and in a rural village setting in Japan. This year, these activities take place during a sojourn in Kyoto, Tokyo, and finally in Tohkamachi, Niigata.

In Kyoto, the project's theme examines the centuries-old Gion Festival and its past/future influence on the architecture of a particular historic neighborhood that is rapidly urbanizing. Design propositions are prepared and delivered at a public presentation in the community center. In Tokyo, a public performance-based event is planned and acted out by the students on the streets of Omotesando, the unique phenomena of hip Tokyo youth culture and high-profile architectural eccentricities all converge. An analogous "continuity/transformation" social & environmental critique will be enacted in the rural expanse of Tohkamachi's rice-paddies.

This is the 13th Japan Design Workshop. The program is directed by Professor Shun Kanda and as in previous years, is held jointly with the graduate students of Kyoto University of Art & Design and this year, with Keio University students in Tokyo and Niigata. Each workshop is conducted in collaboration with local residents, professionals & faculty from the other affiliated institutions. A full documentation of the workshop is prepared by the students in the fall term and made available in publication form.

photo by Yi-Hsiang Chao

AIR, LIGHT, WATER, COMMUNITY AND CULTURE IN MODERN KYOTO
3 LIVING UNITS, 1 LIVE-WORK UNIT AND STUDIO, 6 COMMERCIAL SPACES

PETER DEPASQUALE, MICHELLE HA, MEELENA OLEKSIUK - MASSACHUSETTS INSTITUTE OF TECHNOLOGY

H

KO HOUSE

Peter DePasquale, MArch II, Michelle Ha, MArch II, Meelena Oleksiuk, MArch II

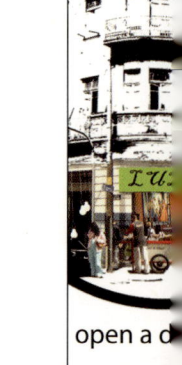

São Paolo
Urban Design Studio

Julian Beinart and John de Monchaux, Instructors
Robert Campos, Jeffrey Fugate, TAs
MArch Level III, SMArchS, MCP Studio 4.163J/ 11.332J
Fall 2006

The MIT urban design studio, in parallel with studios at the University of Sao Paulo and Mackenzie University, had as its client the city of Sao Paulo, who requested help to restore the center of the city of 20 million people which has suffered significant blight through consistent decentralization.

Six studio teams focused on upgrading to the north and east of the center. Two teams chose to redesign the existing Dom Pedro Park. The first saw it as becoming a world-class urban park actively used, ecologically attuned to a restored culverted river on the east, with a new commercial and residential edge to the downtown and out to the Bras neighborhood. The second cleaned out the existing park to make a permanent green bowl as a venue for culture and entertainment, for 20,000 people for sport and festivals, as well as, with temporary infrastructure, for a World Cup soccer venue.

Two teams chose the Luz neighborhood rehabilitation, currently the site of prostitution, drugs and homelessness. Both teams renounced the city's urban renewal direction to retain the area's positive urban qualities: one by proposing a process of slow social and physical reconstruction, the other by linking the neighborhood to existing educational sites in the center. Another team designed the environmental restoration of the presently culverted river on the center's eastern edge. The sixth team saw an opportunity to grow an international fashion industry in the Pari neighborhood where production, design and marketing of sustainable fashion could offer major economic growth to the city's center.

open a d

image by Jessica Berman Boatright, Matt Brownell, and Carey Clouse

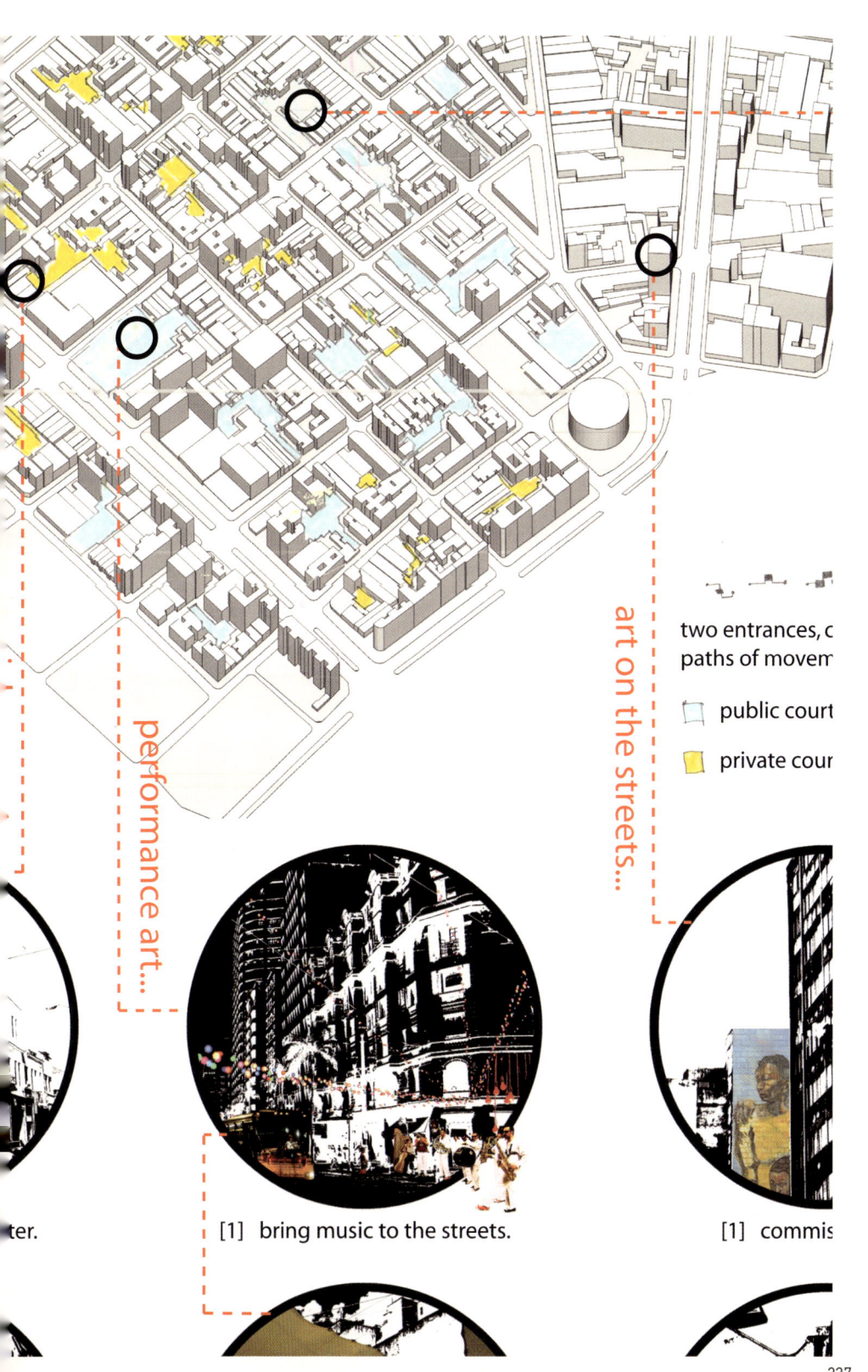

art on the streets...

two entrances, c
paths of movem

public court

private cour

performance art...

[1] bring music to the streets.

[1] commis

ter.

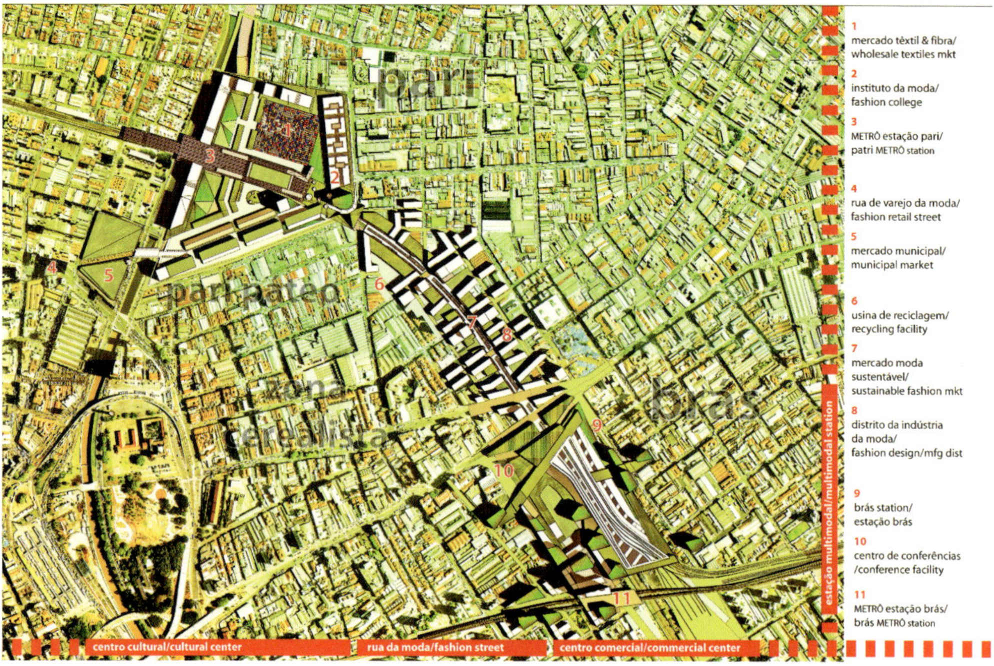
pari
pari pateo
zona cerealista
brás
1
2
3
4
5
6
7
8
9
10
11
centro cultural/cultural center
rua da moda/fashion street
centro comercial/commercial center
estação multimodal/multimodal station
1
mercado têxtil & fibra/
wholesale textiles mkt
2
instituto da moda/
fashion college
3
METRÔ estação pari/
patri METRÔ station
4
rua de varejo da moda/
fashion retail street
5
mercado municipal/
municipal market
6
usina de reciclagem/
recycling facility
7
mercado moda
sustentável/
sustainable fashion mkt
8
distrito da indústria
da moda/
fashion design/mfg dist
9
brás station/
estação brás
10
centro de conferências
/conference facility
11
METRÔ estação brás/
brás METRÔ station

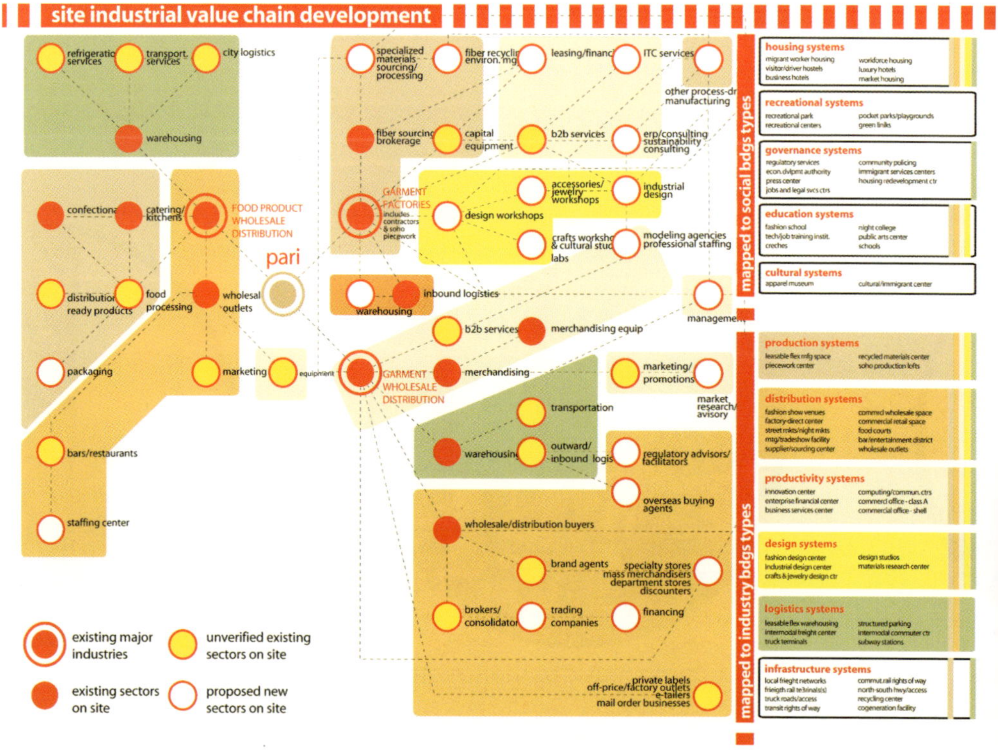
site industrial value chain development
refrigeratio services
transport. services
city logistics
warehousing
confectiona
catering/ kitchens
FOOD PRODUCT WHOLESALE DISTRIBUTION
distribution ready products
food processing
wholesal outlets
packaging
marketing
bars/restaurants
staffing center
pari
equipment
specialized materials sourcing/ processing
fiber recycli environ. mg
leasing/financ
ITC services
other process-dr manufacturing
fiber sourcin brokerage
capital equipment
b2b services
erp/consulting sustainability consulting
GARMENT FACTORIES
includes contractors & soho piecework
design workshops
accessories/ jewelry workshops
industrial design
crafts worksho & cultural stud labs
modeling agencies professional staffing
warehousing
inbound logistics
management
b2b services
merchandising equip
GARMENT WHOLESALE DISTRIBUTION
merchandising
marketing/ promotions
market research/ avisory
transportation
warehousin
outward/ inbound logis
regulatory advisors/ facilitators
overseas buying agents
wholesale/distribution buyers
brand agents
specialty stores mass merchandisers department stores discounters
brokers/ consolidator
trading companies
financing
private labels off-price/factory outlets e-tailers mail order businesses
existing major industries
unverified existing sectors on site
existing sectors on site
proposed new sectors on site
mapped to social bdgs types
housing systems
migrant worker housing
visitor/driver hostels
business hotels
workforce housing
luxury hotels
market housing
recreational systems
recreational park
recreational centers
pocket parks/playgrounds
green linlks
governance systems
regulatory services
econ. dvlpmt authority
press center
jobs and legal svcs ctrs
community policing
immigrant services centers
housing redevelopment ctr
education systems
fashion school
tech/job training instit.
creches
night college
public arts center
schools
cultural systems
apparel museum
cultural/immigrant center
mapped to industry bdgs types
production systems
leasable flex mfg space
piecework center
recycled materials center
soho production lofts
distribution systems
fashion show venues
factory-direct center
street mkts/night mkts
mtg/tradeshow facility
supplier/sourcing center
commrcl wholesale space
commercial retail space
food courts
bar/entertainment district
wholesale outlets
productivity systems
innovation center
enterprise financial center
business services center
computing/commun. ctrs
commercl office - class A
commercial office - shell
design systems
fashion design center
Industrial design center
crafts & jewelry design ctr
design studios
materials research center
logistics systems
leasable flex warehousing
intermodal freight center
truck terminals
structured parking
intermodal commuter ctr
subway stations
infrastructure systems
local frieght networks
frieigth rail te3rinals(s)
truck roads/access
transit rights of way
commut.rail rights of way
north-south hwy/access
recycling center
cogeneration facility

Brazilian center for low-cost garments

+ environmental agenda
+ vertical integration
+ tech-assisted production
+ recycled materials
+ safe fiber treatments
+ revitalized trade
+ global branding
= international center for
sustainable fashion

comparing international fashion centers:

couture

new york
2006

paris
2006

labor driven

tech driven

shenzhen
2006

sao paulo
2006

sao paulo
2020?

mass-market

Pari - Al Wei, MCP/ SMArchS, Lu Ai, SMArchS, Ai Yamamoto, MCP, Raj Kottamasu, MCP

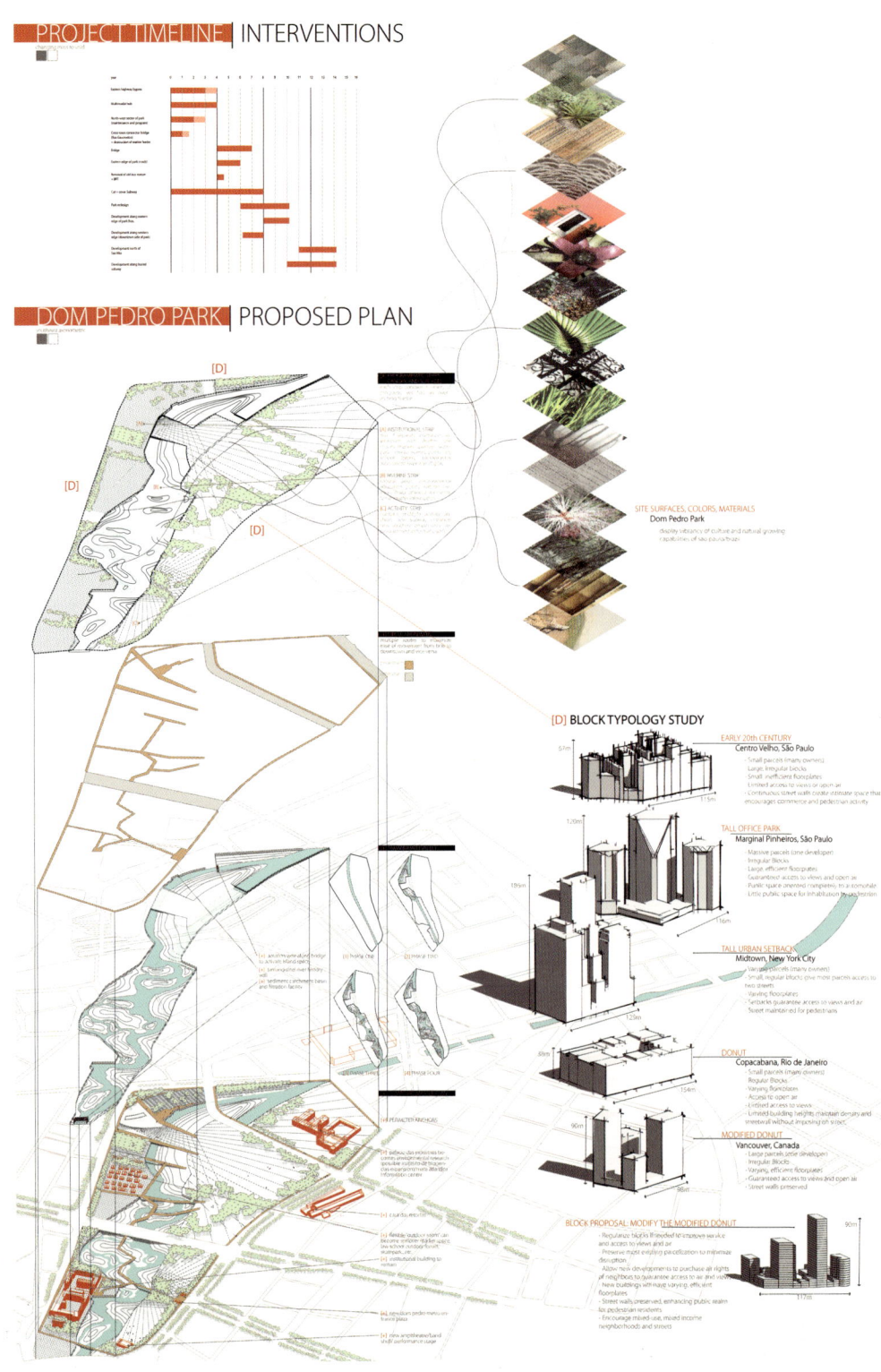

DOM PEDRO PARK | PROPOSED PLAN

SITE SURFACES, COLORS, MATERIALS
Dom Pedro Park

display vibrancy of culture and cultural growing
capabilities of são paulo's forest

[D] BLOCK TYPOLOGY STUDY

EARLY 20th CENTURY
Centro Velho, São Paulo
- Small parcels (many owners)
- Large, irregular blocks
- Small, inefficient floorplates
- Limited access to views or open air
- Continuous street walls create intimate space that
  encourages commerce and pedestrian activity

TALL OFFICE PARK
Marginal Pinheiros, São Paulo
- Massive parcels (one developer)
- Irregular Blocks
- Large, efficient floorplates
- Guaranteed access to views and open air
- Public space oriented completely to automobile
- Little public space for inhabitation by pedestrian

TALL URBAN SETBACK
Midtown, New York City
- Variable parcels (many owners)
- Small, regular blocks give most parcels access to
  two streets
- Varying floorplates
- Setbacks guarantee access to views and air
- Street maintained for pedestrians

DONUT
Copacabana, Rio de Janeiro
- Small parcels (many owners)
- Regular Blocks
- Access to open air
- Limited access to views
- Limited building heights maintain density and
  streetwall without imposing on street

MODIFIED DONUT
Vancouver, Canada
- Large parcels (one developer)
- Irregular Blocks
- Varying, efficient floorplates
- Guaranteed access to views and open air
- Street walls preserved

BLOCK PROPOSAL: MODIFY THE MODIFIED DONUT
- Regularize blocks if needed to improve service
  and access to views and air
- Preserve most existing parcellation to minimize
  disruption
- Allow new development to purchase air rights
  of neighbors to guarantee access to air and views
- New buildings with have varying, efficient
  floorplates
- Street walls preserved, enhancing public realm
  for pedestrian residents
- Encourage mixed-use, mixed income
  neighborhoods and streets

San Pedro Park
Tim Terway, MCP, Rana Amirtahmasebi, SMarchS/ MCP, Luke Schray, MCP

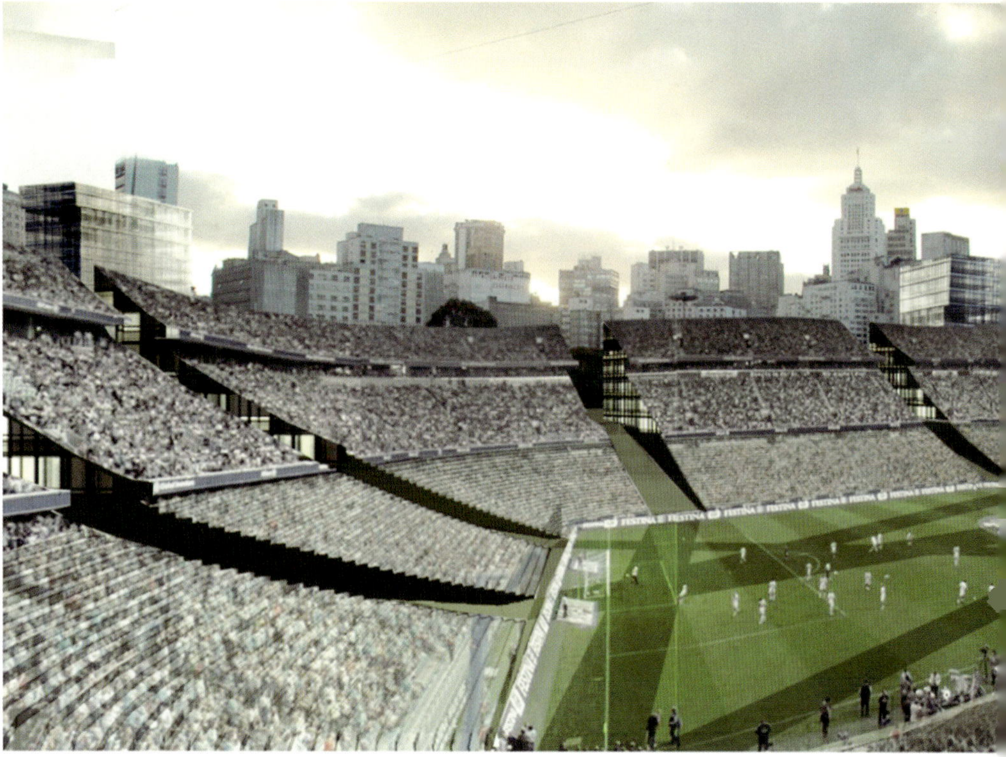

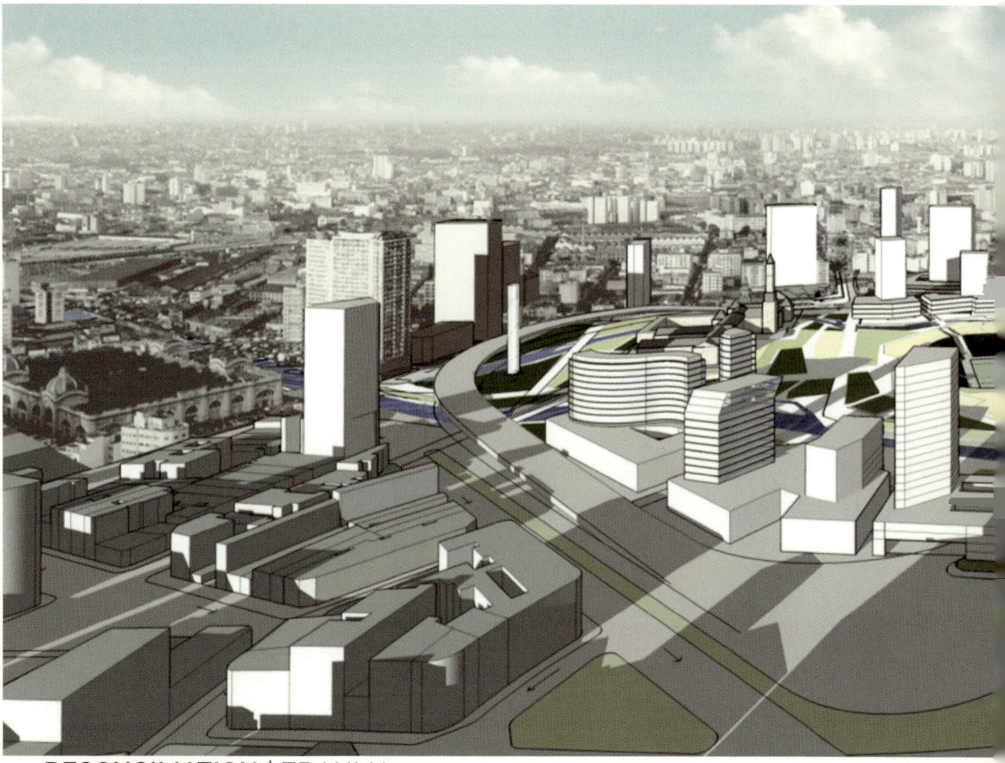

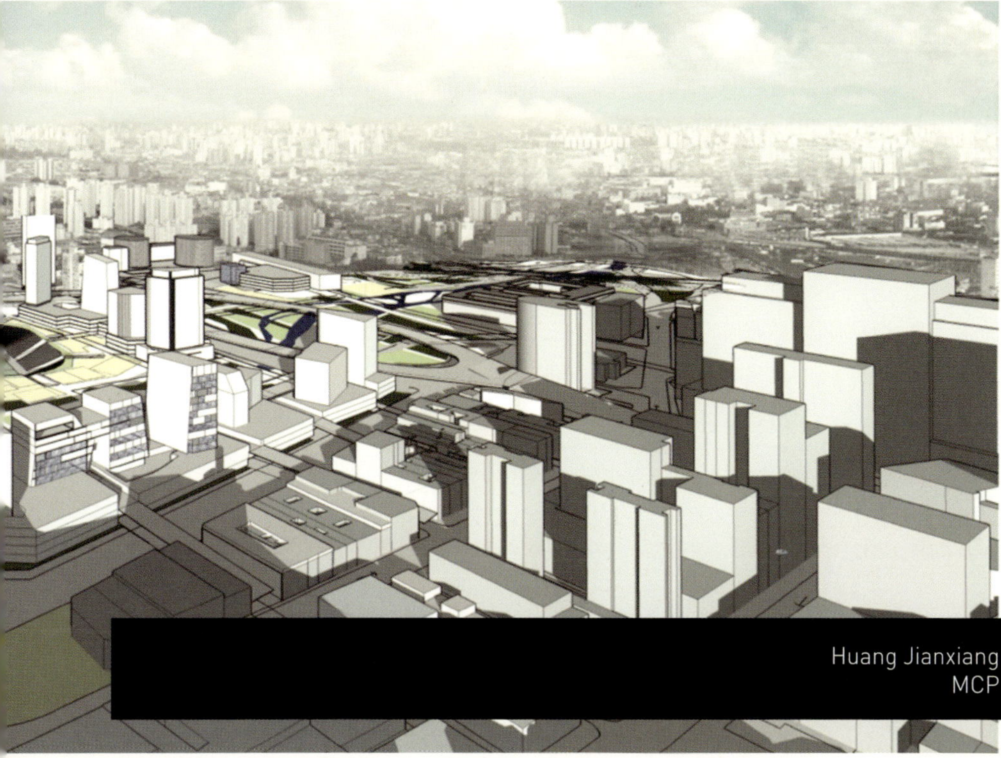

Huang Jianxiang
MCP

TRAUMA

Working Place: A Science Archive at MIT
Fernando Domeyko, Instructor
MArch Level II Studio 4.143

**Ascender : Unfolding Fantasies of Control, Power and
Collapse through Expanded Painting**
Oliver Lutz
SMVisS Thesis

**Sensorium : Embodied Technology, Experience,
and Contemporary Art**
Bill Arning, Jane Farver, Yuko Hasegawa, and
Marjory Jacobson, Curators
Caroline Jones, Editor
Exhibition and Publication

Bridge: An Unraveled Architecture
Ahmed Elhusseiny
MArch Thesis

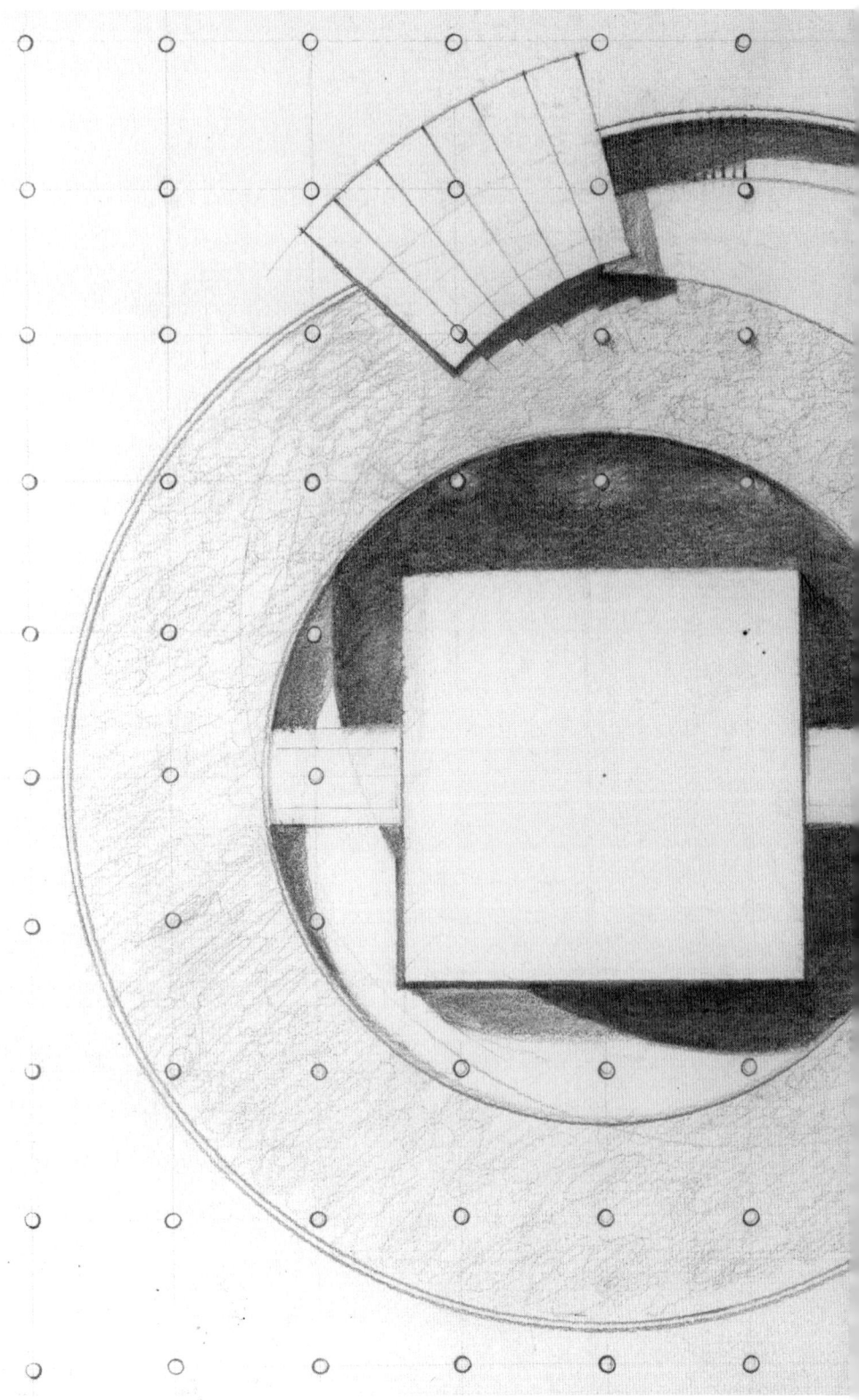

Working Place: A Science Archive at MIT

Fernando Domeyko, Instructor
Jeffrey Anderson, TA
MArch Level II Studio 4.143
Fall 2006

The central objective of this studio project is not the labyrinth-like condition of document storage, but rather the human inhabitation of it.

The studio pushes students to understand the needs of researchers as both individuals and as a community. This dicotomy of the individual versus the collective is central to the architectural investigation, a process of contemplation and making, constantly reformulating the students' discovery.

The specific requirements of the research community are testing the limits of the tangible and virtual configurations of space. The studio will address the needs of both individual researchers and the research community. It will specifically investigate the need for silence and privacy; the cultural sense of specific architectural experiences; the understanding of mental and physical experience of interacting with the "infinite labyrinth" quality of the archive; and the cultural and formal debate between the tactile material and virtual media.

Students will create a series of installations and interactions, with the goal of idenfifying specific problems and creating a specific architectural response. A conceptualization of space will be investigated within the realm of site, landscape, scale, organization, and topology.

drawing by Pholkrit Santhong

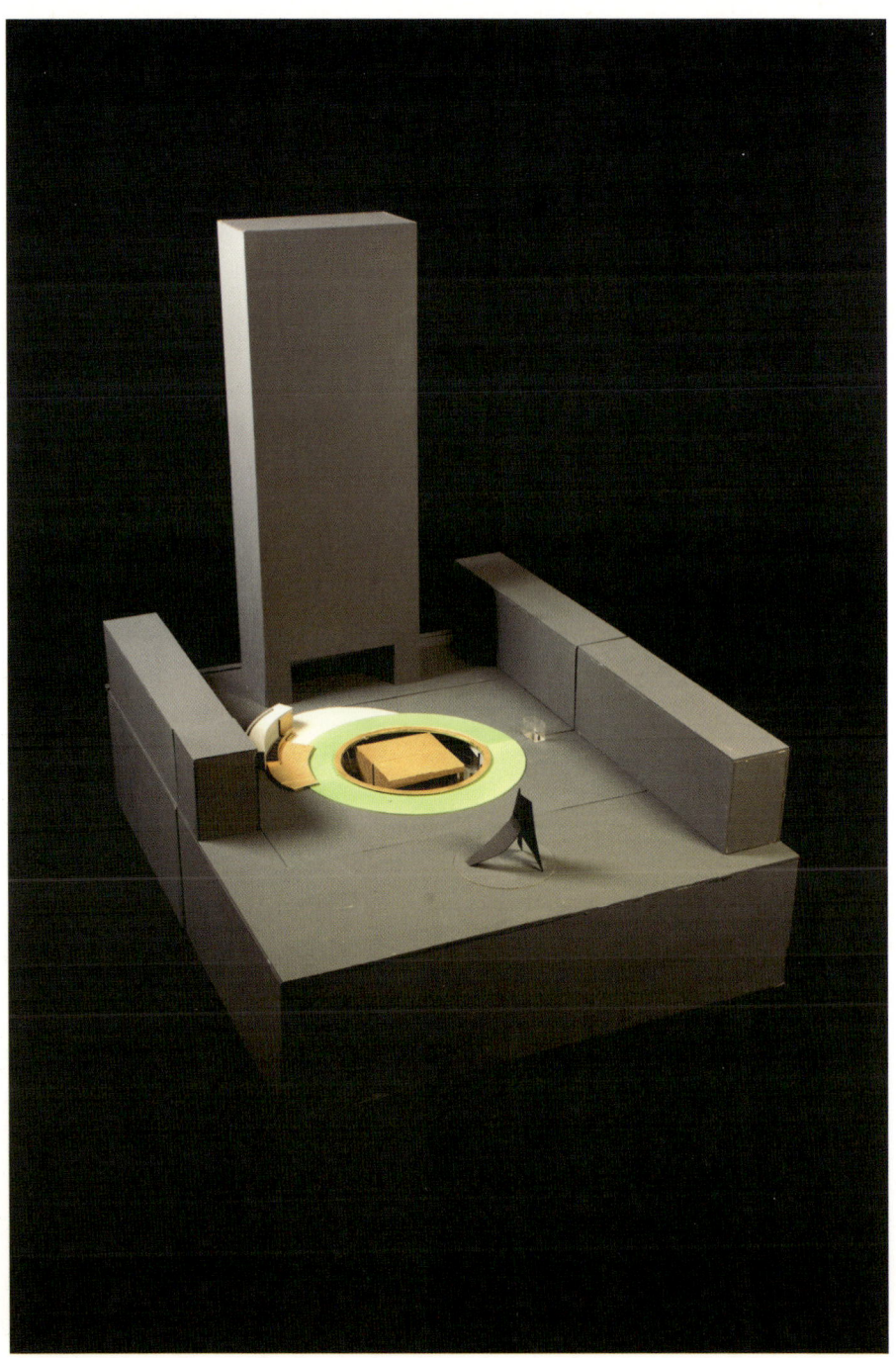

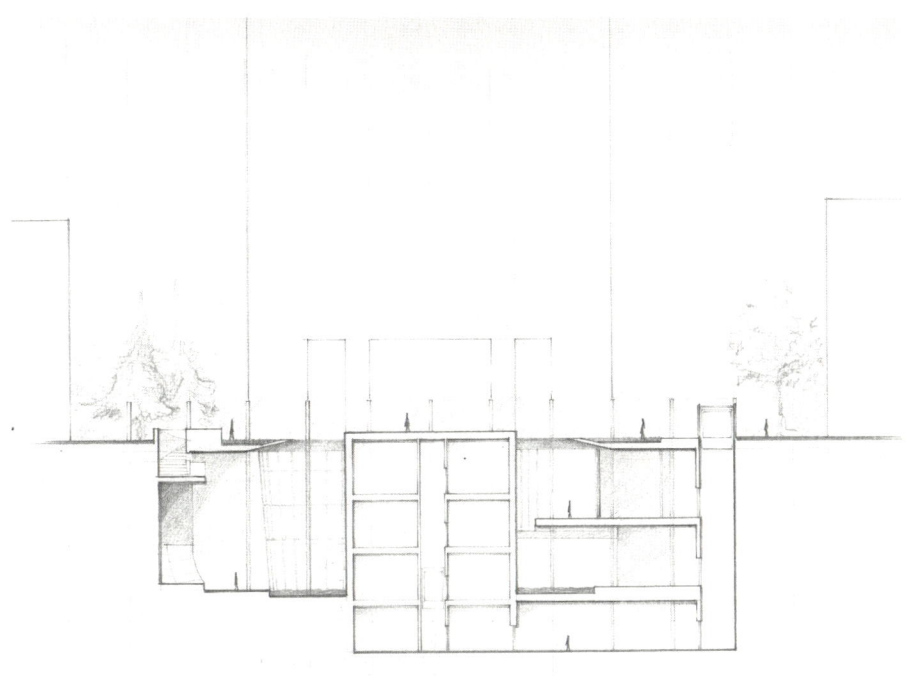

Pholkrit Sangthong
MArch II

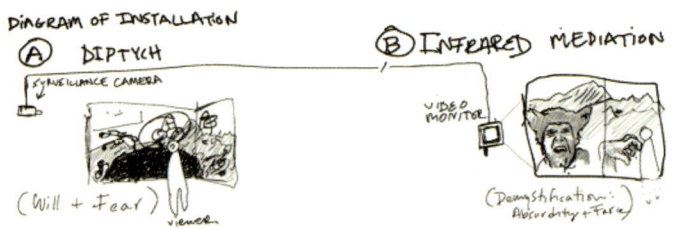

DIAGRAM OF INSTALLATION

(A) DIPTYCH

SURVEILLANCE CAMERA

(Will + Fear) viewer

(B) INFRARED MEDIATION

VIDEO MONITOR

(Demystification: Absurdity + Farce)

Ascender: Unfolding Fantasies of Control, Power and Collapse through Expanded Painting

Oliver Lutz
SMVisS Thesis
Joan Jonas, Advisor
Spring 2006

The "Ascender" artworks are about transcending desires of power, control and collapse through a complex "taking-apart" of the artist's mental model. In a two-part arrangement of artworks the artist explores fantasies of power, control and collapse and the conflation of romanticism with these fantasies through an expanded painting practice. This project is an unraveling of personal mythologies through the application of multiple simultaneous media that include performance, drawing, painting, and installation. This 'unwrapping' of ideologies and narratives of self, this 'unfolding', becomes itself a transcendent act through which the artist's overall vision is conveyed. It is the working through of ideas that becomes the essence of this artwork, whether it is a painting, video, or drawing. This practice also engages the expanded field of painting in terms of direct external influences on the medium such as surveillance technologies and reflectography, as well as methodological influences derived from external practices such as User Experience Strategy that have affected the artist's regard for the viewer.

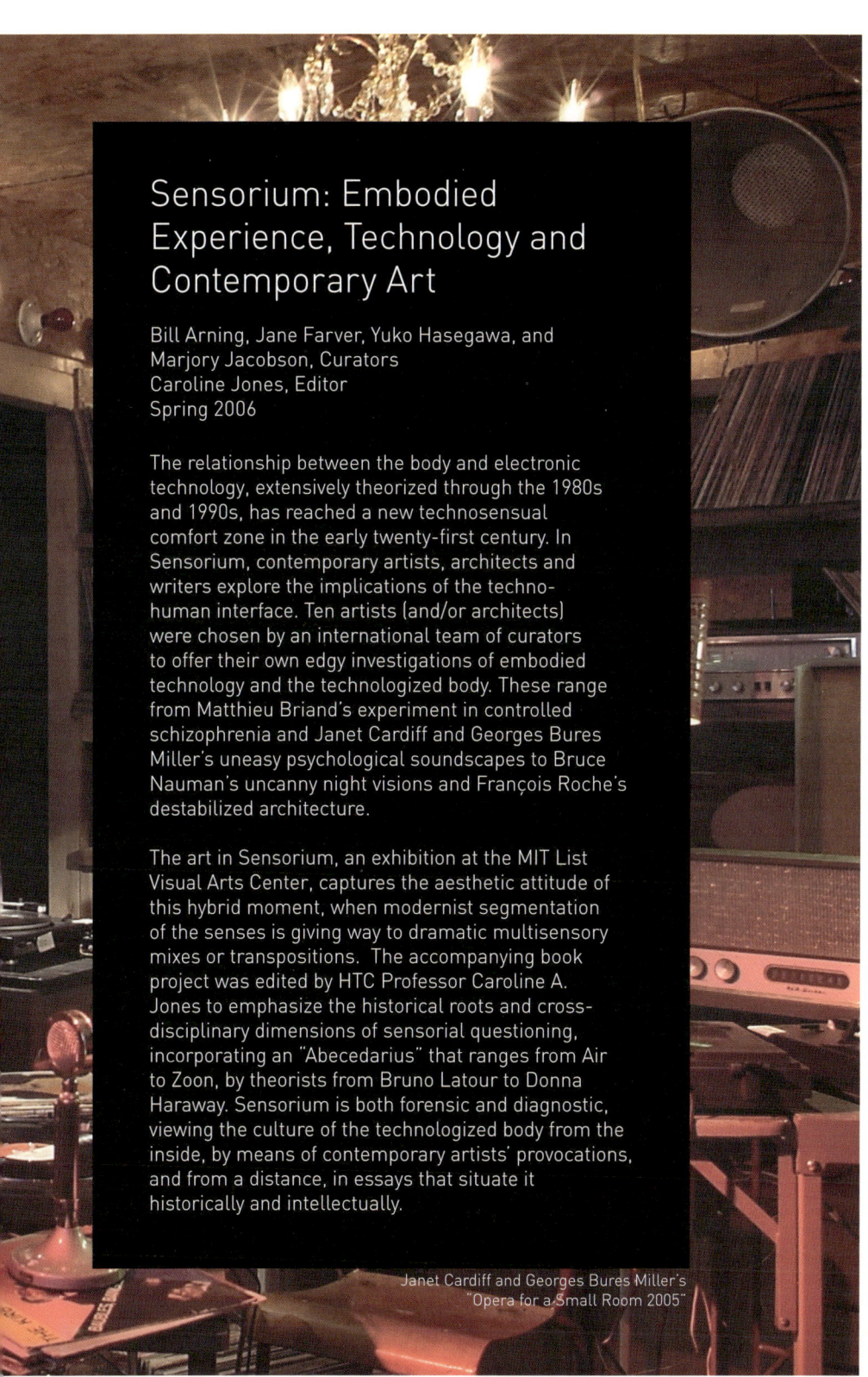

Sensorium: Embodied Experience, Technology and Contemporary Art

Bill Arning, Jane Farver, Yuko Hasegawa, and
Marjory Jacobson, Curators
Caroline Jones, Editor
Spring 2006

The relationship between the body and electronic technology, extensively theorized through the 1980s and 1990s, has reached a new technosensual comfort zone in the early twenty-first century. In Sensorium, contemporary artists, architects and writers explore the implications of the techno-human interface. Ten artists (and/or architects) were chosen by an international team of curators to offer their own edgy investigations of embodied technology and the technologized body. These range from Matthieu Briand's experiment in controlled schizophrenia and Janet Cardiff and Georges Bures Miller's uneasy psychological soundscapes to Bruce Nauman's uncanny night visions and François Roche's destabilized architecture.

The art in Sensorium, an exhibition at the MIT List Visual Arts Center, captures the aesthetic attitude of this hybrid moment, when modernist segmentation of the senses is giving way to dramatic multisensory mixes or transpositions. The accompanying book project was edited by HTC Professor Caroline A. Jones to emphasize the historical roots and cross-disciplinary dimensions of sensorial questioning, incorporating an "Abecedarius" that ranges from Air to Zoon, by theorists from Bruno Latour to Donna Haraway. Sensorium is both forensic and diagnostic, viewing the culture of the technologized body from the inside, by means of contemporary artists' provocations, and from a distance, in essays that situate it historically and intellectually.

Janet Cardiff and Georges Bures Miller's
"Opera for a Small Room 2005"

edited by
Caroline A. Jones

sensorium

embodied experience,
technology, and
contemporary art

'hardly see the propaganda balloons anymore. Its like they're not there. they're actually quite beautiful at dusk, all lil up...

Bridge: An Unraveled Architecture

Ahmed El Husseiny
MArch Thesis
Shun Kanda, Advisor
Nasser Rabbat and Ann Pendleton-Jullian, Readers
Fall 2006

The bridge is an uninhabitable structure housing live/work artists studios, galleries and workshops. It is an urban/architectural/personal intervention that strives to explore issues of latent/ potential narratives within a built form. It accepts a tightly bundled cord of circulation and unravels it as it traverses the water. Each strand becomes an individual opportunity for a sequence of narrative projections that simultaneouly affect and are affected by overlapping, intersecting and parallel strands.

beached

confusion

fliight

Bridge: an Unraveled Architecture
Ahmed El Husseiny, MArch Thesis

259

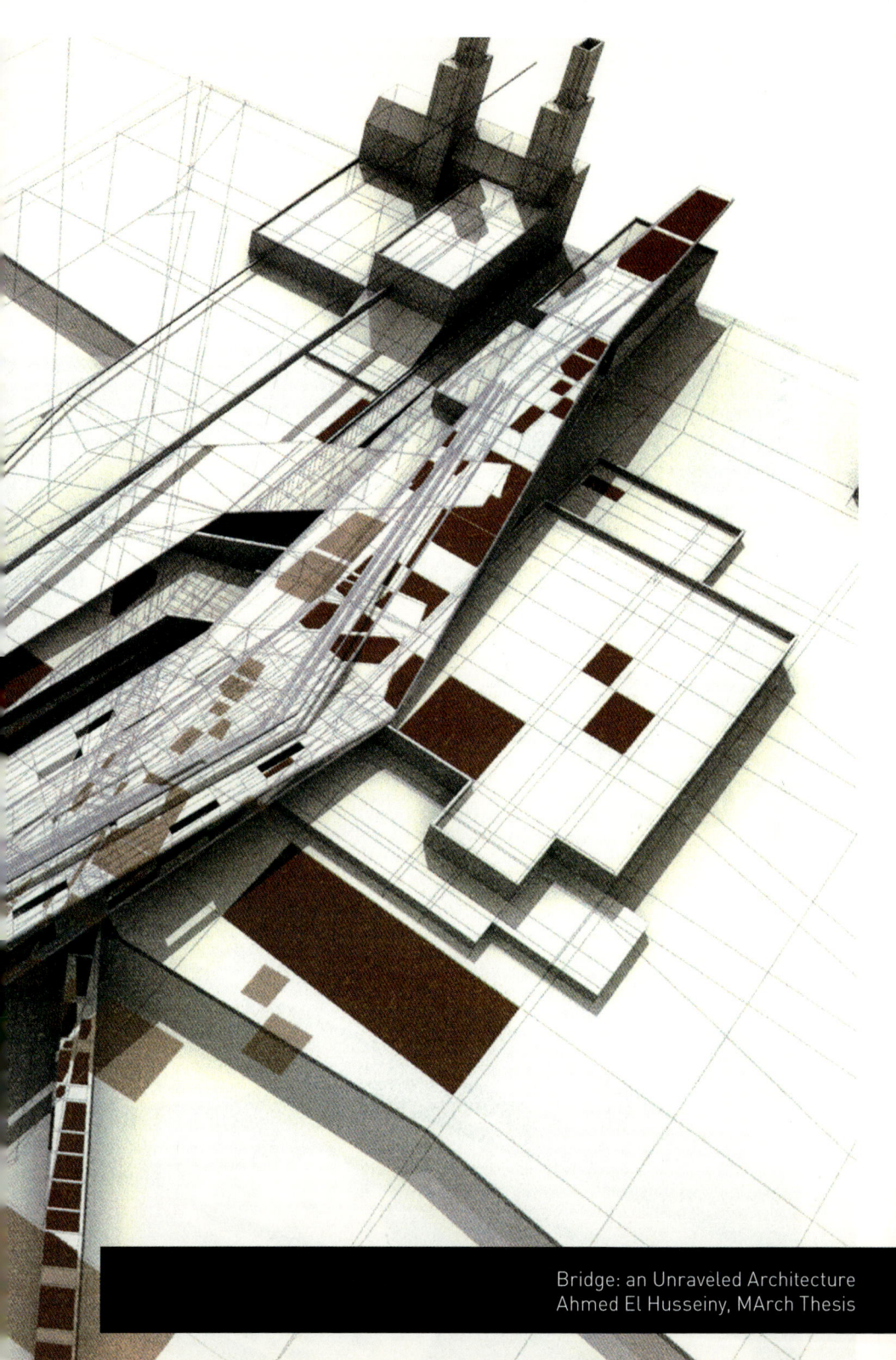

Bridge: an Unraveled Architecture
Ahmed El Husseiny, MArch Thesis

METABOLISM

Metabolism of course not only describes the body as a processor of flows and energy; it also describes a historical moment in architecture when architects wanted to liberate themselves from the bounds of typologies in architecture – categories of architectural objects both historical and modernist – in order to install a completely totalizing, expanding vision of architecture as (according to Kenneth Frampton) 'bee-hives' of human activity, summarized in soaring, grandiose architectures with techno-organicist overtones. A generation of early-postwar Japanese architects in fact proposed Blobs avant la lettre.

In opposition to this, the notion of type finds its roots in post-war Italian discourse, where among others Aldo Rossi developed typology into an architectural language of quasi-structural elements which had become crystallized through centuries of historical development. Type is, however, not per se historicizing. Mies van der Rohe spent his entire life making the same object, so to speak, every iteration better, closer to perfection than the previous one. The ultimate perfect project achieves the type. Type suggests certain unchanging, permanent categories of objects; Metabolism suggests an endlessly changing, metamorphosing system of flow infrastructures.

TYPE

So our last opposition is between 'dynamic' and 'static.' The search for fundamental, unchanging formal templates in architecture versus the search of ultra-dynamic, mobile, systems.

Metabolism sees architecture as a biological system, as a second nature – a proliferating system which is in a sense objective to society as a whole. It takes the individual subject out of the equation. Type, on the other hand, psychologizes architecture. It assumes that within cultures certain fundamental templates and schemata structure the perception of space, and that the crystallization of this is architecture's highest task.

METABOLISM

N=1=NPK=KIMCHI=N
Jae Rhim Lee
SMVisS Thesis

Informed Form
Axel Kilian, Instructor
MArch Level II Design Studio 4.143

Space-Fighters
Winy Maas with Kaustav De Biswas (Phd Computation) and Joris Fach (MVRDV), Instructors
Workshop 4.181

WhoWhatWhenAIR
Philippe Block, Axel Kilian, Peter Schmitt,
John Snavely, Collaborators

N=1=NPK=KIMCHI=N

Jae Rhim Lee
SMVisS Thesis
Joan Jonas, Advisor
Fall 2006

N=1=NPK=KIMCHI=N is a mobile, expandable living unit which consists of a urinal, urine processing system, hydroponic napa cabbage garden, seedling growing area, customized bed, and kitchen table. I tested my urnine, modified my diet to produce urine ideal for growing napa cabbage, grew napa cabbage hydroponically with the optimized urine, made kimchi from the napa cabbage, and fed the kimchi to the public from the living unit.

In this paper I elaborate on the intimate affiliation between the "narcissistic self" and the planet proposed by the N=1=NPK=KIMCHI=N. I synthesize concepts of the self-body, narcissism, death, and ecology to arrive at a methodology for the long-term preservation of the self and planet.

Informed Form

Axel Kilian, Instructor
Joshua Lobel, TA
MArch Level II Studio 4.143
Fall 2006

The studio "INFORMED FORM" is working with
Sullivan Square to develop architectural intervention around the evolving nature of transportation in
the context of Sullivan Square. The area has seen
instances of most transportation systems over the
past 150 years, starting from the Middlesex shipping
canal, to the elevated highway. Previously a site for an
intermodal station for trams and busses recently the
area has been mostly empty. The studio attempts to
develop proposals for Sullivan square envisioning the
next development step at the intersection of architecture and transportation. The studio makes use of
programmed constructs in Processing and Generative Components in order to integrate findings into the
form generation process through digital means.

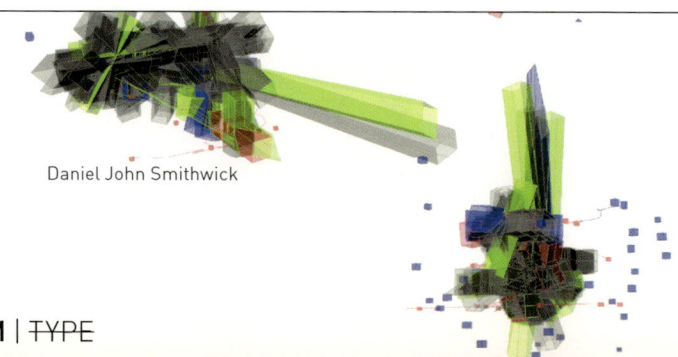

Daniel John Smithwick

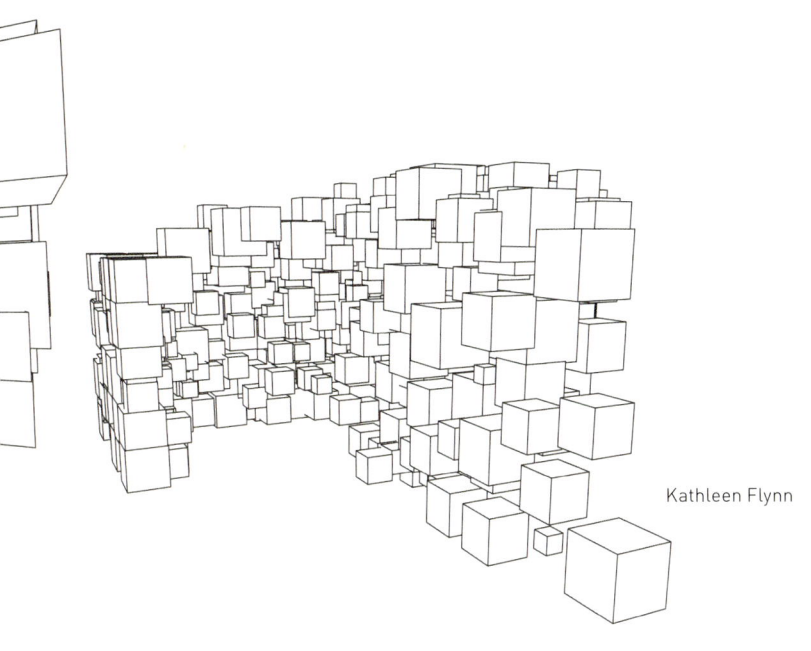

Kathleen Flynn

Simon Schleicher

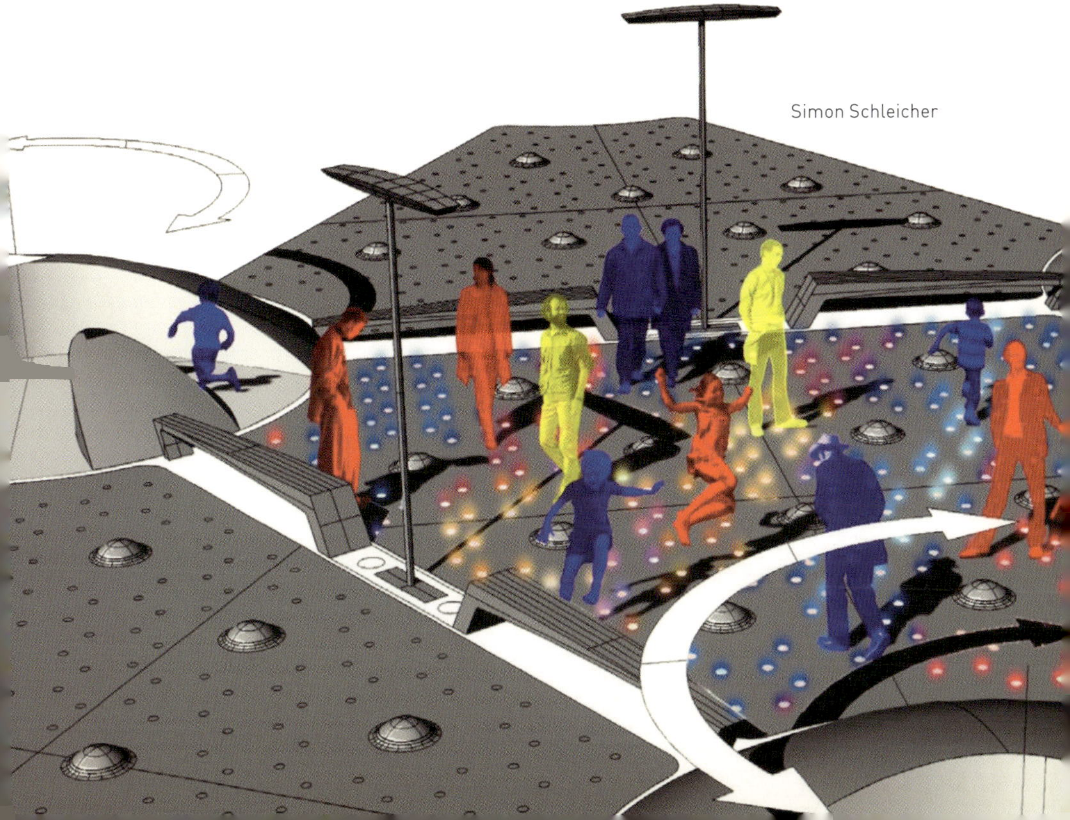

A

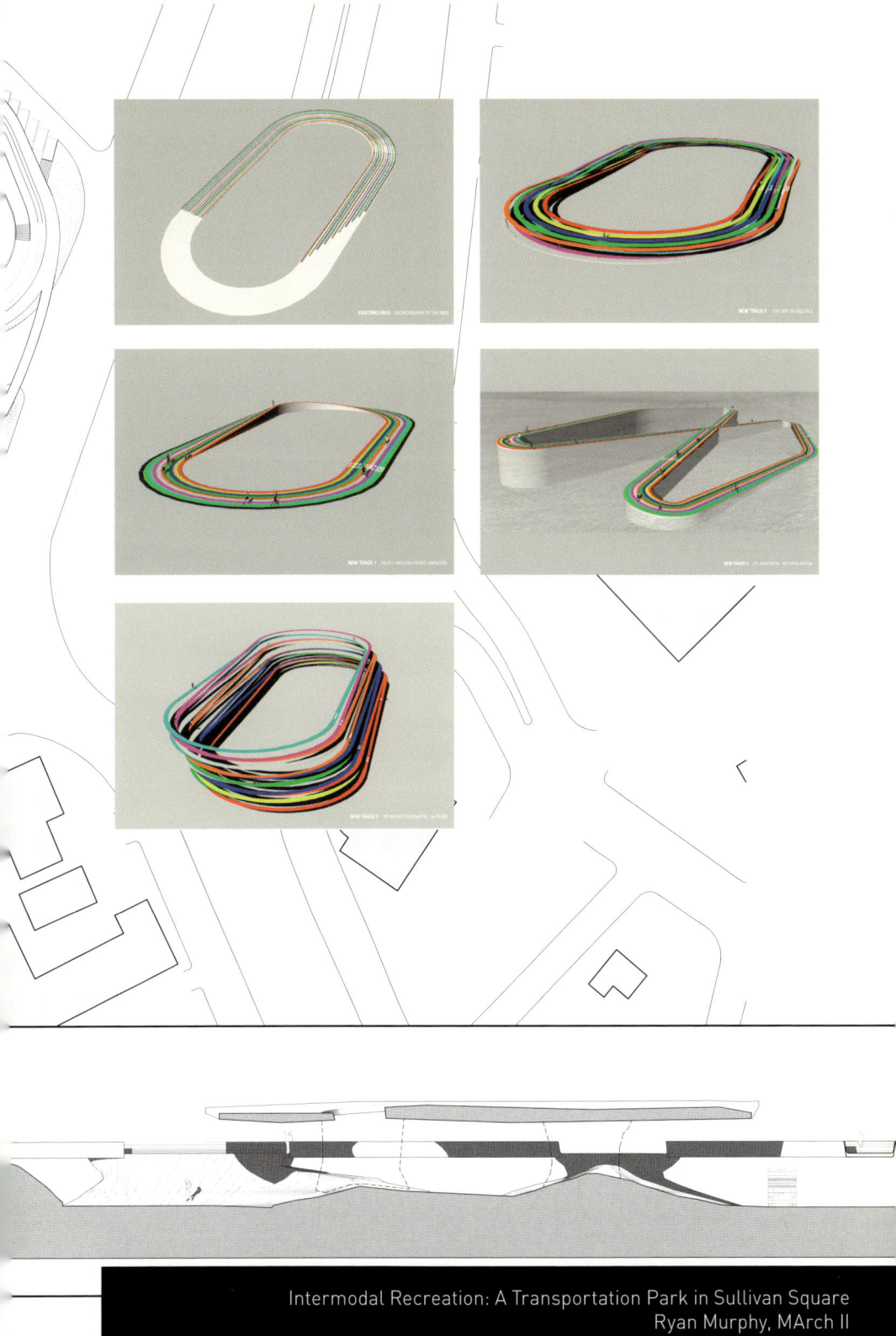

Intermodal Recreation: A Transportation Park in Sullivan Square
Ryan Murphy, MArch II

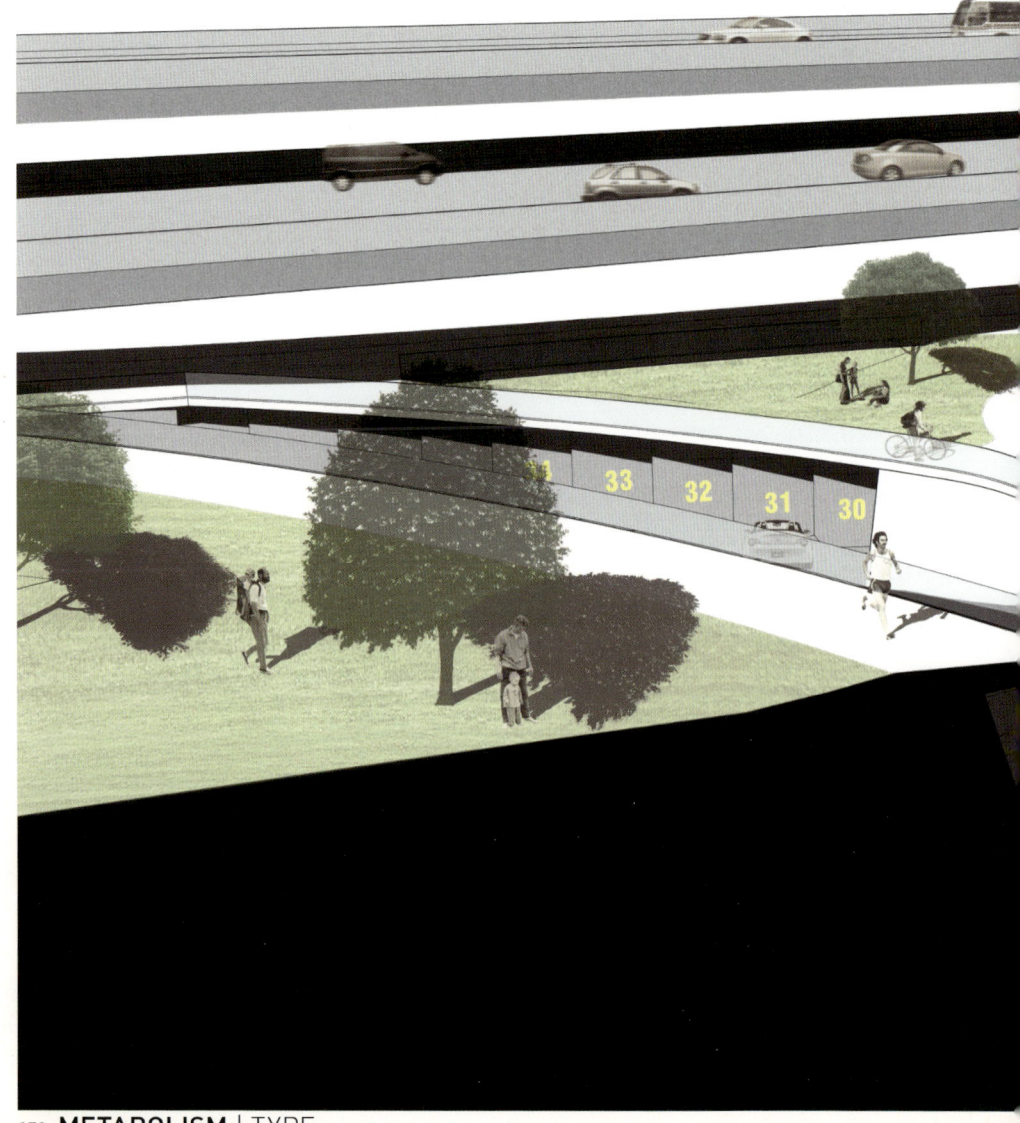

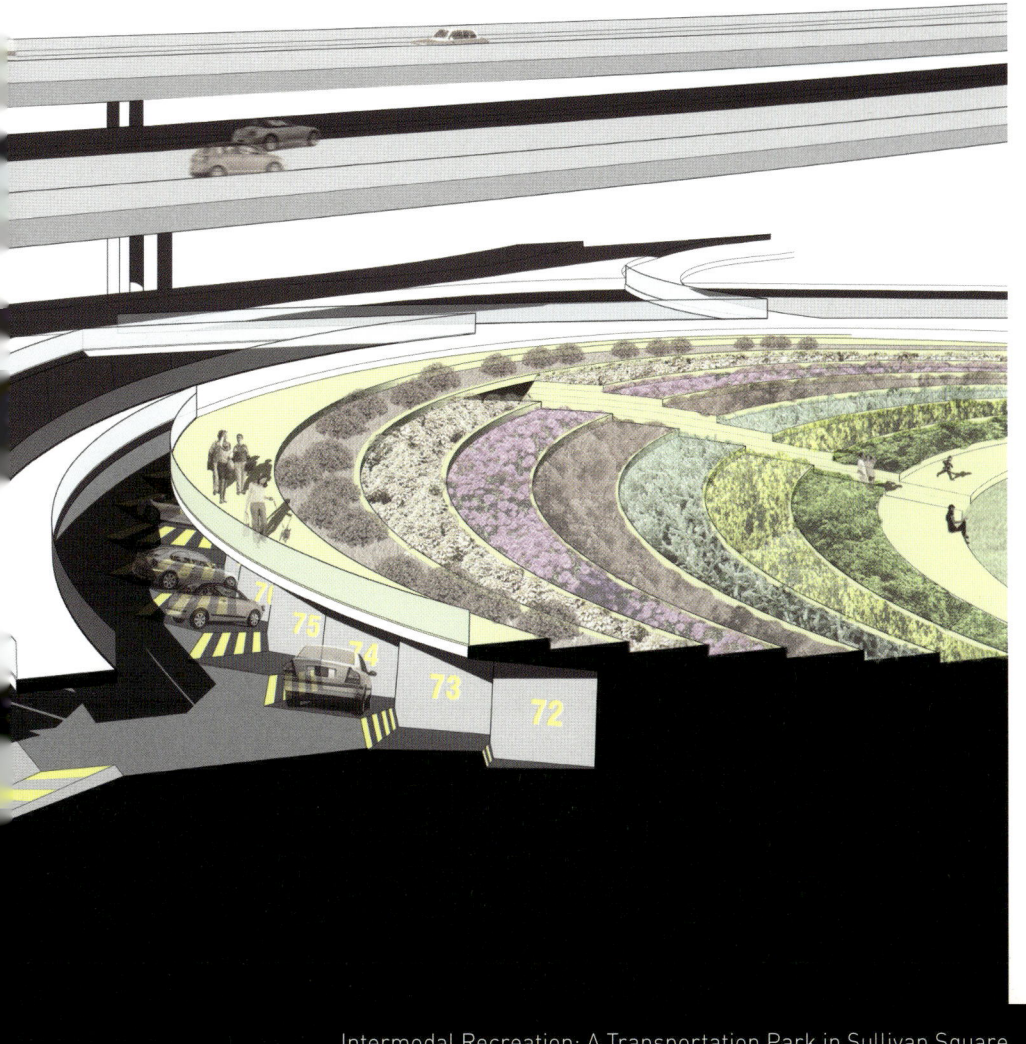

Intermodal Recreation: A Transportation Park in Sullivan Square
Ryan Murphy, MArch II

the tramp
a provocation

daniel john smithwick MIT 2006

the bum
a provocation

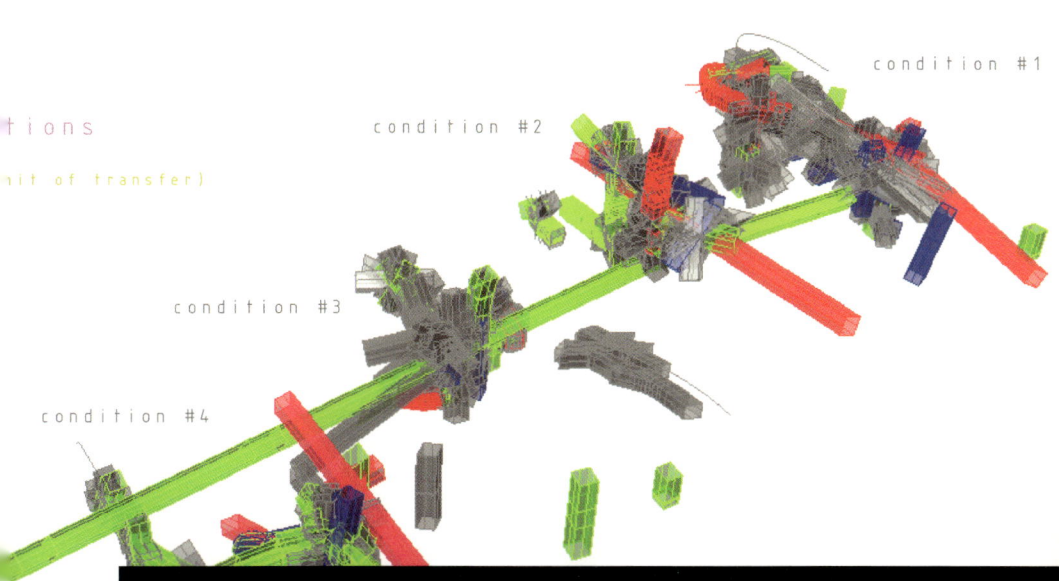

the hobo
a provocation   daniel john smithwick MIT 2006

...tions
(...it of transfer)

condition #1

condition #2

condition #3

condition #4

The Beast: An Intermodal Transit Station for the Bum, the Hobo, and the Tramp
Daniel John Smithwick, MArch II

Space Fighters

Winy Maas with Kaustav De Biswas (Phd Computation) and Joris Fach (MVRDV), Instructors
Workshop 4.181
Fall 2006

The course will explore 'game' as a metaphor for design. The to-be-designed artifact is a city. A wide array of agents from different layers of society follow their own sets of rules and perform local changes to the city form. However, mysteriously, even though no single constituent remains in place, the city still persists.

What enables cities to retain their coherence despite continual disruptions and a lack of central planning? Can the process of design be simulated over time as the work of a multi-agency? When these games are played together, with different players having different 'diagrams'(Energy/Housing/Trade) of the 'to-be-designed' and respective goals but a common goal (a good city?), the players might have to negotiate conflict (game theory) over each generation of the evolution. To the observer this 'process' is the 'city', at any moment!

diagram by Kaustuv De Biswas, Giles Phillips, Ken Cheung, & John Rothernberg

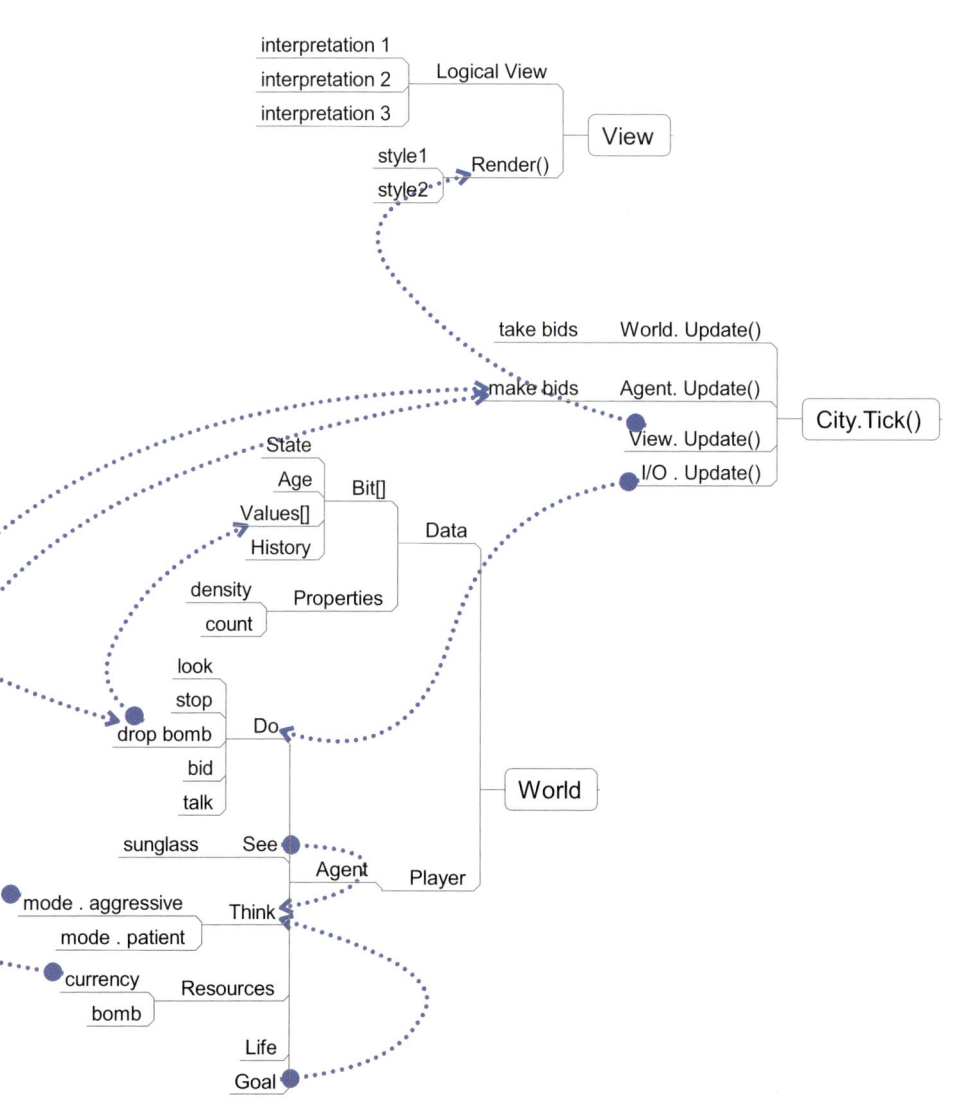

interpretation 1
interpretation 2 — Logical View
interpretation 3

style1 — Render() — View
style2

take bids — World. Update()
make bids — Agent. Update()
View. Update() — City.Tick()
I/O . Update()

State
Age — Bit[]
Values[]
History — Data

density — Properties
count

look
stop
drop bomb — Do
bid
talk

sunglass — See — World

Agent — Player

mode . aggressive — Think
mode . patient

currency — Resources
bomb

Life
Goal

Space Fighter

277

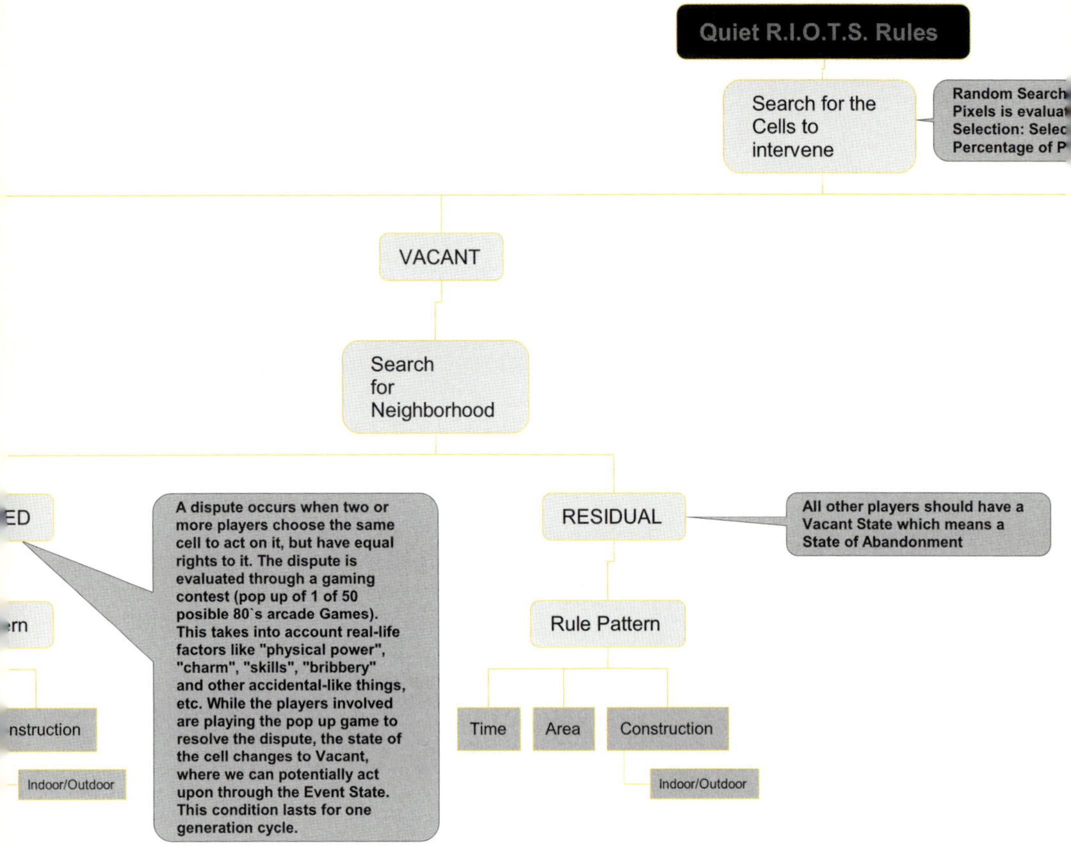

Search for the Cells to intervene

Random Search
Pixels is evalua[...]
Selection: Selec[...]
Percentage of P[...]

VACANT

Search for Neighborhood

ED

rn

nstruction

Indoor/Outdoor

A dispute occurs when two or more players choose the same cell to act on it, but have equal rights to it. The dispute is evaluated through a gaming contest (pop up of 1 of 50 posible 80's arcade Games). This takes into account real-life factors like "physical power", "charm", "skills", "bribbery" and other accidental-like things, etc. While the players involved are playing the pop up game to resolve the dispute, the state of the cell changes to Vacant, where we can potentially act upon through the Event State. This condition lasts for one generation cycle.

RESIDUAL

All other players should have a Vacant State which means a State of Abandonment

Rule Pattern

Time   Area   Construction

Indoor/Outdoor

Visualistion
Casey Renner, MArch III

METABOLISM | TYPE

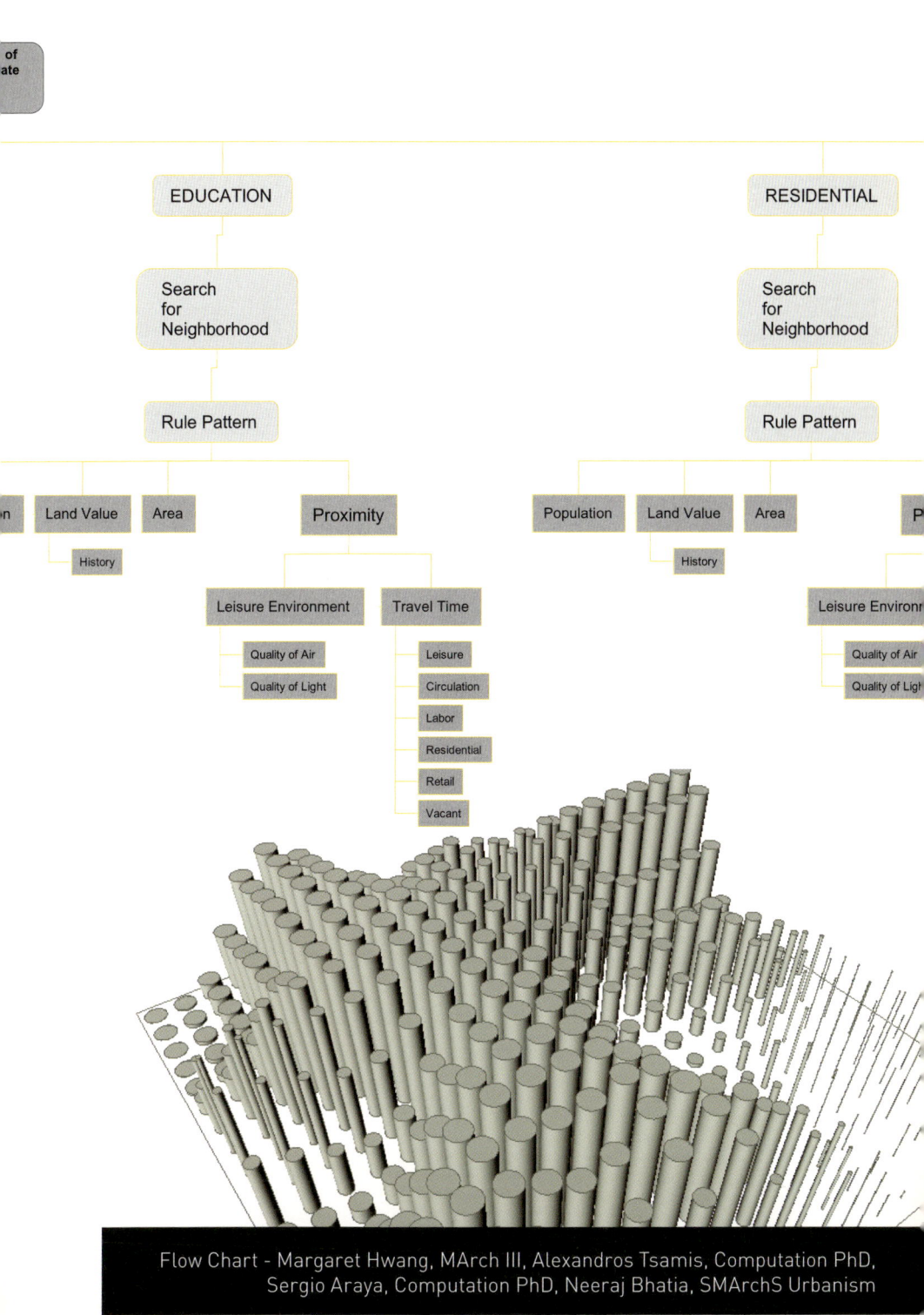

EDUCATION

Search
for
Neighborhood

Rule Pattern

n	Land Value	Area		Proximity

History

Leisure Environment

Travel Time

Quality of Air

Quality of Light

Leisure

Circulation

Labor

Residential

Retail

Vacant

RESIDENTIAL

Search
for
Neighborhood

Rule Pattern

Population	Land Value	Area		P

History

Leisure Environment

Quality of Air

Quality of Light

Flow Chart - Margaret Hwang, MArch III, Alexandros Tsamis, Computation PhD,
Sergio Araya, Computation PhD, Neeraj Bhatia, SMArchS Urbanism

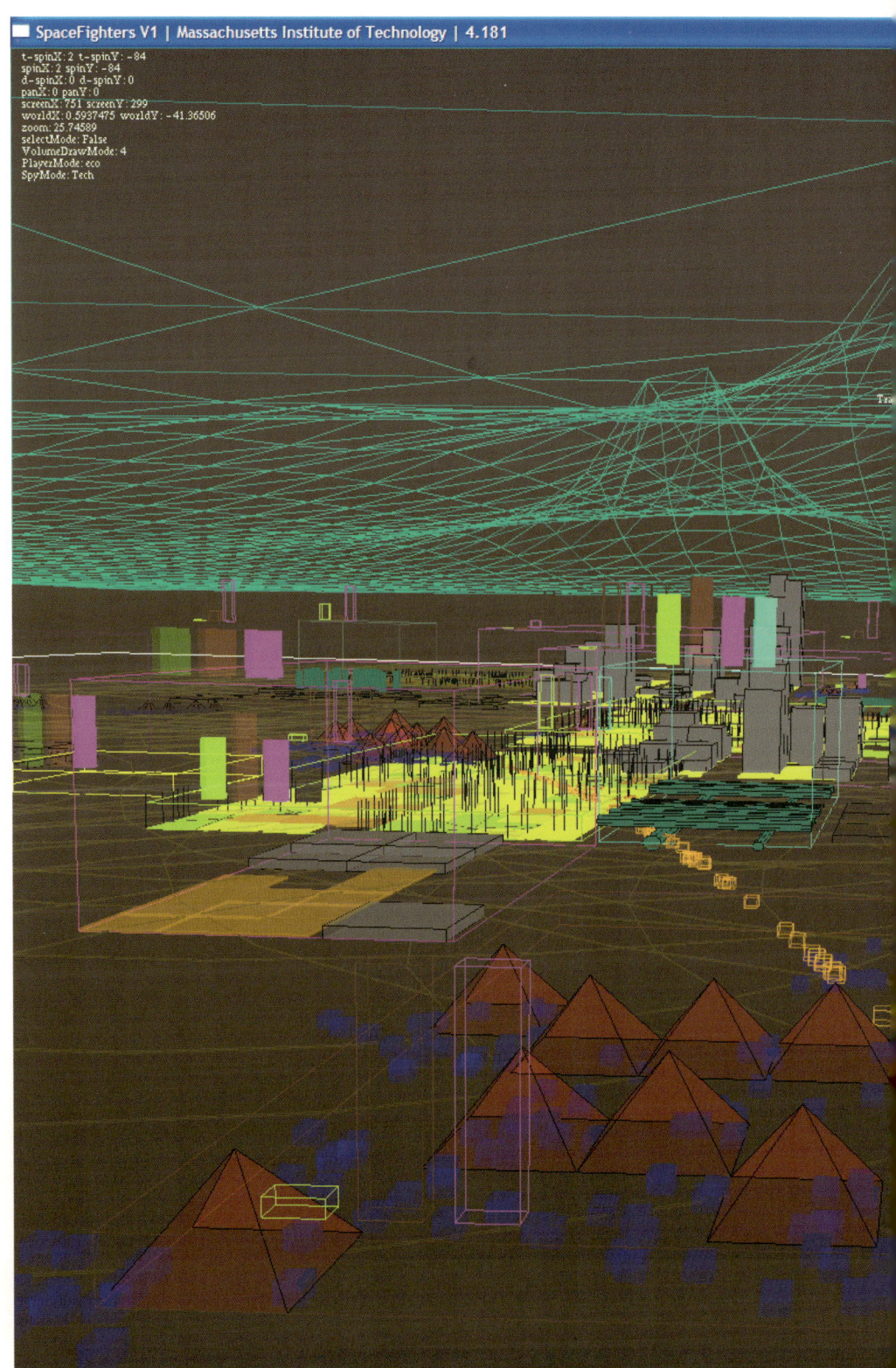

t–spinX: 2 t–spinY: –84
spinX: 2 spinY: –84
d–spinX: 0 d–spinY: 0
panX: 0 panY: 0
screenX: 751 screenY: 299
worldX: 0.5937475 worldY: –41.36506
zoom: 25.74589
selectMode: False
VolumeDrawMode: 4
PlayerMode: eco
SpyMode: Tech

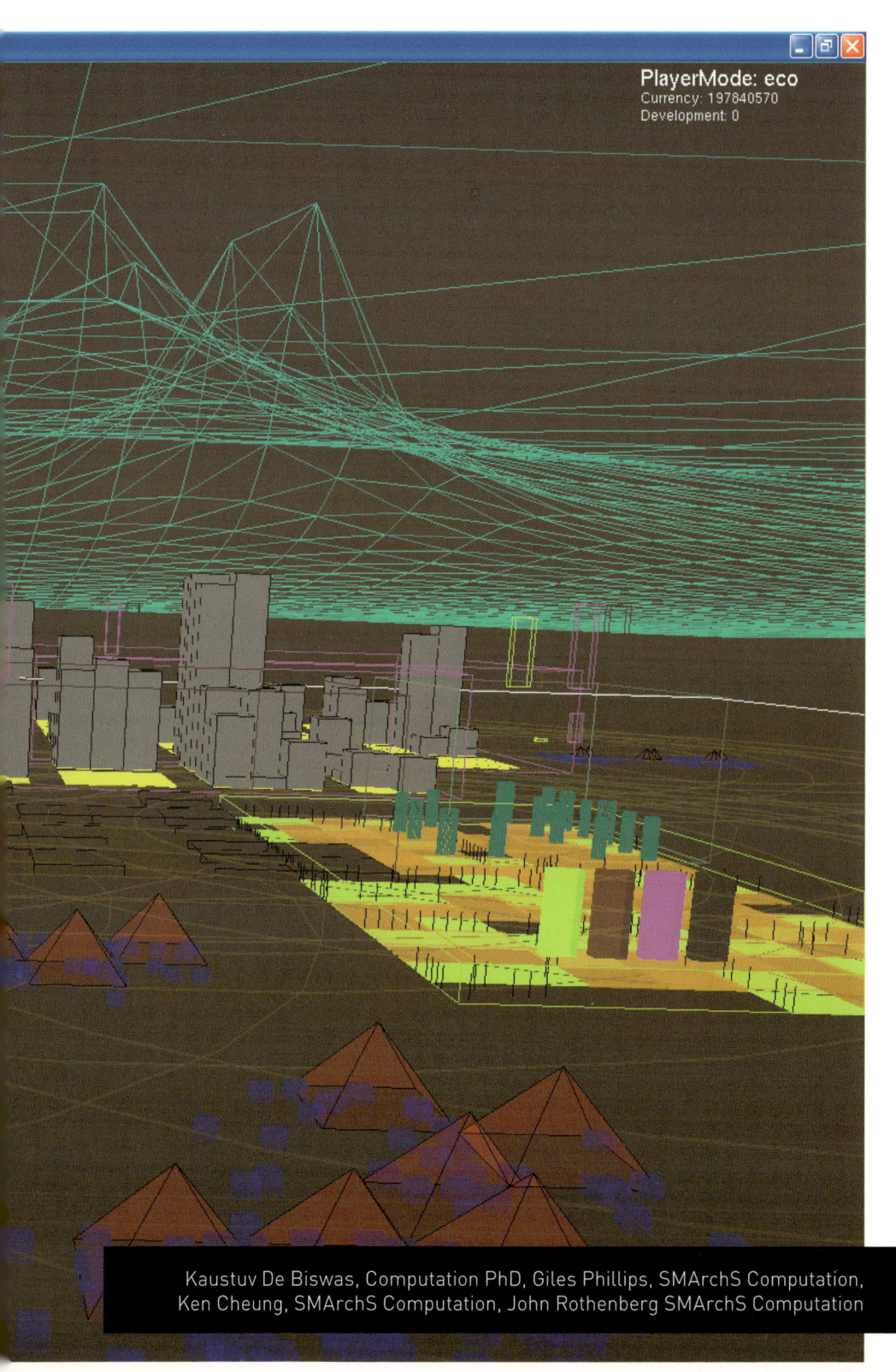

Kaustuv De Biswas, Computation PhD, Giles Phillips, SMArchS Computation,
Ken Cheung, SMArchS Computation, John Rothenberg SMArchS Computation

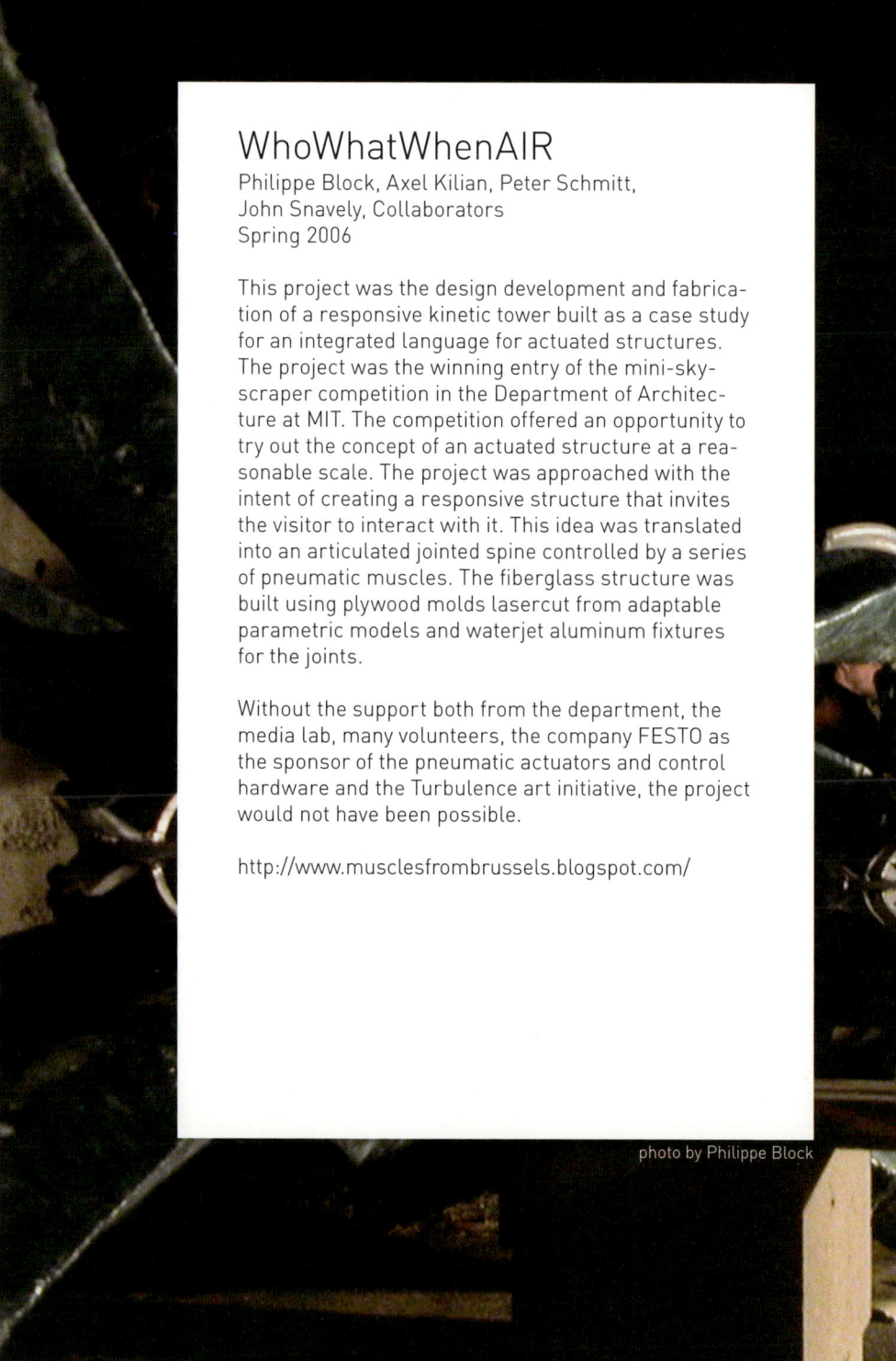

WhoWhatWhenAIR

Philippe Block, Axel Kilian, Peter Schmitt,
John Snavely, Collaborators
Spring 2006

This project was the design development and fabrication of a responsive kinetic tower built as a case study
for an integrated language for actuated structures.
The project was the winning entry of the mini-sky-
scraper competition in the Department of Architecture at MIT. The competition offered an opportunity to
try out the concept of an actuated structure at a rea-
sonable scale. The project was approached with the
intent of creating a responsive structure that invites
the visitor to interact with it. This idea was translated
into an articulated jointed spine controlled by a series
of pneumatic muscles. The fiberglass structure was
built using plywood molds lasercut from adaptable
parametric models and waterjet aluminum fixtures
for the joints.

Without the support both from the department, the
media lab, many volunteers, the company FESTO as
the sponsor of the pneumatic actuators and control
hardware and the Turbulence art initiative, the project
would not have been possible.

http://www.musclesfrombrussels.blogspot.com/

photo by Philippe Block

John Snavely tests the tower's strength.

Peter Schmitt applies fiberglass to a mold.

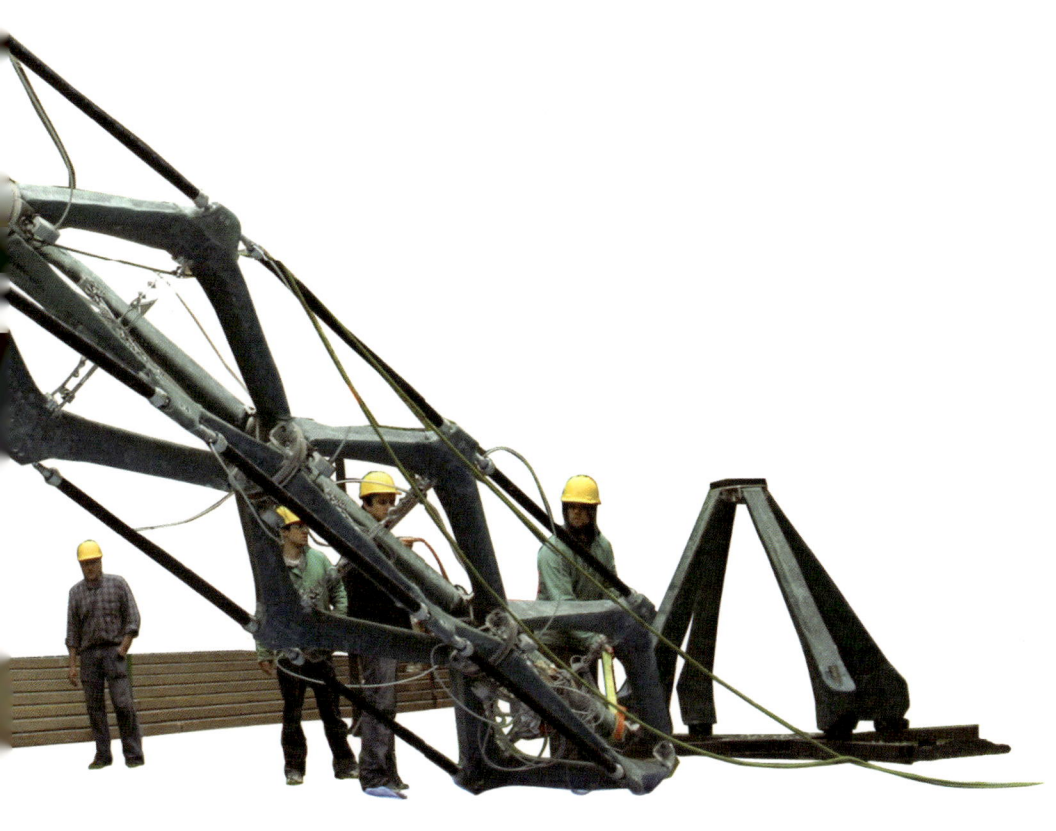

Raising the tower.
photo by Daniel Nagaj

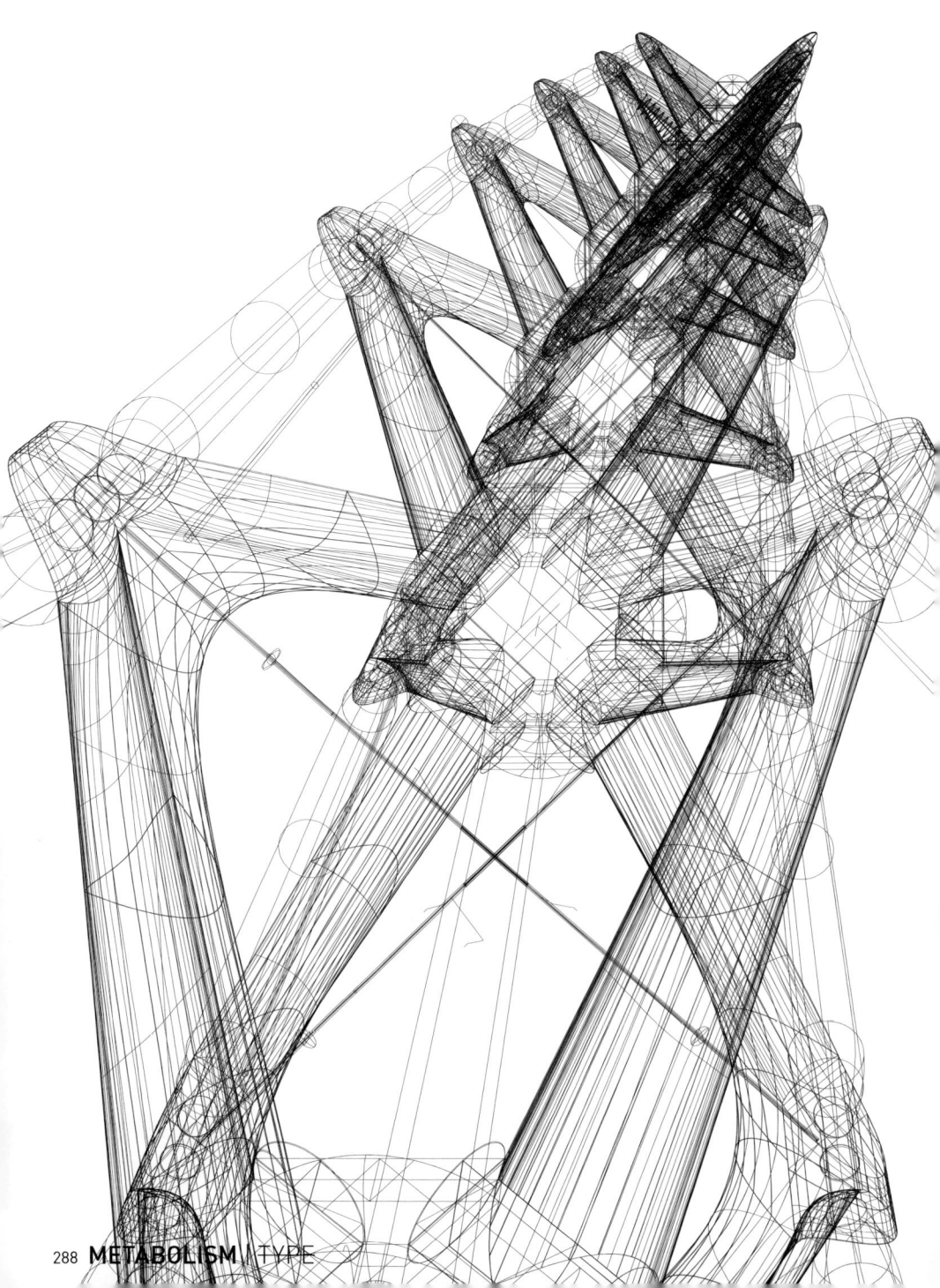

Axel Kilian tests the tower's interactivity.

TYPE

**Urban Morphology, Low- and Mid-rise High-density
Housing Appropriate to Shanghai**
Stanford Anderson and Xiangning Li, Instructors
Shui On Land Ltd, Hong Kong, Sponsor
Workshop 4.667

Instant Cabin
Larry Sass, Instructor

**MALIBU: Design Negotiations with Nature:
Retreat at Sweetwater Mesa**
Andrew Scott, Instructor
MArch Level III Studio 4.155

Urban Morphology: Low- and Medium-Rise High-Density (LMRHD) Housing for Shanghai

Stanford Anderson and Xiangning Li, Instructors
Shui On Land Ltd, Hong Kong, Sponsor
Architecture Design Workshop 4.667
Fall 2006

The intentions for this workshop are to design city-building that would provide an alternative to high-rise urban development. Notions of active street life, diversity of use (indoors and out), vitality of the pedestrian realm, and community facilities inform the work.

Housing stock is the single largest part of the urban fabric. Thus housing must contribute to the making of humane urban life if that ambition is to succeed.

The first half of the workshop is devoted to background in the study of urban morphology, introduction to Shanghai and its development policies, and the identification and analysis of prototype LMRHD housing:

Not for direct imitation
To provoke innovation
To discover suggestive details
Positive urban/street qualities
A range of densities
A range of economic levels
Always to recall that the search is for improved urban life, not the quality of the unit alone.

Realistically, one must acknowledge that it is more likely that LMRHD housing will be achieved for the more affluent residents — and that is part of building a livable city.

However, on an ethical basis as well as in the interest of a good urban life for all, one must pursue the possibility of LMRHD housing for lower economic levels.
We included a high number of Dutch precedent projects for these reasons. The Dutch, for more than a century, have sought to build livable cities while providing housing for all its population. Such housing typically embraces important features:
  Low rise, medium to high density
  Economical plans
  Good light and ventilation
  Shared courtyards, gardens, lanes
  Mixed use
  Attention to privacy of access

In the limited time of the second half of the Workshop, sketch designs of possible LMRHD housing for Shanghai will be undertaken. Some projects will draw on combined features of the studied precedent works.

model by Wenjun Ge

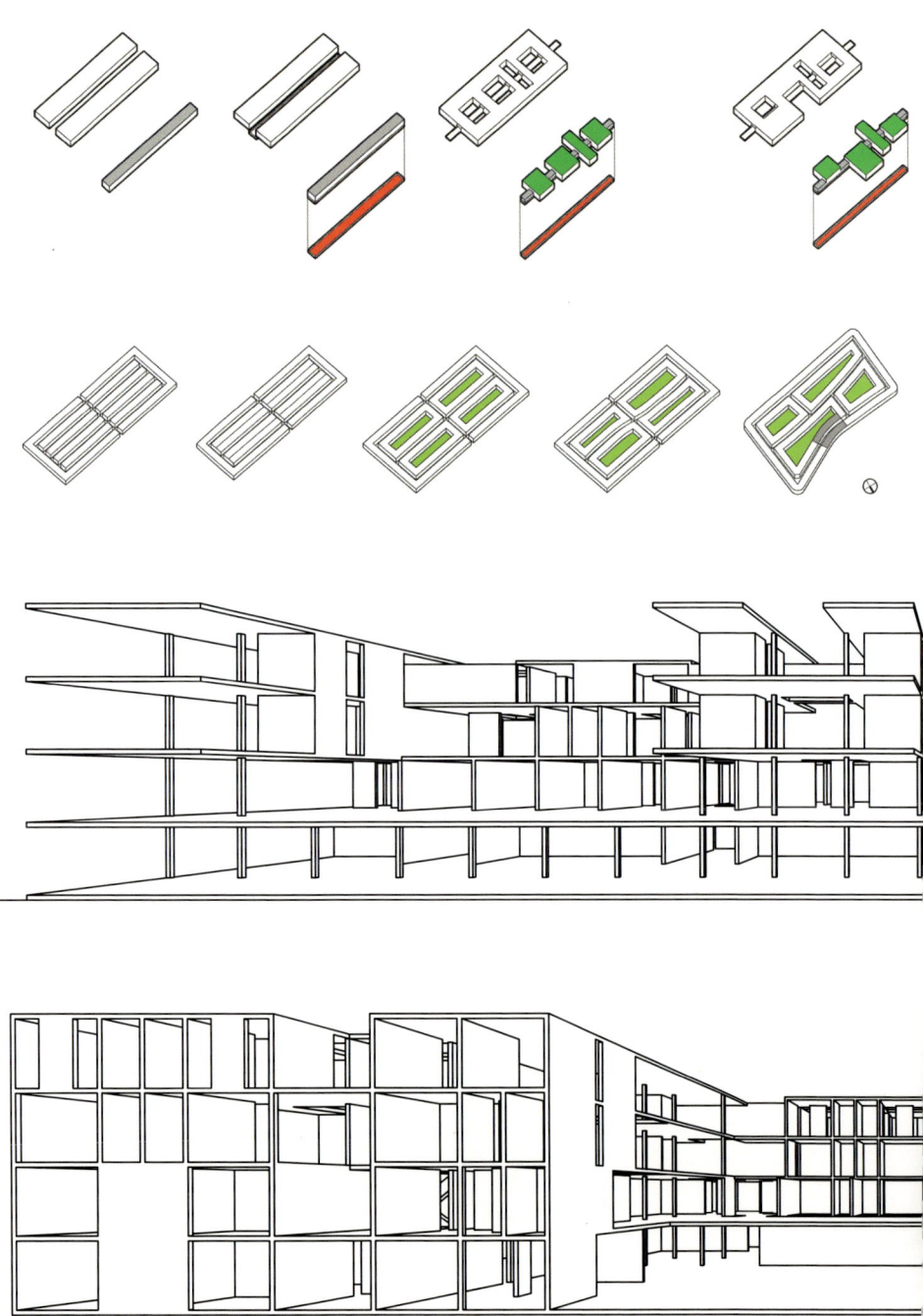

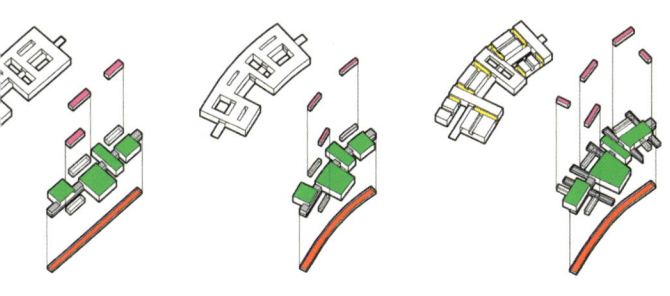

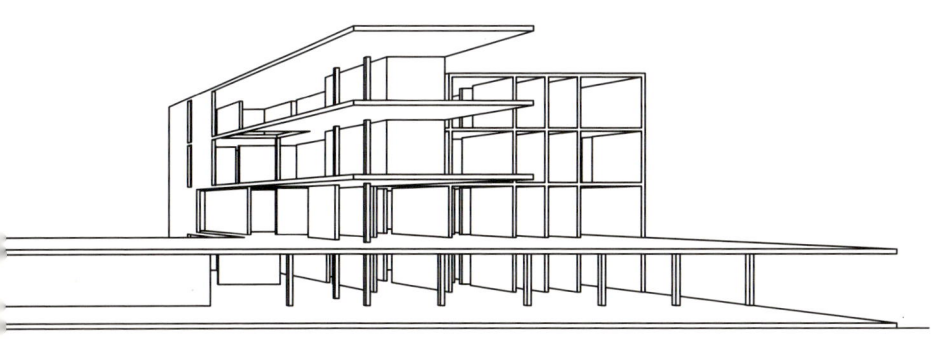

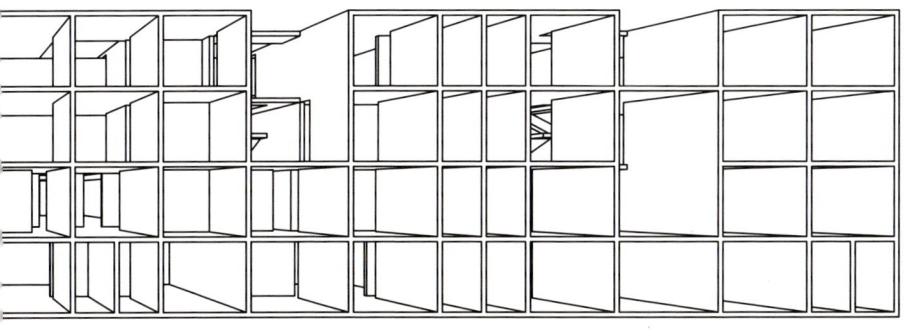

Wenjun Ge
SMArchS Urbanism

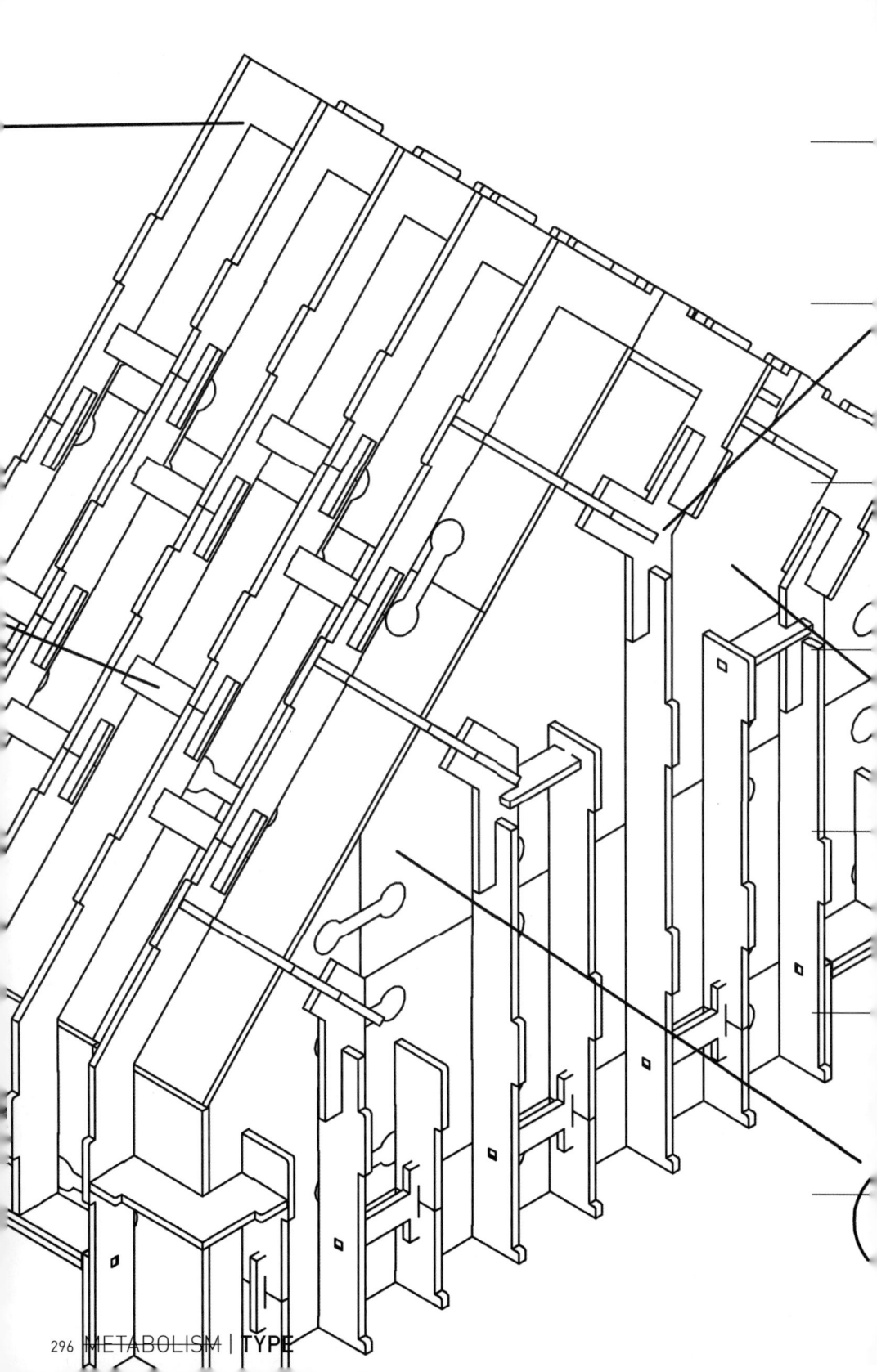

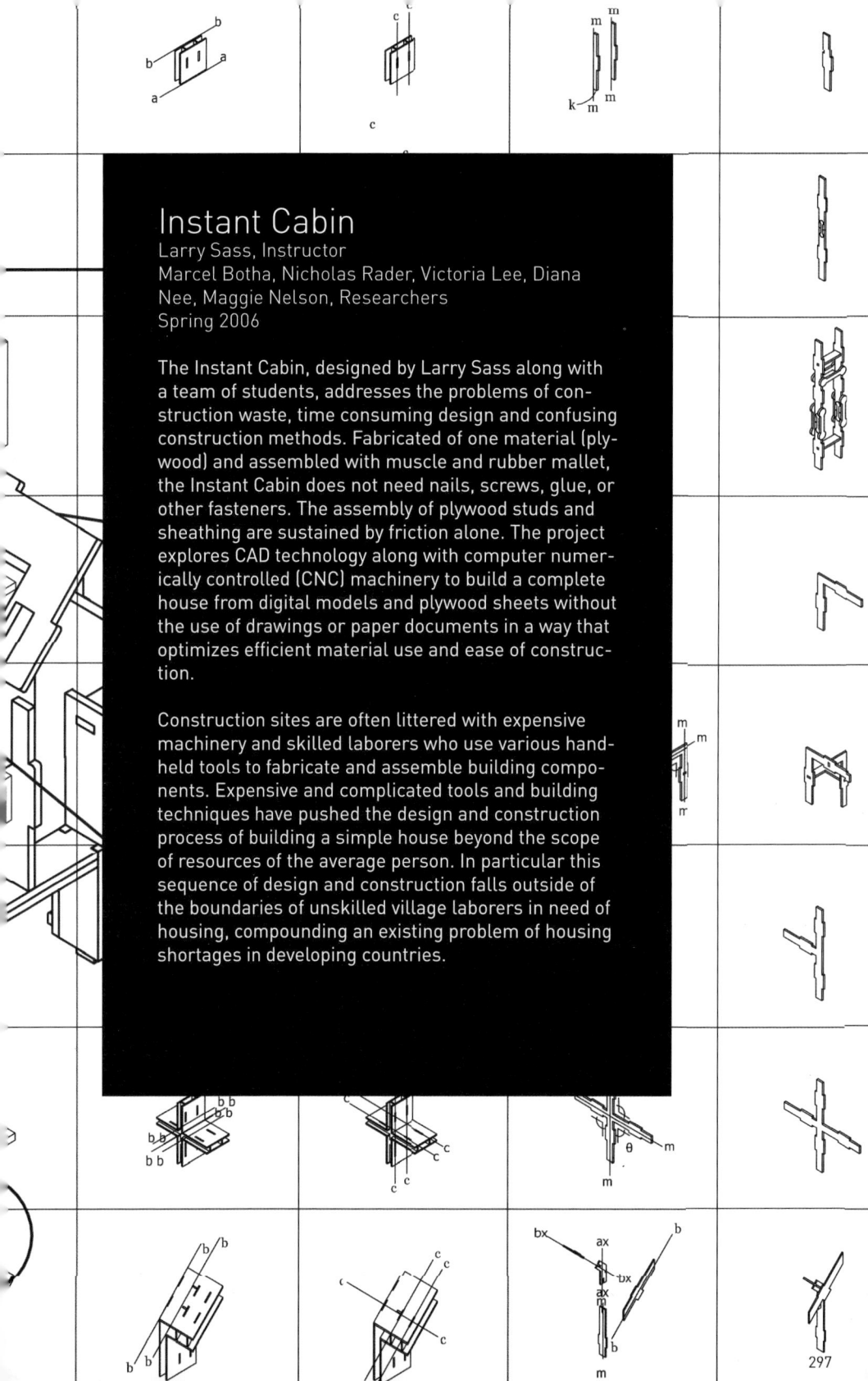

Instant Cabin

Larry Sass, Instructor
Marcel Botha, Nicholas Rader, Victoria Lee, Diana Nee, Maggie Nelson, Researchers
Spring 2006

The Instant Cabin, designed by Larry Sass along with a team of students, addresses the problems of construction waste, time consuming design and confusing construction methods. Fabricated of one material (plywood) and assembled with muscle and rubber mallet, the Instant Cabin does not need nails, screws, glue, or other fasteners. The assembly of plywood studs and sheathing are sustained by friction alone. The project explores CAD technology along with computer numerically controlled (CNC) machinery to build a complete house from digital models and plywood sheets without the use of drawings or paper documents in a way that optimizes efficient material use and ease of construction.

Construction sites are often littered with expensive machinery and skilled laborers who use various hand-held tools to fabricate and assemble building components. Expensive and complicated tools and building techniques have pushed the design and construction process of building a simple house beyond the scope of resources of the average person. In particular this sequence of design and construction falls outside of the boundaries of unskilled village laborers in need of housing, compounding an existing problem of housing shortages in developing countries.

Design team with the completed cabin.

Assembly of 1:1 plywood components with a rubber mallet.

MALIBU: Design Negotiations with Nature: Retreat at Sweetwater Mesa

Andrew Scott, Instructor
Jennifer Ferng, TA
MArch Level III Studio 4.155
Fall 2006

This studio focuses on making architecture on the mountain landscape above Malibu in Southern California. The site, Sweetwater Mesa, is about 160 acres and can be read at multiple scales. Within the site there exist microclimates and varied topography. Looking beyond the site reveals relationships to the Pacific Ocean and Los Angeles.

At Sweetwater Mesa, we will explore an architectural design that challenges the notions and theoretical framework of contemporary sustainability. Working from a position that recognizes the necessity for environmental responsibility at many scales, the studio will develop concepts and strategies that explore how sustainability becomes a critical thought and design process in the emergence of a project. Sweetwater Mesa itself has several systems that can be addressed within the design process, including climatic forces (fire), topography, resources and ecology.

The architectural program requires a residential retreat as part of a series of houses on the land. Each student will develop the program differently by creating a conceptual narrative for living in the site and a subsequent masterplan for the project. The masterplan lays out a strategy for the architecture at the larger scale of the landscape, and establishes the relationships between sub-parts of buildings and their local sites.

image by Stephen Perdue

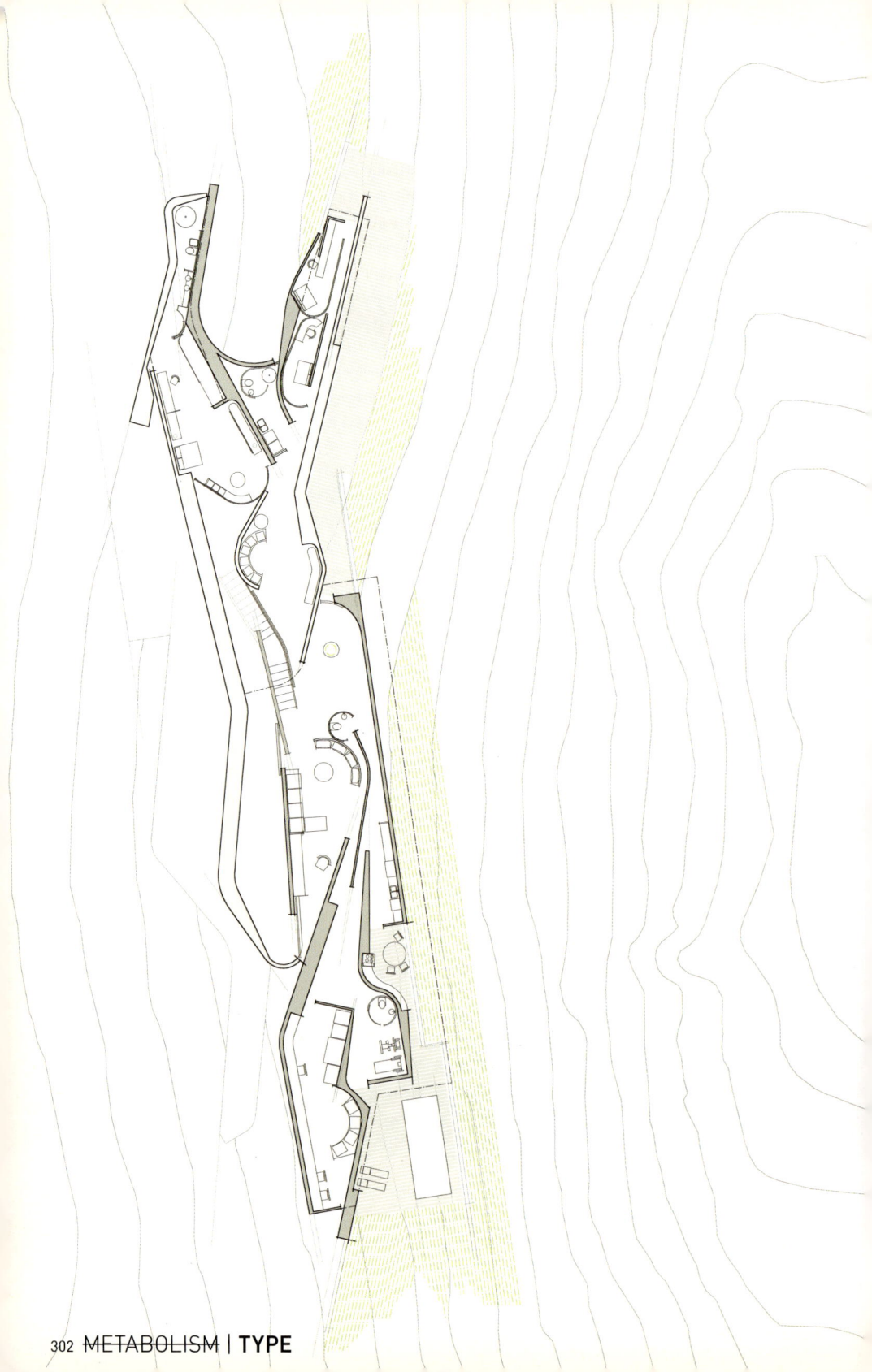

Meghan Green
MArch III

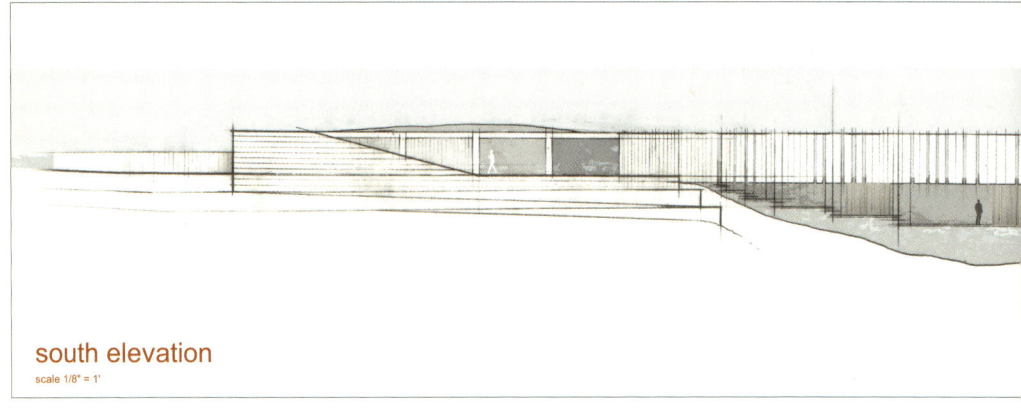

south elevation
scale 1/8" = 1'

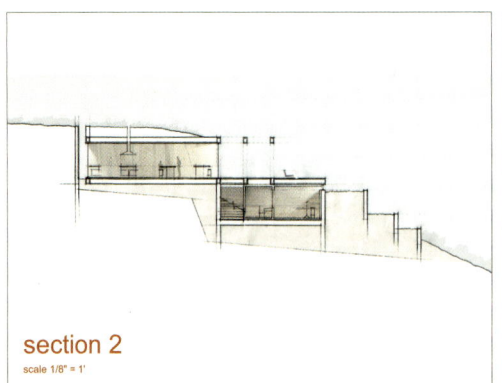

section 2
scale 1/8" = 1'

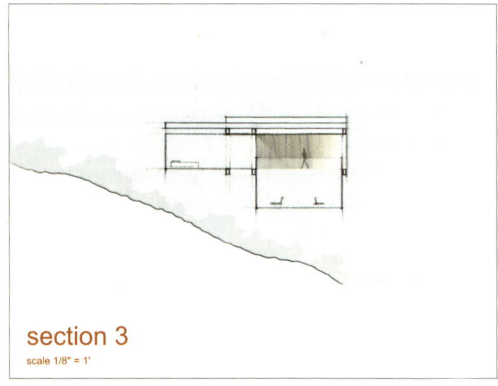

section 3
scale 1/8" = 1'

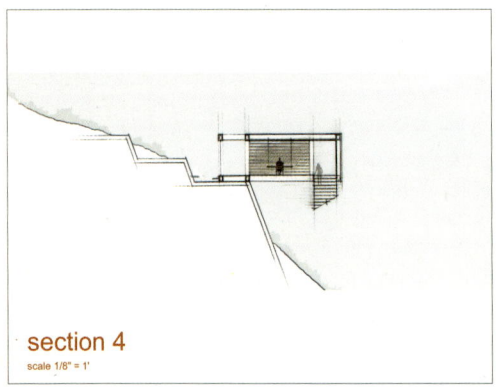

section 4
scale 1/8" = 1'

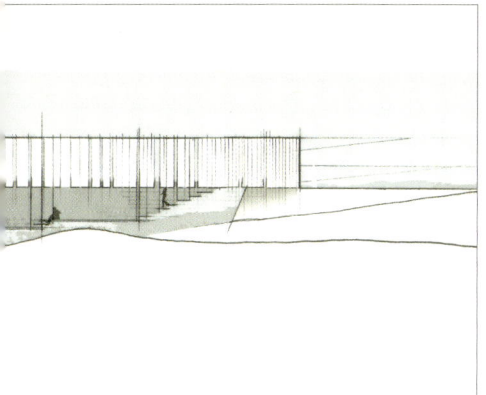

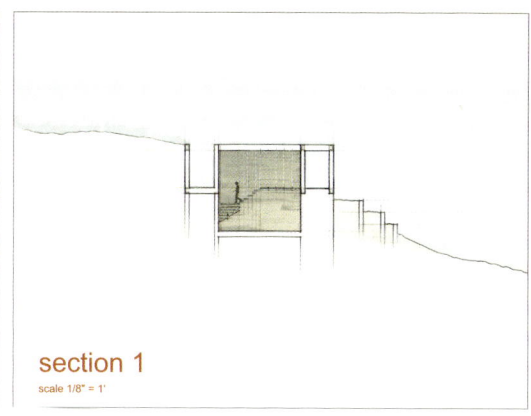

section 1
scale 1/8" = 1'

Stephen Perdue
MArch III

Stephen Perdue
MArch III

Architecture Programs

Degree Programs
Bachelor of Science
Bachelor of Science in Art and Design

Master of Architecture
Master of Science in Architecture Studies
Master of Science in Building Technology
Master of Science in Visual Studies

PhD in Building Technology
PhD in Computation
PhD in the History and Theory of Art & Architecture
Dual Degrees

Non-Degree Programs
Post-Doctoral Fellowships for Research in Islamic Architecture
Urban Design Certificate

Major Research Programs
Computation
Building Technology
History, Theory and Criticism
Visual Arts
Architectural Urbanism

Resources

Libraries

The Rotch Library, housed in an award-winning building by Schwartz/Silver Architects, is one of the nation's premier resources in architecture and planning. The collection offers extensive depth in architecture, building technology, art history, photography, environmental studies, land use, urban design and development, housing and community development, regional planning and development, urban transportation and real estate.

Rotch Visual Collections, an adjacent branch library, holds 350,000 visual images including the Kepes-Lynch Collection, the Kidder Smith Collection and the Aga Khan Visual Archive. Both Rotch libraries are part of the MIT Library System, with more than 2.6 million printed volumes, 17,000 journal subscriptions, 275 online databases and over 3800 electronic journal titles licensed for MIT access.

Access to other libraries is provided through the Boston Library Consortium, a cooperative association of nearly 20 academic and research libraries in the area. Graduate students are also eligible for borrowing privileges at the Harvard College Libraries and at the Loeb Library at the Harvard Graduate School of Design.

Galleries

The Wolk Gallery, in the School of Architecture + Planning, mounts several shows a year in its exhibition space surrounding Frank Stellas phantasmagorical 3-D sculpture Loohooloo. Exhibits are curated

by the Curator of Architecture and Design at the MIT Museum.

The PLAZmA Digital Gallery features the work of students and faculty presented on nine large monitors in the school's public areas; the content overlaps with the Online Portfolio. The screens can also be used for student reviews and presentations.

The MIT Museum frequently features exhibits on architecture and visual studies in its main galleries at 265 Massachusetts Avenue, as well as in its Compton Gallery, located in the heart of campus under the big dome. The Museum's eGallery, a virtual exhibition space and archive, features sites designed specifically as virtual exhibitions, spotlighting museum collections as well as exhibitions no longer on display in its galleries.

The Center for Advanced Visual Studies, an artists' fellowship program sponsored by the School of Architecture + Planning, maintains a gallery in its space in Building N52-390. A working laboratory for interdisciplinary art practice, the Center commissions and produces new artworks and artistic research, often presenting new work in its gallery space.

The List Visual Arts Center, three galleries on the first floor of the Media Lab's Wiesner Building, presents 5-8 shows a year exploring contemporary artmaking in all media. Artists of national and international stature, as well as emerging artists, are featured.

Rotch Library also features exhibits of student, staff and faculty work, as well as shows from its collections, in its space in Building 7-238.

Publications

AGENDAS IN ARCHITECTURE
Is a new vehicle for publications and books about student and faculty research at the Department of Architecture. This book is its first publication.

PLAN
Is the monthly newsletter of the School of Architecture and Planning. Plan is published both on paper and online, at: http://loohooloo.mit.edu/resources/newsletter_plan/

SPEC
SPEC is a weekly tabloid summarizing, exclaiming main talking points brought up during lectures or seminars, fostering hallway debates and corridor conversations.

THRESHOLDS
thresholds is the bi-annual critical journal of architecture, art and media culture produced by editors in the Department of Architecture of the Massachusetts Institute of Technology. Thresholds editors produce two independently themed journals a year. The best submissions from fine arts, design, graphics, media arts and sciences, film, photography, architecture and theory are selected based on their holistic fit around the given theme. Graphic and pictorial works play as strong a role in each journal as do works of critial writing. The thresholds advisory board is composed of internationally recognized figures in various fields of visual culture. The Board provides intellectual support for theme development, and brings forth a large amount of high quality submissions for each issue. As a result, the work of many important, international figures has been featured. (See: Kenneth Frampton and Michael McKinnell in Journal #12; Trinh T. Minh-ha & Jean-Paul Bourdier in Journal #13; Paul Carter, Ignasi de Sola-Morales and James Wines of SITE in Journal #14; The Art Guys and Carol Burns in Journal #15; Bill Mitchell and Mitchell Schwarzer in Journal #16; Charles Correa, Tunney Lee, Cherie Wendelken and Stephen Cairns in Journal #17; Keller Easterling and Mark Jarzombek in Journal #18; Alfredo Jaar and Diane Ghirardo in Journal #19.) Thresholds is held within 150 university art & architecture libraries around the world (ISSN #1091-711x), and is available for sale at 40 locations in the US. thresholds issues can also be aquired individually or on a subscription basis. The cover price is $10 ($13 outside the US).
http://architecture.mit.edu/thresholds/index.html

People

Marilyne Andersen
Stanford Anderson
Ute Meta Bauer
Julian Beinart
Yung Ho Chang
Charles Correa
Dan Chen
Alexander D'Hooghe
John de Monchaux
Michael Dennis
Christopher Dewart
Fernando Domeyko
Arindam Dutta
John Fernandez
Andrea Frank
David Friedman
Joe Gibbons
Leon Glicksman
Reinhard Goethert
Mark Goulthorpe
N. John Habraken
Simi Hoque
Eric Howeler
Bill Hubbard
Stephen Intille
Wendy Jacob
Mark Jarzombek
Joan Jonas
Caroline Jones
Alan Joslin
Shun Kanda
Terry Knight
Kent Larson
Rebecca Luther
William Mitchell
Takehiko Nagakura
Erika Naginski
Leslie Norford
John Ochsendorf
Ann Pendleton-Jullian
William Porter
Nasser Rabbat

Carl Rosenberg
Adèle Naudé Santos
Lawrence Sass
Andrew Scott
Anne Spirn
George Stiny
Joel Turkel
Jan Wampler
Angela Watson
Krzysztof Wodiczko
J. Meejin Yoon
Joe Zane

Visitors, Lecturers, Guests

Tetuzi Akiyama, Gannit Ankori, Wiel Arets, Gustavo Artigas, Stuart Bailey, Keith Bargaheiser, Judith Barry, Siobhan Barry, Arthur Beale, Gordon Bell, Michael Bell, Paul Bertram, Peter Beinart, Carol Bier, Can Bilsel, Abbe Bjorklund, Petra Blaisse, Michael Blum, Magali Bodart, Frank Borelli, Louise Borque, Michael Boucher, Ole' Bowman, William Craft Brumfield, Angelo Bucci, Katherine Carl, Nathan Carter, Jae Cha, Marian Chertow, Mel Chin, Barbara Clausen, Chris Carbone, Rey Chow, Wasma'a Chorbachi, Karl Chu, Lise Anne Couture, Bill Daniel, Michael Deane, Xaveer De Geyter, Laura De Lorenzis, Andrea Deplazes, Christian Derix, Stan Douglas, Juan Du, Deborah Dunning, Craig Dykers, Ana Dzokic, Christopher Eamon, Keller Easterling, John Ehrenfeld, Olafur Eliasson, Karen Fairbanks, Harrell Fletcher, Kenneth Frampton, Andrew Freear, Philip Freelon, Robert Frosch, Sou Fujimoto, Mario Gandelsonas, Ivan Gaskell, Finn Geipel, Heidi Gilpin, Jack Glassman, Geoff Goats, Terence Gower, Tom Graedel, Dabney Hailey, Andrei Harwell, Mahmoud Hawari, Stefan Heidenreich, Walt Henry, Juan Herreros, Tad Hirsch, Steven Holl, Walter Hood, Eric Howeler, Ying-Chun Hsieh, Sheng-yuan Hwang, Dorothee Imbert, Toshio Iwai, Jessica Jaques, Karen Jones, Rick Joy, Lydia Kallipoliti, Greg Kelley, Sheila Kennedy, Greg Keoleian, Bernard Khoury, Charles Kibert, Nico Kienzl, Axel Kilian, Kent Kleinman, Rem Koolhaas, Ivan Kucina, Stanford Kwinter, Miwon Kwon, Lynne C. Lancaster, Jonathan Lavery, Noel Lawrence, Pamela Lee, Lianne Lefaivre, Thomas Y. Levin, Bruce Lindsey, Steven Lockley, Winy Maas, Daria Martin, Reinhold Martin, Ian MacDonald, Joseph MacDonald, John Malpede, Scott Marble, Thom Mayne, Matthew Mazzotta, Scott McCloud, Anne Arden McDonald, Alex McDowell, Rahul Mehrotra, Edward Melendez, Partha Mitter, Regina Moeller, Helen Molesworth, Philippe Morel, Petia Morozov, Catherine Morris, Sandy Mulkern, Matt Mullican, Senadin Musabegovic, Nicholas Negroponte, Marc Neen, Guy Nordenson, Carmen Oquendo-Villar, Franz Oswald, Trevor Paglen, Kyong Park, Alix Pearlstein, Antoine Picon, Victoria Powers, Jerry Pucilio, Ali Rahim, Kuroda Raiji, Vic Rawlings, Roger Reed, David Reinfurt, Damon Rich, Milda Richardson, Charles Rose, Constanze Ruhm, Matthias Ruth, Jessica Rylan, Yousuf Saeed, Julia Schimmelpenningh, Paul Schlapobersky, Gunther Selichar, Leith Sharp, John Shnier, Michael Smith, Doris Sommer, Simon Starling, Julius Orion Smith III, Marianne Staniszewski, Hadas Steiner, Roslyn Sulcas, Sarah Sze, Nader Tehrani, Joseph Tanney,

Diana Thater, Jacob Wagner, Edward Walsh, Gili Weinberg, Srdjan Jovanovic Weiss, Ai Weiwei, Silke Witzsch, Peter Welz, Sarah Whiting, Gregory Williams, Daniel Winkert, Kyu Sung Woo, Jon Wybar, Ethel Sara Wolper, Nina Yuen, Waclaw Zalewski, Mel Ziegler, Zhengyou Zhang, Claire Zimmerman

Thank You

Michael Ames, Julian Beinart, Aaron Bennett, Scott Campbell, Rebecca Chamberlain, Yung Ho Chang, Maryann Czerepak, Annette Horne-Williams, Mark Jarzombek, Anne Simunovic, Jack Valleli, Puritan Press, and all the students and professors who contributed work.

Colophon

Editor
Alexander D'Hooghe

Student Editor & Graphic Designer
Sarah Dunbar

Introductions to research projects were provided by the instructor of the class or studio and in the case of theses, by the thesis student. In the case of special projects, participants in the project provided the description. All texts have been edited by the editorial team. Introductions to each chapter were written by Alexander D'Hooghe.

Layout
Peter DePasquale, Sarah Dunbar, Casey Renner

Book Team
Peter DePasquale, Sarah Dunbar, Rebecca Edson, Kathleen Flynn, Coryn Kempster, Marika Kobel, Stephen Perdue, Morgan Pinney, Casey Renner, James Shen

Publisher
SA+P Press
Cambridge, MA 2007

Printing
Puritan Press

Contact
Certain Agendas in Architecture
Room 7-337, MIT
77 Massachusetts Avenue
Cambridge, MA 02139-2307

ISBN
978-0-9794774-0-9